Theological educators worldwide have greater opportunities to teach interculturally than ever before, especially through distance learning options that are increasing daily. Even with the greatest of intentions, many educators still lack an adequate understanding of their students' contexts. *Teaching across Cultures* is a timely tool which offers critical ways to examine educational contexts in advance and depicts real-life insights from numerous local voices. Please do not set foot into another culture's classroom without this teaching resource.

Michael A. Ortiz, PhD
International Director,
International Council for Evangelical Theological Education

Any given chapter in this book is worth the price of the book. Such is the quality throughout. The authors deliver a penetrating critique of the frequent unconscious cultural assumptions and blinders accompanying the cross-cultural teacher. Insights flow liberally and coherently from these global veterans shedding light on more sensitive cultural teaching leading to more desirable outcomes. Reinforcing themes emerge from the insights, but perhaps the most compelling is the need for humble listening for those aspiring to teach in another culture. The distinctive last section, "Local Voices," contains faculty from thirty countries offering insightful points for cultural understanding for anyone teaching in that respective region. The authors reveal a passionate and urgent desire that the gospel of Jesus Christ be heard clearly within one's own cultural framework. Their wisdom guides us to that end . . . for the glory of God. Highly recommended.

Duane H. Elmer, PhD
G. W. Aldeen Professor of International Studies, Retired,
Distinguished Professor of Educational Studies, Emeritus,
Trinity International University, Deerfield, Illinois, USA

For those willing to learn with humility as they serve and equip others, *Teaching across Cultures: A Global Christian Perspective* will prove to be an invaluable resource and insightful guide for effective cross-cultural teaching ministry. The book makes a unique and strategic contribution by providing theological educators with the tools they need to navigate the complexities of language, culture and context generally, as well as specific guidance regarding what to do and what to avoid when teaching in more than thirty representative cultures from across the Majority World.

Paul Branch, PhD
President, Central American Theological Seminary (SETECA)
General Secretary,
Latin American Association for Evangelical Theological Education

At last there is a book written by four top-notch theological educators that will help those who wish to teach across cultures. With the increasing internationalization and globalization of theological education, Christian higher education institutions across the world will welcome students and faculty members from different cultures. Many institutions will engage in cross-cultural faculty exchange programs. This book is certainly a must-have resource for all serious educators.

David Tarus, PhD
Executive Director, Association for Christian Theological Education in Africa

Teaching across Cultures is an exciting and valuable resource that will help cross-cultural teachers hear what Majority World educators say they need to know. They will hear how crucial humility is and see what it looks like in practice. Wherever they plan to go, this volume has a representative regional voice. Commencing with a powerfully told story that illustrates common faux pas and redemptive steps, this book has useful questions for reflection at the end of each chapter. This book will help cross-cultural teachers navigate the borderland between cultures. It will be an essential resource for Theologians Without Borders as we orient scholars before short-term visits for teaching across cultures.

Ian Payne, PhD
Executive Director, Theologians Without Borders

Teaching across Cultures is more than a book about theological education or simply about education. It is a necessary resource for everyone who undertakes a cross-cultural task, whether teaching, missions, or business. The central objective is "humble listening." Both the testimonies and theoretical developments on cross-cultural education from the first chapters, as well as the contributions of thirty-one global contexts, constitute a unique conceptual and experiential richness. But the great contribution is to insist on listening as a first step. Those of us who teach are tempted to try to have all the answers, when the important thing is to know how to listen to all the questions. *Teaching across Cultures* is a scholarly and testimonial work, but above all, it is an invitation to a change of attitude.

Norberto Saracco, PhD
Rector Emeritus,
Facultad Interamericana de Estudios Teológicos (FIET Theological Institute)

Here – at last! – is a gently instructive "manual" for teaching with the mind of Christ: with humility. Its surprise feature is a "Lonely Planet" equivalent for sensitive and successful teaching as a "foreigner" right across the continents. Great is the kingdom value in this wise guide! Those setting off from anywhere to serve in seminaries anywhere, shouldn't leave without it in their backpacks.

Havilah Dharamraj, PhD
Head of the Department of Biblical Studies,
South Asia Institute of Advanced Christian Studies, India

This book is timely planned, thoroughly researched, and concisely written to fill a huge gap in theological education as it attempts to be more globally relevant in the borderless world we live in now. The authors have skillfully shared theory and knowledge, and their genuine experiences in this regard, and further took time to listen to theological educators from around the world so as to provide a model of "humble learning" which promises greater transformative impact for both teachers and students for the common goal set before us. It is a must-read book for theological educators if they want to be effective for their calling in cross-cultural contexts.

Jung-Sook Lee, PhD
Church History Professor and fifth President,
Torch Trinity Graduate University, Seoul, South Korea

Majority World theological institutions have been blessed by having visiting professors, especially coming from the West. But in several

Teaching across Cultures

A Global Christian Perspective

Perry Shaw, César Lopes, Joanna Feliciano-Soberano, and Bob Heaton

Series Editors
Riad Kassis
Michael A. Ortiz

ICETE International Council for Evangelical Theological Education
strengthening evangelical theological education through international cooperation

Langham
GLOBAL LIBRARY

Taiwan 161

Korea 165

India 173

North-East India 179

Sri Lanka 183

Pakistan 187

Bangladesh 191

Lebanon 195

Africa 199

Kenya 203

Ethiopia 209

Francophone Africa 215

Benin and Togo 217

Nigeria 223

Zambia 227

Zimbabwe 235

Mozambique 243

Guatemala 249

Costa Rica 253

Caribbean 259

Colombia 263

Andean Peru 267

Brazil 271

Paraguay 275

Greece 277

Czech Republic 281

Ukraine 285

Afterword 293

For Further Reading 295

Author Biographies 305

Introduction

The past fifty years have seen major changes in the landscape of the global Christian movement. The strength of the church has moved from the West to Africa, Asia, and Latin America, and with this has come an accelerating need for quality leadership training across the Majority World. Demand for training programs has far exceeded supply, even with the maturing of theological colleges. Although there are growing numbers of highly qualified and insightful national faculty, many schools continue to look for outside faculty to support their leadership development endeavours.

With a notable tightening of visa restrictions in much of the world, the opportunities for long-term service in cross-cultural teaching are diminishing. This, with the desire to have the core of the curriculum taught by local faculty, has led to an increase in short-term cross-cultural teaching stints – often in brief intensive courses. While these can be a great blessing to the school and church community, too often cross-cultural teachers come with substantial "baggage" that undermines their credibility and their teaching.

Hence this collection. The purpose of this text is to provide cross-cultural teachers with good theory and practical insights that can guide them towards making their educational endeavours personally transformative and relevant for the students and those whom they serve. While the primary target audience is cross-cultural theology teachers, most of the material given in the collection relates equally to anyone teaching cross-culturally. In whatever role you hope to serve, we trust this collection will be of value.

The focus of our collection is on providing practical guidelines. However, good theory undergirds quality practice. Consequently, we have begun the collection with eight chapters that look more generally at what it means to teach theology cross-culturally.

The collection opens with a story. George wants to make an impact for God's kingdom in a cross-cultural context and so offers to teach a course on leadership. He starts badly, but his willingness to listen humbly is rewarded with

1

appreciation from the school. This theme of humble listening runs through the collection, and while there is so much more that this text can offer, you will go a long way on the path of transformative service if you approach your teaching with a humble listening ear.

Too often the practice of theological education is "neither theological nor educational."[1] In order to provide you with a genuine theological framework for your cross-cultural teaching service, our second chapter investigates pathways for a biblical understanding of teaching and culture. What do the Scriptures have to say about teaching, and how might the Bible shape the Christian educational endeavour? How do theology and culture intersect, and what are the implications for teaching cross-culturally?

There are many insights offered by the field of cultural anthropology, and chapters 3 and 4 present a number of lenses for the practice of teaching cross-culturally. Three key cultural parameters that are addressed repeatedly in the literature are summarized in chapter 3: the extent to which a context is collectivist or individualist, the way in which power and authority are distributed in a society, and the ways in which culture shapes thought processes. Each of these has huge implications for when you teach in another cultural context.

Particularly in cross-cultural education it is essential that you understand the diversity of communication patterns across the world. Chapter 4 delves into the topics of high- and low-context communication and intercultural rhetoric, and the implications for teaching cross-culturally. Many who teach theology in another country do so through translation, and the second half of chapter 4 provides a swathe of practical advice gleaned from experienced translators. Your teaching through translation will be strengthened through incorporating these suggestions in practice.

One of the greatest challenges in teaching theology cross-culturally is the diversity of understanding as to what good work looks like. From our joint experience we have discovered that assessment is one of the greatest frustrations experienced by visiting teachers in our theological schools. Consequently, we have devoted the whole of chapter 5 to investigating pathways to the development of more effective assessment strategies in cross-cultural teaching.

---

1. P. Sanders, "Evangelical Theological Education in a Globalised World," presentation delivered at Centre for Theological Education, Belfast, Northern Ireland, 17 November 2009.

In the past, theological education in the Majority World was largely a male domain. Over the past few decades the number of women in theological education – both teachers and students – has grown dramatically. However, there is still a long way to go, and in many parts of the world women are limited in what they can and cannot do. In the classroom there are often unspoken expectations that hinder the extraordinary contribution that women have to offer. Chapter 6 looks specifically at the topic of gender in cross-cultural teaching. Joanna begins by poignantly telling her own story and the stories of other women she has encountered in the Asian context. The chapter then moves to practical advice, based on the comments of thirty-six women from around the world who are in leadership in theological education. We hope that this contribution may in some small way better strengthen the voices of women in the world of theological education.

Chapter 7 is the most complex chapter in the text, but one of the most important. As a cross-cultural teacher you will inevitably carry a large amount of cultural baggage with you, not simply in content, but also in the way you think, your assumed norms, and your relative wealth. The educational encounter is always "political" in the sense that the teacher is vested with "power" and the students are in a relative position of "weakness." The key to enabling transformative learning to take place – for both you and your students – is to create a safe "third space" where the history and cultural background of your students is brought into healthy and humble dialogue with the substance of your field of expertise.

This theme is developed further in chapter 8. Throughout our collection there is an emphasis on humility and learning, but the exercise of humble learning becomes more challenging when our theological premises are questioned. And yet, if you reach the end of a stint teaching theology cross-culturally and none of your presuppositions has been challenged, it is probable that your teaching has been irrelevant to your students' context and you yourself have lost the opportunity for transformative growth. How much better it is to come with theological humility – a recognition that what is perceived as normative in your home community in both dogmatic content and theological methodology may be limited and limiting. From the position of theological humility there is potential for genuine growth.

1

Teaching Cross-Culturally ... Did I Learn More Than My Students?

Bob Heaton

I had come to this Bible school from my home country after some twenty years of teaching experience, wanting to make an impact for God's kingdom in a cross-cultural context. I thought my zeal to impart information – especially related to the Bible and the Christian faith – would be enough, together with the Holy Spirit's help. But I was wrong.

I'd prepared a course on leadership based on the character and life of David from 1 and 2 Samuel. I assumed that the leadership principles I'd taught at home, the illustrations I'd used, and the experiences I'd shared would have the same impact here as they did at home. But I was wrong. I assumed that everything would be understood the same way all around the world – including the way I taught and the way students learned. But I was wrong.

I had done some research on the Internet about the country, its peoples, customs, and traditions. I'd even taken the time and trouble to speak to some missionaries I vaguely knew. I wanted to get their opinions and a general idea about what I should expect and what to do and not do. I had bought a pocket language dictionary and begun to learn some basic greetings and phrases. I thought I was fairly well prepared. But I was wrong.

So here I was, on the afternoon of the third day of the course, about to enter the principal's office to share my concerns – and frustrations – about why the class wasn't responding to me very well. I took a deep breath, knocked on the door, and waited for the invitation to come in. Nothing. I knocked again, a little louder and longer this time. Eventually, a genial invitation came . . .

"Come in," said Dr. Smith, the Principal. "Hello, George. Please come in. Have a seat. How are you anyway?" he asked, pointing to a comfortable sofa. We both sat down.

"Thank you, sir," I said, still a little nervous.

"It's good to see you. I'm glad you've come. What can I get you – tea, coffee?" He stood up to pour. "Milk, sugar? Tell me," he added, "how's the family?"

That came as a surprise. I hadn't come to talk about my family at all, but about my teaching.

"How's Shirley doing?" he continued, seemingly genuine and interested. He had met me at the airport three days earlier and had asked about my family. "And what about Alan and Tom – what's happening with them at school?" he asked about my two teenagers.

"Oh, they're fine," I said rather matter-of-factly. I was glad that he had asked about them, but my primary business and concern right now was my teaching. It wasn't going very well.

"Yes, coffee, please; milk and one sugar," I answered. "Thanks. Shirley has a little cold, but the boys are enjoying school." I thought that would end that conversation and I could get on with the real issue at hand. But I was wrong.

As he handed me the cup, he asked again. "You said Alan's about to finish high school, is that right? What's he going to do after graduation?" he went on. It was obvious he wanted to know even more about my family.

"Oh, he's not sure yet. He's been thinking about becoming a pilot." I thought that would end the interrogation. Once again, I was wrong.

"Well, what about Tom, what does he want to do when he's finished with school?"

"Mmm, I think we're way too early for that," I said. "He's only just turned fifteen. Right now, he doesn't know whether he wants to play tennis or soccer," I added, laughing, hoping that would kill the conversation. It didn't.

"So, he's into sports, is he? Oh my," Dr. Ted said, pausing to reflect. I was about to jump in to change the subject to my teaching when he continued:

"I remember when I was his age. I couldn't decide whether I wanted to be a swimmer or to run the marathon." He laughed as his mind wandered back.

"Eventually, I settled on triathlon as a compromise. But that only lasted three or four years." He laughed again. "I hope your Tom makes up his mind soon," he said, looking over me to the window, rather whimsically.

After another long, reflective pause, he turned and asked,

"So, how's the leadership course going, George?"

I wanted to narrate the last three days of teaching. "Well, Dr. Smith, I – "

"Please," he quickly interrupted, "do call me Ted – all my friends do." He was working hard to put me at ease. I realized that was part of the reason for all the questions about my family. He wanted a relationship, not just a formal conversation about my work.

"Thanks, Ted." With another sip of coffee, I began to relax. "I must admit it's not going as well as I expected." I sighed.

"Why?" he asked, puzzled and genuinely concerned at the same time. "Our first-year class are a good bunch of students and, overall so far, they're doing very well academically. What's the problem?"

"Well, for one thing, I'm punctual, but only a few of the students are. Most come casually into class – sometimes fifteen minutes late! Some apologize, but others don't. I feel offended. After all, I've made the effort to prepare the course, I've come all this way, and besides, there's a lot to cover. The timetable says the lessons start and finish at certain times. So that's what I expect from the students.

"On top of that, I don't seem to be able to get their attention. For another thing, a couple of them are rude and disrespectful. They're gazing out of the window instead of taking notes. Some are whispering to each other. And then, when I ask questions for feedback, they all just keep quiet.

"It's so frustrating!" I added, rather exasperated. "Most times they only write what I write on the board: a few key words here and there. How do they expect to take effective notes like that? And yesterday I gave them some homework to do. None of them did it, and when I remonstrated with them this morning – because it meant having to slow down on what I wanted to cover today – they got all sullen and refused to say anything.

"I'm sorry, Ted," I concluded, "this class may be good for you, but compared with my classes back home, it's terrible! This is the third day, but I've covered only a quarter of what I need to. I'm not getting through, and it's almost as if I'm wasting my time here."

"Well, no, I didn't. I've got so much to get through, I didn't think I could waste time with that."

"No, no, no, George!" I sensed yet another problem coming up. "In our culture," Dr. Ted said, "not only is it rude not to introduce yourself well, it's also impolite not to ask others about themselves. Remember, George, relationships, relationships, relationships! These are not just robots into whom you are stuffing information. They are real, living people, with feelings, likes and dislikes, struggles and joys. They need to connect with you as another human being who thinks and feels as they do! Your failure even to ask their names – even if you couldn't remember all of them at once – told them you don't care about them. They likely then concluded, 'Well, if he doesn't care about us, why should we care about him?' That's 'switch-off time.'" Dr. Ted shook his head at the thought of the difficulty.

"Oops," I said again, now starting to feel totally useless as a teacher.

I think he felt my increasing embarrassment. "Don't worry, George. This is as much a learning opportunity for you as it is for the students," he said, trying to put me at my ease again. "There's a third thing you need to appreciate, too. This culture is an oral culture; the students are oral learners. You see, oral learners learn mainly by listening. The whole way they process and internalize material is different from learners who read. For you, not taking notes seems foolish. But I can guarantee you that the students were listening, and some may even surprise you with what they can repeat of what you said. All they need is a key word here or there to remember what you said."

"Oh!" I exclaimed. I thought everyone learned the same way. "I'll have to research that," I thought to myself.

"But there's more, George," Dr. Ted went on. "When you remonstrated with that student in front of the others, you really did blow it! Again, in our culture, you simply *never* criticize someone in public. And even though it was meant generally for most of the class, the fact that you pointed to and named a specific student means he was belittled in front of his classmates. He was thoroughly embarrassed and the others were embarrassed for him. In our culture, that is rude. As far as they are concerned, you have lost respect as a teacher. It no longer matters whether what you're teaching them is sound and worthwhile. Your credit as a teacher has been turned into a debit, I'm afraid.

And that's going to be a little harder to fix." Dr. Ted pursed his lips as if to emphasize the problem.

"Yes, there are times when you have to tell someone that they've made a mistake, but it's when, where, and how you do it that matters," he continued. "If you reckon the whole class is at fault, you have to choose your words very carefully without fingering anyone in particular. That way, no one feels they are being singled out especially."

"Oh dear . . . So what do I do now?" I asked, feeling thoroughly foolish and embarrassed myself.

"W-e-l-l," said Dr. Ted, thinking aloud. "You will need to apologize both in public to the class and in private to the student. It may also help if I say something to them as well. But that explains the negative response you got about not doing the homework – which, in turn, was a response to yesterday's issue."

It seemed Dr. Ted was piling up the problems. I certainly didn't feel like the expert teacher any more!

"And by the way, George," Dr. Ted continued, seemingly on a roll, "is what you're wearing now what you had on in class?" He was looking at my short trousers, loose T-shirt, and open sandals.

"Yes," I answered. "In this hot weather, this what I'm comfortable with."

"Unfortunately," Dr. Ted replied, "in our culture, that is unacceptable for a teacher – no matter how hot it is. A teacher is someone to whom students expect to look up. Shorts are for outdoors on the sports field, and T-shirts and sandals are for lounging around in the house." He made me blush as he looked at my knees. "That's not proper teacher attire for the classroom, I'm afraid. It means another withdrawal from your teacher credit account." He smiled at me with a nod to emphasize the point.

"I'm sorry," I stuttered, "I didn't know."

"That's OK," Dr. Ted said, patting me on the shoulder reassuringly. "Tell you what," he offered, "I'll come to class a couple of minutes early tomorrow and talk to them before you casually walk in a few minutes late. I'll explain to them that you didn't mean to offend them. You just didn't know.

"But here's what you'll have to do tomorrow," he went on. "You'll have to apologize to start with, both to the particular student and to the class in general. But then take some time to tell them about yourself: your teaching, why you enjoy it, and what some of your students have said about your teaching.

That's not to boast, you understand. It's just that it's important in our culture that people get to know each other so they can connect relationally. The class hasn't connected with you because they don't know you. Be casual. This is an important part of your teaching.

"Then talk about your family. Explain how you met your wife, Shirley, and why you married her. Tell them something about your two teenage children – what they like, how they messed up and you had to discipline them. And some of the fun things you've done with them. What do you enjoy doing as a family?

"And then explain why you teach courses on leadership – why does it interest you in particular? How does studying leadership help in ministry, and what do you think the students can gain from this course? You may think you're wasting valuable teaching time. Trust me, you won't be. Once you've apologized and spent some time chatting informally about yourself and your family – and answered some questions, of course – you'll find the class much more receptive and responsive. And the teaching will go much quicker."

"I hadn't thought about that," I said apologetically. "It's not that the students were being rude or impolite yesterday," I added quickly. "I really think they're trying."

"Yes, they will be, George. That's another cultural aspect to be aware of. But that doesn't mean they like the way you're doing things. They just won't tell you directly," Dr. Ted explained.

"And one last thing," Dr. Ted added as he wrapped up the conversation. "To get the class to think a little more, ask them to discuss some set questions in small groups – say twos or threes – and then ask one member of each group what they discussed. The rest of the class can chip in for a broader conversation. As each group presents, you can be asking questions as a prompt for the class to be thinking about things the students may have left out.

"At the end of the whole discussion, ask for an assessment of what they learned in the groups and how discussing the issues together helped them to think things through. You'll need to constantly encourage them to be thinking beyond just what you say. Get them to think of their own questions to ask each other. To begin with, you'll probably find those questions will have to do with content rather than alternative opinions – because, again, seeming to contradict or correct a fellow classmate is perceived as rude and improper. Get them to share in groups their own personal experiences of what you have been teaching them. You'll find that this will help them remember the content and will be a first step to getting them to think more critically about the content.

"You'll need to reduce your content to give them space for discussion and thinking about how the material works in practice. Slowly, as they practise, they will get a clearer sense of the difference between criticism and critique. The more they practise questions, the more they'll distinguish between negative, critical questions and positive, affirming ones. Sadly, because of our school system, that's a long process. You won't finish the job in one course. But at least, after you're gone, we can continue the work."

"Well, thanks, Ted, that's been very helpful," I commented, standing up to go. "I've learned a lot this afternoon. I appreciate your being frank with me. I'm sorry I offended the students in so many ways, but let's see if I can repair the damage tomorrow."

"We'll work on it together," Dr. Ted said, walking to open the door for me. "It's been good chatting, George. I'll be praying for connection with the class in tomorrow's lesson. By the way," he asked, "why not come to our place again for dinner tonight? My family would love to get to know more of you, too!"

"Well, thanks, I'd enjoy that," I said, grateful for the invitation to enjoy some more delicious home cooking from Ted's wife. "What time?"

"Oh," Dr. Ted said rather matter-of-factly, "about 7:00 p.m. would be great. See you then."

"Sure."

At dinner that evening at the Smiths' home, I had the opportunity to raise a couple of other concerns I had.

"Ted, you suggested this afternoon that I prod the class with questions. I do keep asking questions to get them to think critically, but all I get back is blank stares. I don't know if they don't want to answer, or if they don't know how to. The day before yesterday, I gave them a short assignment – just to see if they'd been following, you understand – and all they did was regurgitate what I'd written on the board. There was no critical thinking or self-expression at all! It was almost as if they didn't want to express their own opinions."

Dr. Ted smiled knowingly as his wife handed around the dessert.

"Our educational system here is very rote-oriented," he explained. "It focuses on students passing exams. So the emphasis is on getting the material.

2

Thinking Theologically about Teaching and Culture

Bob Heaton

Perhaps you believe God is calling you – either short-term or long-term – to teach in a different cultural context. Or it may be that you are thinking that a one-time stint teaching cross-culturally would be a good experience and an opportunity for you to learn and grow. Alternatively, perhaps you are already teaching cross-culturally. However you have come to this point in your teaching ministry, it is likely that you have a myriad of practical questions related to teaching and learning, living in another culture, and those you hope to serve.

Although the practical questions are important, we can only hope to be effective cross-cultural Christians if we grasp the biblical and theological foundations for (1) Christian teaching, and (2) the diversity of cultures and what it means to serve in another culture. Hence, in this chapter, we will explore very briefly the two complementary elements of the theology of teaching and the theology of culture.

All cultures are human constructs. Theology is also a human construct. Hence, culture both establishes or sets the "rules" for living in society and interprets God (and Scripture) theologically within that culture. At the same time, all human endeavour is tainted by the fall. Thus, every culture has both godly and ungodly elements. And our theology – that is, our understanding of God, his ways and purposes – is also a human construct affected by the fall. Even our application of Scripture varies from culture to culture. Indeed, our culture shapes our interpretation of Scripture, and, for the Christian, Scripture shapes our culture. The two elements are complementary. Yet, at the same time, our expectations from culture and our interpretation of Scripture are not uniform across the globe. That is why there are divisions and differences of opinion as to both our interpretation of Scripture and our practice of Christianity in our cultures. Both our culture and our interpretation of Scripture, then, impact our teaching cross-culturally.

Further, for the Christian teacher, there is the added dimension of our understanding of the gospel. The gospel comes not just to forgive sin, but to transform thinking, speech, habits, traditions, behaviour, and culture that is ungodly. The gospel should transform both the individual and the community in the individual's culture. But this can happen for the Christian teacher only if there is an awareness of the transformative purpose of the gospel in his or her teaching. Because the gospel is central to both what we teach and why we teach, we must first explore what teaching – for the Christian teacher – means *theologically.*

Theology of Teaching

We must begin by drawing an important distinction: there is a difference between theological education (that is, teaching theology, or theology *in* education) and a theology *of* teaching. The term "theological education" is often and typically used to refer to the process and content of what is normally taught in seminary, university, college, and even Sunday school. It is commonly understood to involve doctrines, hermeneutics, biblical studies (Old and New Testaments), and a range of subjects under the general rubric of "practical" or "applied" theology.[1] All this, typically, is to prepare students for various forms of vocational ministry.

---

1. The terms "practical" and "applied" theology, although common, are an unfortunate misnomer. The study of theology – God and humankind's relationship to him – must always be practical and applied. For disciplines and departments to be labelled in such ways implies that some disciplines and departments are not practical or should not be applied. That, of course, negates the word of God which is given precisely so that we can practically relate to God. All ministry, by definition and intent, must be practical, otherwise it serves no meaningful purpose. The question must always be "So what? What does this information mean for ministry – that is, practically?" If that question is not answered, it implies that the information has no meaningful purpose for ministry. Hence, all theology must be applied in one way or another.

Such training, of course, is not limited to vocational ministry. Christians seeking to exercise their spiritual gifts in their local churches through, for example, Sunday school, youth ministry, Bible studies, and so on, can also benefit. As with vocational ministry, so-called "lay" people should also be aware of educational issues such as human development, lesson preparation, the role of ministry in the life of the local church, and so on. Crucially, of course, both training contexts must also cover the "philosophy of Christian education" (as opposed to secular education). Although all this might be termed "theology *in* teaching" or teaching theology (in its broadest sense), it is not theology *of* teaching.

Although Christian teachers – and particularly those involved in vocational training – may think theologically about their lesson content (the "what"), it is not necessarily typical for Christian teachers to think theologically about how (or even why) they teach the way they do. The issue here, then, is not so much about teaching theology, but, rather, about teaching *theologically*. In other words, what is the theological basis for our teaching (irrespective of the subject)?

How and why should the Christian teacher teach "Christianly"? How and why should a Christian teacher teach any subject? The difficulty here is that we tend to think in terms of subjects or disciplines. But asking, "How (or why) do I teach X (subject)?," although an important question from a praxis point of view, is actually not the first question to ask. Nor, perhaps, is another obvious question at this point: "What does this *subject* have to do with theology?" That is not the primary question either. Instead, the right question is: "How do I teach this subject *theologically*?" That is, how do I teach this subject with God's purposes in mind?

This is not to say that there is some theological doctrine in every subject, so that we need to teach that as well as the subject. Nor is it to suggest that every lesson must be evangelistic. Rather, we should consider our *teaching* theologically. In other words, what is the *theological* reason for why I teach what I teach? To put it another way: am I aware of *how* what I teach and *why* I am teaching it helps to promote God's plans to transform society? The point here is not so much about the subject – the "what" – since, for the theological educator, the "what" should be clearly linked to our theology. Rather, and in addition, we should be equally clear as to what it means for a *Christian* to teach (any subject). What is the theological basis of my teaching (as a profession)? Why and how should I teach? Is teaching "Christianly" merely a matter of Christlikeness in the classroom? Am I teaching Christianly if I simply start my lesson with a prayer? How much of my Christian *philosophy* (not just what I believe doctrinally) should I, or do I, bring into the classroom – and why? In short, what does "teaching theologically" or a theology *of* teaching look like? To answer these questions, let's explore some other, basic ones first.

- What does the Bible have to say about teaching?
- Who is to teach? Who is to be taught?
- What is to be taught?
- Why, when, where, and how?
- What does God's interaction (the incarnation, the death, burial, and resurrection, his global, eternal plan) with humankind mean for teachers and teaching?
- What is the role of the gospel (i.e. transformation) in teaching?

What Does the Bible Have to Say about Teaching?

If we are going to teach as Christians, and if we are going to understand our teaching theologically, we must start at the beginning. What does the Bible – God's word – say about teaching? Helpfully, there is much to chew on! From the very beginning of the Scriptures, in Genesis 2:16–17, we see God "teaching" Adam about obedience and the consequences of disobedience. God taught Adam by telling him something he didn't know before. In Genesis 4, we see the first murder, which arose because of Cain's bitter disappointment at God's apparent rejection of his sacrifice. Where did the two brothers learn the ideas for their sacrifices in the first place? Someone must have taught them. Then, in response, God questioned Cain's wrong attitude, pointing out that he wasn't interested in what was brought, but why it was brought (4:5–7). Here God tried to teach Cain, but to no avail; Cain *didn't* learn the lesson and ended up killing Abel because Abel *had* learned the lesson! So, from the beginning, we see from these biblical incidents that teaching involves learning something new, and in these cases, as in many cases in Scripture, the key issue is learning right from wrong. An important point to note here is that people needed to learn about God because they didn't already know much about him.

Indeed, as we work all the way through Scripture, from Abram learning about God through Isaac's birth, Moses learning about God at the burning bush, the giving of the law at Mount Sinai, God teaching Israel through the prophets and kings, through to the New Testament, with Jesus's teaching, the letters of Paul, Peter, and John, to Revelation 22, throughout the Bible we find that God is teaching about himself and his ways. Sometimes he teaches positively, sometimes in discipline – and all because we need to know something about him. This is a principle that applies to everyone who wants a meaningful relationship with God. He needs to teach us, and we need to learn.

What are we learning? We should be learning about God, his world, and our place in it – but not everyone does. We should be learning about life – but not everyone does. In short, teaching itself – at least for the Christian – *is* theological because it's ultimately all about God.

At the same time, there are many Scripture passages that speak directly to teaching. For instance, the well-known passage Deuteronomy 6:5–13 outlines, briefly yet significantly, what should be taught, when, where, and to whom. However, we should notice first that, before giving the content of instruction, Moses explains *why* they are to teach: "that your days may be prolonged . . . that it may be well with you, and that you may increase exceedingly as the Lord God of your fathers has promised you" (6:2–3 AMP). Here we see that the Israelites were to teach in order to receive God's blessings in obedience. Moreover, these blessings should not be construed merely as spiritual blessings only; they are general enough to apply to all of life in any context. In effect, Yahweh was saying, "Here's the right way to live; do it this way and you will enjoy life. If you don't want to do it my way, and choose to do it your way, there will be consequences."

The political and spiritual history of Israel, the prophets, the Proverbs, and the Psalms all teach us. On another level, Jesus himself was called "Teacher" (Matt 19:16; John 3:2) and was recognized as one who taught with authority (Matt 7:29; Mark 1:22). Then, after Christ's resurrection, there came the Paraclete, the Holy Spirit, to teach us "all things" (John 14:26). Then there are the epistles of Paul, James, Peter, and John that teach other practicalities of living with and for God. And, lastly, there is Revelation to teach us about the future. So it is clear that the task of teaching is ordained by God, was initially directed by God, and was about him so that "*adam*" – that is, all of us in humanity – could know him and our place in his world.

However, all these examples illustrate teaching from and about God. You might be asking yourself, "Does this mean that I am expected to proselytize or evangelize in every lesson or mention God in every second sentence?" No, that's not the point. The point here is simple: *why* are you teaching? As a Christian teacher, you should teach primarily for theological reasons: God has designed his world to work in certain ways, and we need to understand those ways so that we can understand him in those ways. In other words, thinking theologically about *why* you teach gives a deeper, more significant *motive* for teaching.

What Is to Be Taught?

God's mandate to Adam (Gen 1:28–30) was to steward his creation. Obviously, to do that wisely and well, we must learn how God's universe works: so, what happens when we mix two chemicals together? How do we get iron to make implements? What can we do with wood and other plants? How can the animals, birds, and insects help us? What do we need to be careful with? How do we interact with each other? What does "living" in society mean? How do we treat illness and disease? What skills do we need to do all this work, anyway? And so on. In simple terms, if 2+2 did not equal 4 consistently all around the world, very little in our lives would work. Hence, 2+2=4 is not just a mathematical statement, it's also a theological statement! The universe works the way it does because that's the way God designed it. And, if we are to fulfil our mandate to steward it, we must learn how and why it all functions the way it does. Hence, we need to learn – which means someone must teach us. From this, we can see that the common secular–sacred divide is actually false. Everything about God's creation needs to be learned so that we can learn about God. That means that, from a learning perspective, learning chemistry or mathematics is just as important as learning theology. That's not to downplay the eternal significance of theology, but just to put all teaching into a right perspective.

In addition, because we are *Christian* teachers, what we teach must be linked – at least philosophically – to God's purposes for his kingdom rule. That means we must also teach with the gospel in mind. Unfortunately, many who teach theologically related subjects see the gospel very narrowly as either "preaching" or "evangelism." This is unbiblical. As we noted earlier, the primary function of the gospel is transformation. Hence, a fundamental question for all theological educators must be: is what I teach transforming lives because I have the purpose of the gospel in mind? So, whether I teach Hebrew or homiletics, Greek or Gnosticism, Chronicles or counselling, what transformational difference will that information or skill make in the lives of my students and those to whom they minister? That leads us to the next question . . .

What Does God's Interaction (the Incarnation, the Death, Burial, and Resurrection, His Global, Eternal Plan) with Humankind Mean for Teachers and Teaching?

It should be clear by now that, as a Christian teacher, my subject is not the only issue to consider. Correctly understanding my broader role as a Christian teacher means I must recognize the link between the gospel and what I teach, and why: our teaching as Christian teachers requires us to consider the broader purpose of the gospel.

Part of the difficulty here, unfortunately, is that many Christians think of the gospel narrowly as "merely" the death, burial, and resurrection of Jesus to redeem us from sin. Proclaiming this message is all too often thought to be something that a pastor or evangelist must do, and therefore others are exempt. However, although this narrow definition is important, as noted above, the more comprehensive purpose of the gospel is to *transform*. This is often ignored. Our thinking, speech, behaviour, habits, traditions, and worldviews that have been fouled up by the fall need to be transformed from being ungodly to being godly. That transformation can only begin once we have dealt with our sin problem.

Thus, dealing with the sin problem is just the beginning; it is not the end. There is much, much more to the gospel than just our repentance and God's forgiveness. Hence, the Christian teacher has an obligation to view his or her teaching as transformative, not just the imparting of plain information. Yes, we need the information, but the deeper question is, what should we do with it? Sadly, in many contexts, the answer to that question is simply, "Pass an exam!" Yet, without a "gospel understanding" of how a subject fits into God's desire for transformation, the Christian teacher will miss a fundamental purpose of that information. It should be stressed, though, that such theological understanding does not mean that the Christian teacher must teach theology in every course. Rather, Christian teachers should be *philosophically* and *theologically* clear about *why* they are teaching, that *what* they teach fits into God's transformative agenda, and *how*. Thus, again, the secular–sacred divide is unhelpful theologically. So, whatever subject you teach, as a Christian teacher, you should be clear about how your subject fits into God's broader purposes. Crucially, such understanding will give you a motive for teaching beyond the mere existential and you will gain a sharper perspective on how to teach.

When, Where, and How?

What, then, does all this say about when, where, and how we are to teach? The Deuteronomy 6 passage which we discussed earlier, although primarily concerned with teaching the Israelites about God's laws, emphasizes when, where, and how we are to teach. Verse 7 (Amplified Bible, Classic Edition) says,

> You shall whet and sharpen them [these words] so as to make them penetrate, and teach and impress them diligently upon the [minds and] hearts of your children, and shall talk of them when you sit in your house and when you walk by the way, and when you lie down and when you rise up.

In other words, we are to teach all the time: at home, travelling somewhere, last thing at night, and first thing in the morning. We are to teach at every opportunity, and we are to teach diligently and effectively. Although this was in the context of teaching the Torah, it nevertheless gives an outline of when and where instruction should happen.

Then again, we have Jesus's example: he taught wherever he was – in homes, by the lake shore, on a mountainside, by a well, around a fire cooking fish. His teaching was not limited to a fixed place or time. In short, if I understand the theological purpose of my teaching, I will not see my teaching as limited to the classroom and the set syllabus. Rather, I will see every interaction with a student as a learning opportunity – and thus a chance for growth. I can teach many things in addition to my formal subject – if I correctly understand what God wants me to teach and why. Hence, our teaching goes beyond the subject; it also involves our *time* and *philosophy* about (or theology of) teaching. That is why reflecting on Scripture passages about teaching and then devising a personal statement expressing a theology of teaching is an important exercise.

This helps to clarify our motive(s) for teaching and gives extra impetus to our calling. Why should God be involved in our teaching anyway?

And now to the other side of the coin: theology and culture . . .

Theology of Culture

Learning takes place in two basic ways: through personal experience, or through someone telling us (either through writing or through speech). Either way, what we learn is culturally presented. This is true for the Christian faith. Thus, for the Christian teacher wanting to teach cross-culturally, apart from understanding his or her teaching role theologically, it is also important to understand culture theologically.

If Christ is the Lord yet at the same time I live within the demands of my culture, what is the relationship between Christ and my culture? Or, how do I practise my Christian faith faithfully within my culture? And, crucially for cross-cultural teaching, what does my understanding of "my" Christian faith mean for others in a different culture? The fact is, whatever I teach must be done with my culture as an interpretative base because that is the only way I can understand God and his relationship to me and those around me. Again, though, as with our theology, our culture is also a human construct. Hence, my culture shapes my theology. It also means my culture is similarly affected by the fall. Therefore, I must be aware of my own cultural impact on my theology. Then, in a cross-cultural setting, I must both recognize and refer to the culture of my students if they, in turn, are to make sense of "their" Christian faith through my teaching.

But, first, what is culture? Lingenfelter and Mayers suggest that "culture is the anthropologist's label for the sum of the distinctive characteristics of a people's way of life . . . Culture, then, is the conceptual design, the definitions by which people order their lives, interpret their experience, and evaluate the behaviour of others."[2] They go on to speak of culture on various levels. First, there is personal culture, taught in families, often in the first six years of childhood; this is the foundation of our cultural heritage. But culture, they

---

2. S. Lingenfelter and M. Mayers, *Ministering Cross-Culturally: An Incarnational Model for Personal Relationships* (Grand Rapids: Baker, 1986), 17–18.

viewpoints you firmly hold are completely wrong."[5] It is important in a cross-cultural setting to appreciate that, just as my theological perspective may be different, so too will be my way of seeing and doing things culturally – that is, my worldview. In fact, because of the fall, I might have got it wrong! Thus, my way is not the only way; that what I judge to be "right" and "proper" may be completely different from my cross-cultural students' perspective. Moreover, I should recognize that they have as much right to their view (provided it is theologically sound, of course) as I do to mine. Further, I need to be empathetic and humble towards my cross-cultural students. That is, that they are capable of thinking, interpreting, and concluding as much as I can. Therefore, let me first listen and understand *why* they believe what they believe, say what they say, and do what they do. Only when I am able to summarize an understanding of that, to their satisfaction, will I be in a position to comment and, perhaps, encourage them to critique.

Conclusion

Teaching in any context is not easy. Teaching cross-culturally has even more difficulties. The task can be made somewhat easier, though, by carefully reflecting on our theology of teaching and our theology of culture. What is it about God and his purposes that constrains us to teach? As Christian educators, do we have a good sense of both the narrow (that is, salvation from sin) and the broad (that is, the transformational) purposes of the gospel? Are we clear on why God's desire that we understand these purposes provides a correct motive for our teaching? Are we sensitive to other people groups' theological and cultural perspectives? How aware are we that our theology might be distorted (as was Job's and that of his friends, and Jonah's)? How open are we to consider other people's cultural beliefs and practices as interpretations of their theology? And are we willing to be proven wrong so that we, too, can learn?

These and similar questions are the foundation for the main question of this book: how should I approach my teaching in a cross-cultural context?

---

5. "Edman's Classroom Rules for Critical Thinkers," taken from an adapted PowerPoint presentation, "Thinking Critically," by Jennifer Zimmerman, Assistant Director, Academic Resource Centre, Mercer University, https://slideplayer.com/slide/3932290/.

The chapters that follow explore related educational issues to further assist in answering this main question. The second section of the book gives very helpful practical tips on a country-by-country basis from different regions around the world.

For Reflection and Discussion

1. Consider the story of George in chapter 1. Reflect on how his experience and the advice he received from Dr. Ted may help you in a similar cross-cultural situation. From the material presented in this chapter, list two or three theological questions that still remain in your mind and that you would like to answer about your own cross-cultural teaching opportunity.

2. Identify three cultural practices that have influenced your theology. Using Lingenfelter and Mayers' application of Philippians 2:6–7, how might you approach students in a different cultural context from your own?

3. Choose at least four scriptural passages on teaching and culture. Then, with reflection on the material presented in this chapter, construct a statement expressing your basic theology of teaching cross-culturally. How does this help you to clarify your motive(s) for teaching?

4. Reflecting on the entire chapter, what do you think are some of the most important theological principles that you personally need to bear in mind as you teach cross-culturally?

3

Three Key Cultural Parameters

Perry Shaw

Teaching cross-culturally can be a rich, transformative experience, but it begins with a choice. And that choice is to enjoy and learn from other cultures. The good creation described in Genesis 1 points to God's pleasure in diversity. However, valuing and learning from that diversity can be a challenge: as limited created beings embedded within our own time and place, we tend to filter our understandings through our own experiences. Every culture reflects something of the character of God and something of the fall, and too easily we can become focused on "fallen" elements in another culture while seeing only the "good" in our own. Recognizing that our own culture is far from perfect and seeing what is good in other cultures is the starting point for teaching cross-culturally to become a richly transformative experience.

Along this transformative journey it is valuable to have a few "hooks" on which to "hang" your understanding. While culture is deeply integrated, it can be helpful to examine significant elements of a culture. This chapter will introduce you to three key cultural parameters: collectivism versus individualism, power distance, and thought processing. In the following chapter we will address a fourth parameter: direct versus indirect communication. I have found that if you can grasp these four cultural elements and learn to enjoy the difference, you will be well on the way to effective cross-cultural teaching.

It is important to note at the outset that no community and no individual completely fits into a set pattern. While we will be presenting these four parameters through dichotomistic lenses a more accurate portrayal would be to see them as tendencies, with people at different places on the spectrum. Also, while there are national tendencies there is also a tendency in every context for urbanized people to be more individualistic than those from rural contexts, and globally there has been found to be statistically significant differences between men and women.

This chapter is simply an introduction to a vast field of study, and you are encouraged to read further from the list of recommended readings at the conclusion to this book.

Collectivism and Individualism

> I am because we are, and because we are I am.[1]

The "individualism–collectivism" spectrum refers to the extent to which the relationship ties between individuals are loose or strong. So much of who we are finds its source in the extent to which we see ourselves as individuals or members of extended communities.

Collectivist societies have tight social networks in which the individual's identity is found primarily in relation to a wider group. In collectivist societies individuals corporately have extensive mutual obligations to the group, but the individual can also expect widespread support and help from the group.[2] Communal harmony is considered of primary importance, and there is an emphasis on "shame" and "face": when communal rules are broken, whether by the individual or by another towards the individual, that individual will feel ashamed and humiliated due to the infringement of the collective obligation.[3]

In contrast, individualistic societies have loosely knit social frameworks in which ultimate concern rests primarily on oneself and one's immediate family.[4] In such contexts speaking one's mind is seen as a virtue, and addressing

---

1. John Mbiti's response to Descartes's "I think, therefore I am."
2. G. Hofstede and G. Hofstede, *Cultures and Organizations: Software of the Mind*, 3rd ed. (New York: McGraw-Hill, 2010), 92.
3. Hofstede and Hofstede, *Cultures*, 110.
4. Hofstede and Hofstede, 106–7.

issues with clarity and directness is seen as the characteristic of a sincere and honest person.

The extent to which a person embraces collectivist or individualist bases for life has widespread repercussions. For example, in more collectivist societies hiring in the workplace is done largely on the basis of one's group, even if training or background is inadequate. Nepotism is standard and even seen as a positive approach, the assumption being that you can trust only those from your own group.[5] In contrast to the practice of collectivist societies, individualist societies encourage employment on the basis of ability, any semblance of nepotism generally being regarded as undesirable, perhaps leading to a conflict of interest.

If you come from a more individualist society to teach in a more collectivist society, you may encounter any or all of the following:

- Students may be reluctant to give an individual opinion in class in case their opinion creates disharmony in the community. It is often best not to have whole-class discussion, but rather to have students work in groups answering key questions. The group then appoints a spokesperson who can represent the group's opinion. Particularly where students are encouraged towards personal expression within their small group, the end result can be a high level of synergistic creativity.[6]

- Often you will find that students and faculty are related to well-known Christian leaders, or you may find several siblings attending the college at the same time or students who are related to faculty members. "Nepotism" is a very Western concept and in most parts of the world the practice of favouring members of the family is so normal that there is no term in the language to describe it. You need to be particularly circumspect in any perceived criticism of existing church leadership as you are likely to have students in some way related to these leaders.

---

5. K. Shaw, "All in the Family: Nepotism and Mission?," *Evangelical Missions Quarterly* 49, no. 4 (Oct. 2013): 134–35.

6. H.-S. Choi, J.-G. Seo, J. Hyun, and M. Bechtoldt, "Collectivistic Independence Promotes Group Creativity by Reducing Idea Fixation," *Small Group Research* 50, no. 3 (2019): 381–407.

- Equally you should be cautious of Western notions of "critical thinking." Your students are likely to be members of communities with elders and leaders who are less educated or even illiterate. Your students are at the school to strengthen the community rather than critique it, and consequently a notion of "constructive thinking" is preferable.[7]

- Grades may be perceived relationally rather than objectively. That is, if you give students a high grade they will understand it as "The teacher likes me," or a low grade as "The teacher hates me," rather than as an assessment of the quality of their work. You may consequently encounter local faculty who habitually give very high grades to students, even for substandard work.

- You may experience great reluctance from the school to expel or suspend a student, as such an act would be seen as disruptive to the life of the college community or may have broader repercussions in the wider church community.

- You may find that the school has employed incompetent teachers because they are members of the community the school serves. Equally, many schools have numerous superfluous staff who are employed because of community connections. You would do well to put aside your "professional" scruples and enjoy the relationships that are the foundation of the school.

- Students will tend to look for a patron. Students come from contexts with the assumption of patron–client relationships, and many students will seek to ingratiate themselves with those they perceive as having power, including visiting instructors. You should therefore be extremely cautious of flattery, and view students' affirmation of your teaching circumspectly. Students who are stronger in English will sometimes talk up a foreign teacher as a potential patron for emigration or ongoing financing. This is generally very destructive and most schools discourage the practice.

---

7. P. Shaw, "Moving from Critical to Constructive Thinking," *Evangelical Review of Theology* 45, no. 2 (2021): 128–140.

Plueddemann observes that while individualism affirms personal freedom and responsibility, it also promotes self-centredness.[8] The cure for self-centredness is the strengthening of community relationships and group consensus, but this can lead to conformity and slow decision-making, which then takes one back to individualism. It is noteworthy that the Scriptures transcend both individualist and collectivist perspectives, in that we are seen as unique individuals in community. Unity in diversity is essential to the biblical narrative, and an affirmation of both the individual and the community is essential to Christian identity.

Vertical and Horizontal Power

One of the most widely researched aspects of culture is that of vertical versus horizontal leadership patterns of decision-making. Hofstede and Hofstede have used the term "power distance," pointing to the extent to which the less powerful members of organizations and institutions (including families and schools) accept and expect that power is distributed unequally, the extent to which a leader can determine the behaviour of the follower, and the extent (or lack thereof) to which the follower can influence the leader.[9]

Power distance is pervasive, influencing everything from politics and the business world to churches, schools, and families. For example, more than once I have had pastors in the high-distance context of the Middle East articulate a laudable sense of responsibility for the churches where they serve. In reality this means that they need to be informed of everything, and they reserve the right to override any decision made by any committee in the church. The end result is often a pastor who is always exhausted and has significant health problems, while the lower levels of leadership know they are powerless and have lost any desire to take initiative.[10]

---

8. J. E. Plueddemann, *Leading across Cultures: Effective Ministry and Mission in the Global Church* (Downers Grove: IVP, 2009), 114.

9. Hofstede and Hofstede, *Cultures*, 61.

10. The debilitating effect of high power distance is discussed in some depth in R. Hodgetts and F. Luthans, *International Management: Culture, Strategy, and Behavior*, 5th ed. (Boston: McGraw-Hill, 2003), 161.

These vertical patterns of leadership stand in sharp contrast to the more horizontal patterns of many Western cultural contexts – particularly those of the Netherlands, the UK, and Scandinavia. The predominantly British organization which facilitated our ministry in the Middle East for some years functioned comfortably with no international director, operating with a matrix leadership of seven (perfect, of course!) and a chair who led the meetings but carried little if any executive power. While this was quite comfortable for most of the Westerners, more than one Middle Eastern leader expressed frustration with the lack of a single person with whom negotiations could be made.

A related issue is that of patronage. In many communal societies the leader of an organization becomes the personification of the organization, representing the organization to the outside world, bearing the responsibility of bringing credit to the organization, and protecting and caring for those under his or her patronage. This may include enabling visas and advocating for teachers coming from elsewhere in the world. In such contexts we do well to recognize and honour these patrons who often sacrificially facilitate our work and service.

If you come from a lower power-distance society to teach in a more high-power-distance society you may encounter any or all of the following:

- Decision-making in the school. You should not expect the decisions of faculty committees or even deans of a school to be applicable, as generally the final word rests with the principal or president. You should determine where the ultimate authority lies and ensure that you make no statement or decision without that person's approval.
- Titles. Students will want to use honorific titles such as "doctor" – even if you have not completed a doctorate. If you are older you may be called "uncle" or "grandpa." In the West these titles often imply that you are out of touch and irrelevant. However, in high power-distance societies they are signs of respect which point to your life experience and wisdom. Given that collectivism and high power distance often go hand in hand, you will often find that students will want to use your first name (relationships) with an honorific (respecting power distance): Dr. Joanna or Grandpa Perry rather than Dr. Soberano or Grandpa Shaw.

- Students will tend to keep a certain deferential distance from teachers, even outside class. In many societies the ideal teacher is something of a surrogate mother or father, and students will give you the same high honour that their society expects them to give their own parents.

- Dress code. The English saying "You can't know a book by its cover" is seen as invalid in much of the world, where the Arabic "You know a book by its title" is more operative. In high power-distance cultures your standard of dress matters. For men this may mean a coat and tie and for women modest dresses and skirts, which would be seen as "over the top" in many Western classrooms. A general "rule of thumb" in most high power-distance classrooms is to dress more formally than your students.

- Deference. In high power-distance contexts those "below" never publicly disagree with those "above." Consequently, you should not place students in a situation where they are expected to disagree with you, nor should you publicly critique students as this will be perceived as an attack on their honour. In many high power-distance contexts female students are expected to defer to male students, and if you want to hear the often-distinct voice of women you would do well to have separate men's groups and women's groups in the classroom. You may also observe that younger students will defer to older students, and you yourself may need to show greater honour to older students – especially if they are older than you.

- In high power-distance contexts teachers are often seen as "gurus" whose role is to transfer their knowledge and wisdom to the next generation. In these contexts students may resist expressing their own opinions. "I am too young to know." "My elders have so much life experience." "My teachers know so much more than I do." "Who am I to express a personal opinion when others know better." Joanna will be looking at the issue of "plagiarism" in a subsequent chapter, but is it genuinely "plagiarism" when students naturally see it as correct to absorb and own the ideas of the guru-teacher, repeating them as their "own" in exams and assignments? The contrast is stark with low power-distance situations where teachers are perceived

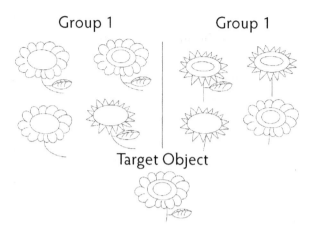

Figure 3.1

These differences exist for many reasons, but the most important factor appears to be the extent to which people grow up in individualist or communal environments. Children growing up in highly networked relationships view reality more through interconnected wholes than through individual details, and certainly correlations are evident between relationality and holistic thinking. Multiple factors influence a relational and holistic emphasis: in general, it would seem that collectivist societies are more relational than individualist societies, rural contexts more relational than urban contexts, and women more prone to holistic relationality than men. Being aware of the diversity that may exist among the group you are teaching can enrich the learning of all.

If you come from a more individualistic and rationalist–empiricist environment to teach in a more relational and holistic environment you may encounter any or all of the following:

in *Advances in Experimental Social Psychology*, ed. M. Zanna (Orlando: Academic Press, 1992), 1–65; H. C. Triandis, "The Self and Social Behavior in Differing Cultural Contexts," *Psychological Review* 96 (1989): 506–20; J. Na, I. Choi, and S. Sul, "I Like You Because You Think in the 'Right' Way: Culture and Ideal Thinking," *Social Cognition* 31, no. 3 (2013): 390–404.

- A desire for lots of practical illustrations. For many people abstract theory is worthless unless it is grounded in life.[16] Western-style systematic theology does not resonate in contexts where lived theology is the preferred pattern for understanding God and his ways – a pattern which is the norm in most of the Scriptures. The use of case studies is greatly appreciated as a means of grounding theory in practice.

- A reluctance to work on narrow research topics, preferring rather to engage a large topic broadly but perhaps with less depth. In the West we are trained to see the starting point for quality writing in the establishment of a clear research question which can be addressed meaningfully in a limited space. A good example would be "What is the connection between Christian unity and incarnation in the first two chapters of Paul's letters to the Philippians?" In many parts of the world this is seen as inappropriate, even insulting to rich theological affirmation. Rather the students might, for example, prefer to look at two or three aspects of the incarnation, perhaps seemingly unrelated. Is there space for this sort of broad engagement in your assessment practices?

- Explanation by story. Communal societies often find stories to be the most effective vehicle for binding diverse ideas into a holistic understanding. Consequently, you may find that in answer to a very specific question a student responds by telling a long and convoluted narrative, only a small part of which is directly related to the original question. The story is the means by which the student is seeking to connect the specific question into its broader context. Likewise, you may encounter protracted faculty or leadership meetings in which the discussion largely comprises a series of stories to illustrate the point.

---

16. H. M. Chan and H. K. T. Yan, "Is There a Geography of Thought for East–West Differences? Why or Why Not?," in *Critical Thinking and Learning*, ed. M. Mason (Oxford: Blackwell, 2009), 44–64.

Reflecting on her own experiences in Latin America, Marlene Enns observed:

> I am learning to recognize the validity of holistic ways of reasoning and starting to realize that:
> - It may be just as important to discern the driving forces behind a narrative as it is to discern the rationality of the narrative.
> - Pushing back boundaries in research may happen just as much through weaving together existing topics with a different pattern and the pursuit of missing relationships as through the pursuit of new topics and of missing pieces.
> - Inter-disciplinary and "broad" research may be just as necessary as intradisciplinary and "deep" research.
> - To point out mystery and complexity without need to come to a resolution – at least not for now – may be just as important as to explain and predict.[17]

Conclusion: Appreciating and Embracing

Cultural diversity can be a source of great conflict and distress, but it also has potential for rich and creative benefit and mutual learning. Effective teaching across cultures is able to both appreciate and embrace culturally different patterns. In this regard I conclude with the following key suggestions which can help facilitate the process of learning and growing together:[18]

1. *Recognize your own ethnocentrism.* We all like to think that our culture is the best culture in the world. But if we are to grow personally and corporately, we must first recognize that such judgments are a matter of opinion, not fact, and that a person from *any* other culture is most likely not to agree with you.

2. *Avoid criticizing anyone else's culture.* Be sensitive to the ethnocentricity of people from other cultures. They, like you, are proud of their

---

17. M. Enns, "Theological Education in Light of Cultural Variations of Reasoning: Some Educational Issues," *Common Ground Journal* 3, no. 1 (Fall 2005): 76–87.

18. Adapted from J. McCroskey and V. Richmond, *Fundamentals of Human Communication: An Interpersonal Perspective* (Prospect Heights: Waveland, 1995), 289–91.

culture. You gain nothing by making negative references to another person's cultural views or practices. Such references will serve only to create enmity and ruin your chances for establishing effective intercultural communication.

3. *Demonstrate respect for others and their culture(s).* If you show respect and sensitivity to others and their culture, it is more likely that you will be shown similar respect in return. Remember: you do not need to like another person's cultural orientations, but you do need to be sensitive to them and show respect for them if there is to be effective intercultural communication.

4. *Be empathetic.* Try to see things from the position of the other person's culture. If you can empathize with others and understand why they have a different view from your own, it is more likely that the two of you can reach some common ground for communication.

5. *Develop a higher tolerance of ambiguity.* If you develop a high tolerance of ambiguity, you are more likely to presume that there is some good reason for what is perceived as strange behaviour, go along with it, and find out later what was going on.

6. *Reduce the level of evaluation in your messages.* Be descriptive: "That seems somewhat strange to me; can you explain why it is done?," rather than "I hate the way you all . . . "

7. *Be sensitive to both differences and similarities.* In intercultural encounters it is easy to become overly focused on the differences between people. While it is important to recognize these differences, it is equally important to recognize the similarities between yourself and the other. Commonality is essential to any form of effective communication, and intercultural communication is no exception. A small number of important similarities will go a long way towards overcoming problems caused by less important differences. We as brothers and sisters in Jesus Christ should be uniquely equipped to recognize in one another our one faith and one Lord over all.[19]

8. *Never forget that meanings are in people, not in cultures.* Remember that people in any culture do not all behave alike. Therefore, while it is fine

---

19. Eph 4:5–6.

context carries far less value. The meaning is primarily carried in the actual words: you say what you mean, and clarity of speech is seen as a great virtue.[2]

Some of the key differences between HCC and LCC are shown in table 4.1.[3]

Table 4.1

	High-Context Communication	Low-Context Communication
Information location	Most of the information is either in the physical context or internalized in the person	Most of the information is vested in the explicit code of the actual words spoken
Precision and ambiguity	Tends to be imprecise, seeing ambiguity as a means of communication	Tends to be precise, seeking to avoid obscure expressions, ambiguity, excessive verbosity, and disorganization
Type of word use	Use of qualifier words such as "maybe," "perhaps," and "probably"	Use of categorical words such as "certainly," "absolutely," and "positively"
Relationship between communication and feelings	Speakers are expected to communicate in ways which maintain harmony in their ingroups, perhaps transmitting messages that are inconsistent with their true feelings	Speakers are expected to communicate in ways which are consistent with their feelings
Dealing with conflict	More likely to assume a non-confrontational, indirect attitude towards conflicts	More likely to assume a confrontational, direct attitude towards conflict

There are two types of HCC: elaborate and succinct.[4] In elaborate HCC societies (such as the Middle East) there is a high quantity of talk, most of which is designed to affirm the other and build relationship. Excessive flattery, repetition, and exaggerated niceties are used to ensure that each party feels good about the other. There tends to be much talk, and the substance is often embedded in passing comments. More important than the management of business is the communication of relationship. East Asians, on the other hand, have succinct HCC: it is in the form and timing of silence that much communication takes place. Very often the most powerful person in decision-

---

2. D. C. Ramos, "High Context" and "Low Context," in *Encyclopedia of Diversity and Social Justice*, ed. S. Thompson (Lanham: Rowman & Littlefield, 2014), 389–90, 492–95.

3. Summarized from W. Gudykunst, "Individualistic and Collectivistic Perspectives on Communication," *International Journal of Intercultural Relations* 22, no. 2 (1998): 107–34.

4. W. B. Gudykunst, S. Ting-Toomey, and T. Nishida, eds., *Communication in Personal Relationships across Cultures* (Thousand Oaks: Sage, 1996), 30.

making is the one who speaks least, and the essence of the communication may come in a slight nod from the major power broker. In all forms of HCC cultures territory is all-important: the person in whose home the communication takes place carries the greater power.

Monocultural people from each of HCC and LCC cultures can easily misinterpret the intent and nature of the other: more than once I have heard a Westerner describe all Arabs as "liars" because they say one thing when they mean something else; likewise I have heard Arabs describe Westerners as rude, arrogant, and offensive because they don't show appropriate honour and respect, and their forthright speech breaks relationships.

Given that the Scriptures were written in the HCC environment of the Middle East, it is not surprising that there is a predominance of HCC styles evident in the Bible, seen, for example, in the indirect approach taken by Jesus in his parables and his discussions with people such as Nicodemus (John 3:1–15) and the Samaritan woman (John 4:7–26). However, it is striking that there is also a call to greater clarity in speech than is the norm in HCC situations: "Let your yes be yes . . . " That said, neither LCC nor HCC can be said to be more "biblical" than the other. Each has its strengths and weaknesses, reflective of both God's character and the fall.

If you come from a society that tends towards direct speech (LCC) to teach in a more indirect context (HCC) you may encounter any or all of the following:

- Students will seek to make you feel valued and appreciated through affirmation and compliments. Particularly in elaborate HCC you may well be told, "This was the most significant class I have taken," or "You are the best teacher we have ever had," when in fact the students have understood very little of what you have said. This pattern is particularly prevalent in situations where students see you as a potential donor. You should not take the flattery seriously, while enjoying the students' desire to have a good relationship with you.
- Be cautious in your use of Western Aristotelian approaches to direct and "robust" discussion. What is seen as clear and logical argument in the West is perceived by many in the Majority World as aggressive and arrogant.

- Because of the LCC emphasis on clear and direct speech, and the HCC emphasis on the promotion of relationships, in mixed gatherings there is a tendency for HCC participants to let the LCC participants have their way, but then to resent it. For those from an HCC environment very few issues are worth the loss of relationship. I continue to be dismayed that in spite of the decline of the church in the West and the rapid growth in much of the Majority World, the agendas of international Christian gatherings continue to be dominated by Western voices. The interface between HCC and LCC participants in the decision-making bodies is no doubt a key factor. As you meet with nationals, be they faculty peers, office staff, or students, listen long and carefully before you speak.
- Rhetorical patterns are profoundly shaped by culture.[5] Traditional Middle Easterners will tend to repeat themselves (as is pervasive in biblical poetry). East Asian students will talk in spirals, gradually moving from the big picture towards more specific issues. Many Africans will answer questions with a long and convoluted story, generally without giving the point of the story: they expect the hearer to have enough intelligence to get the point, or perhaps the point is more about building relationships than developing an argument. Latin and Slavic peoples are often comfortable with more meandering rhetorical approaches, with regular tangential discussion. Each of these patterns finds precedence in Scripture. Enforcing a Western approach to writing may well be unintentionally training students for irrelevance in their ministry contexts. Giving strict word counts may well be restricting students in their ability to write in culturally resonant ways.
- Much of the Majority World remains oral, preferring story to text. With the proliferation of technology in the twenty-first century new generations of Westerners are equally drawn to visual and aural rather than textual communication. In more oral settings students

---

5. S. Black, "Scholarship in Our Own Words: Intercultural Rhetoric in Academic Writing and Reporting," chapter 7 in *Challenging Tradition: Innovation in Advanced Theological Education*, eds. P. Shaw and H. Dharamraj (Carlisle: Langham Global Library, 2018), 127–43.

tend to learn best through material that has practical connection through stories. Image and personal experience are perceived as more authentic than coldly rational logic. In these settings you would do well to choose classroom texts which include plenty of practical illustrations. While syllabi remain a valuable and often required part of teaching, oral learners are unlikely to read the syllabus, preferring you to guide them relationally through the course requirements.

Teaching through Translation[6]

Teaching through translation can bring many rich benefits to students but it also presents many challenges. This section provides guidelines and advice to instructors for maximizing clarity of communication and quality of student learning through the translation process.

Understanding the Translation Process

The starting point for teaching through translation is to understand that quality translation aims to *transfer meaning in context*. It is not just a matter of word transference from one language to another; translation seeks to bring whole concepts from one language to another. Consequently, a translator must personally understand the material in order to translate well. Word-for-word correspondence is rare between languages, and so as you teach you need to find a pathway for getting whole ideas across to the translator and in turn to the students.

A number of common linguistic features are worth noting:

- *Sentence structure* varies from language to language. For example, in Arabic the sentence begins with the verb, while in English it tends to start with a noun as the subject. Other languages place the verb at the end of the sentence. Some languages embed pronouns into the verb. Consequently, it is rarely adequate to give a translator a clause or half idea if he or she is to translate accurately.

---

6. I owe many thanks to Abed El Kareem Zien El Dien, Walid Zailaa, and Rabih Hasbany, three highly experienced translators at the Arab Baptist Theological Seminary, who generated much of this material in a round-table discussion held at ABTS on 16 April 2019.

- Many languages do not have *prefixes and suffixes.* So be particularly careful when you use long words with multiple prefixes and suffixes or create words with prefixes or suffixes. Your translator may need to unpack the complex word through a whole explanatory sentence.
- *Prepositions* are the most difficult part of a language to master. Each language has its own idiosyncratic way of using prepositions. For example, while in English we are "near to" something, in Arabic you are "near from" something, and there are Arabic prepositions that have no English equivalent.
- Many languages give a *gender* to every noun, and in some languages the verb also has gender. In many languages adjectives and nouns need to match in gender. If you come from a language where gender is a relatively insignificant component of the language the impact of this issue may be overlooked. For example, if you say "my friend," is it a male friend or a female friend? The difference in gender may impact nouns, adjectives, and verbs in the sentence.

Awareness of the basic grammatical structure of the host language is very helpful for quality translation to take place.

The Instructor–Translator Relationship

Keep in mind that the translator is the "bridge" between you and the students. Consequently, good translation is founded on trust between you, as the instructor, and the translator. It is important that you establish a friendly relationship with the translator. Having a meal together in advance enhances the quality of translation and gives you the opportunity to talk through the translation dynamics. If you teach a second or third time with the same translator you will discover that your particular ways of thinking have become known and the translation process will run more smoothly. The translator learns to anticipate what you are thinking and where you are going, and this smooths the translation process.

You should stay close enough to your translator so he or she can hear you and you can hear him or her. Try not to offend your audience by looking at or speaking to the translator. Look at the students, not the translator.

When the translator has studied in the field this will also smooth the translation process. If the translator doesn't know the field you will need to be more patient. It is helpful to ascertain the translator's academic background and areas where he or she may or may not be comfortable.

Before You Begin

Quality teaching through translation needs preparation. It can make a difference for the translator even just to have a clear outline of your lesson in advance. This is particularly helpful if you make clear the flow of your thinking and the main words you will be using. The outline also helps you to communicate more clearly and systematically. Translators have great difficulty translating for instructors who meander or who do not seem to have a clear understanding of where they are going in their teaching; the translation becomes disjointed and the audience rapidly gets lost.

Be aware that different translators have different translation styles. It is crucial that you agree in advance with your translator the preferred approach. In particular you should determine the preferred approach to "blocking" the material: some translators prefer to go in sentence-by-sentence blocks, while others prefer larger blocks which are more idea-by-idea.

You should also take time in advance with the translator to talk about the general process, and the respective roles you each should play in the class. If the translator is an experienced instructor at the school you may wish to give him or her greater freedom to play a teaching role in the process. If the translator is younger or less experienced you, as the instructor, will probably need to take a stronger hand in classroom dynamics.

Presenting Your Material

As you present the material in class the most essential principle is to use simple language as much as possible. If you need to use complex vocabulary or technical words you should define or explain the terms you use or offer an alternative term – *before* asking the translator to translate. The definition or explanation can help the translator choose the right word. Giving examples of what the word might mean in practice is also very helpful.

Give technical words to the translator in advance so that he or she has the opportunity to look up options for translation of these words. You cannot expect the translator to have your level of expertise in the field; otherwise, he or she would be teaching the course, not you! Often words that are transferred directly from language to language are of the more technical variety and will need explanation. For example, simply because the European term "metaphysics" is also used in Arabic does not necessarily mean that students will understand its meaning. When using technical terms like this you should check whether the students understand the meaning; if they don't, then you should clarify. There are many biblical terms and names that the translator may not find familiar, especially the way Old Testament names are translated into English. Words with several meanings should be avoided whenever possible.

Speak in nuggets of complete thought. Short sentences with meaning are best as these are less exhausting for the translator than longer sentences. However, don't cut an idea in two: a longer sentence which gives the whole idea is preferable to a short sentence with only half an idea. Translated phrases do not generally convey meaning. Simply translating words does not translate meaning. You should not be afraid to repeat yourself. In translation this can often bring greater clarity.

Allow time for the translator to finish what he or she is saying before you start to speak again. However, don't resume your teaching simply because the translator has paused: the translator might still be figuring out how best to express what you've just said.

Learning a few phrases of the local language helps build rapport with your listeners. However, you should use the phrases only at the beginning or at the end of the talk. Suddenly using poorly pronounced local phrases can confuse your translator because he or she is expecting one language, and then hears another. Or the translator might think that you are still speaking your own language because you have slaughtered the local language so badly.[7]

You need to agree in advance with your translator as to how much freedom he or she has to expand on what you say for clarity. This is particularly an issue for translators who are already knowledgeable in your field. You don't want to be losing a substantial amount of time with the translator doing extensive

---

7. K. Dahlfred, "Ten Tips on Teaching through Translation," Karl & Sun Dahlfred, 16 February 2011, accessed 5 March 2019, https://www.dahlfred.com/en/blogs/gleanings-from-the-field/440-ten-tips-on-teaching-through-translation.

elaboration of your material. On the other hand, there are times when it is best to give a brief summary to your translator and let him or her do the bulk of the "teaching."

Most importantly, be willing to laugh at yourself. Misunderstanding is bound to happen at some point during the translation process, and not taking yourself too seriously goes a long way towards building rapport with your listeners.

Classroom Discussion through Translation

Classroom discussion is always valuable but it is particularly helpful for sustaining student attention and engagement when a lesson is being translated. However, conducting discussion through translation presents a number of unique challenges – in particular, the extent to which you as the instructor need to be involved in the discussion, and what role the translator should play. If you want a translator to play a role in leading the discussion you should make public to the students that you are giving him or her this right.

You obviously want to be a part of the discussion but also want the students to enjoy smooth and engaged discussion. Often it is best for the translator to whisper in your ear the main ideas being talked about in the class discussion.

When a translator is known and respected by the students you can give him or her greater freedom in leading the class as the translator will probably have greater vested authority with the students. If the translator is less experienced, younger, or unknown by the students you will need to take a stronger leadership role in the classroom. However, where a translator is known and respected locally, particularly if he or she is a teacher at the school, you may find the students deferring to the translator rather than to you as the teacher. It is important that you retain your leadership role in the class – for example, in soliciting student responses rather than having the translator do this. Particularly if things are getting unsettled it is your responsibility to take control of the discussion, rather than expecting the translator to do so. Negotiating with your translator is very important as you seek the best means for smoothing classroom dynamics.

You should be very cautious with students who are bilingual. If they communicate with you in your language you may be excluding the rest of the class. It is often better to insist that they speak in the language of the other students, and then to leave the translator to do all the translating. Do not allow a conversation between you and the bilingual student to run without frequent stops for the translator to enable the rest of the students to know what is being said. You don't want the translator left trying to translate a conversation. "Dr. Philip said . . . , and then Morris said . . . , and then Dr. Philip responded . . . " is very annoying for the rest of the students, who will likely feel shut out of the discussion.

What to Avoid

For translation to be effective there are certain practices you should minimize or exclude as much as possible:

- Do not speak quickly. At all costs resist the urge to speak as quickly as possible to cram more in because your time is limited.
- Avoid figures of speech, alliterations, puns, jokes, and any points that depend on understanding the language you are speaking.
- Do not use idiomatic terms or slang. If you find yourself using idiomatic or slang terms you should carefully explain the meaning to the translator. Remember that most translators have studied only formal language, not slang.
- Proverbs and jokes generally do not translate from language to language. The notion of what is funny varies from culture to culture. Many societies have no understanding of sarcasm or irony.
- You need to be sensitive as to what is culturally acceptable or unacceptable. For example, certain jobs are despised in one culture but worthy of respect in another. Animals that are kept as pets in one culture are seen as dirty in another. In particular, "dog" is seen as an insulting term in many parts of the world.
- Avoid illustrations that are foreign to your audience. If you are teaching in a hot, tropical country, that brilliant illustration about shovelling snow will fall on deaf ears.[8]
- Be very cautious in the use of sports metaphors. Check with the translator in advance to determine whether they would be

---

8. Dahlfred, "Ten Tips."

understood by the local audience. The language of baseball or American football will not be understood in most of the world. However, cricket metaphors would generally be appreciated in South Asia.

- Do not publicly compliment the translator. This places the translator in a very difficult situation.

Simultaneous Translation

The general advice given above for classroom teaching assumes consecutive translation. If you are invited to speak at a conference or in a chapel service you may encounter simultaneous translation. Trying to hear and speak at the same time is a very challenging task for a translator, and if you want a quality translation you need to be sensitive to the needs of the translator. In particular, it is virtually impossible to translate simultaneously a person who speaks quickly. It is particularly important in these contexts that you speak slowly and enunciate clearly.

When there is simultaneous translation, you should give as much material as possible in advance. It is virtually impossible to translate a lecturer who reads a paper which the translator has not received beforehand. It is best to have a full manuscript in the hands of the translator well in advance of the presentation. Even if you don't follow the manuscript exactly, the translator will have had time to go through the material and perhaps clarify certain terms with you. This is particularly important for deep and complex material.

If you are planning to take an interactive approach with plenty of explanation along the way, then an outline may be adequate – but even this should be sent beforehand. It is important that you include key terms in the outline and ensure that the flow of your presentation is clear. As far as possible you should seek to follow the flow of your outline in your actual presentation. However, even if the translator has an outline, you need to be aware that if you then read word for word from a manuscript, translation is virtually impossible.

Be aware of the need to minimize distraction for the translator. If you can find an isolated and quiet situation for the translator you are more likely to get quality translation. The best place is a designated soundproof booth.

Some Final Words on Teaching through Translation

Be aware that your time will be cut in half by translation. If you present complex material that needs explanation in the translation you may have even less than half the time. You therefore need to significantly reduce the quantity of material you would normally seek to cover in class. Save time by having the translator read a Bible passage without you reading it in your own language first. Group discussions are a good use of time, especially if you can eavesdrop with the help of the translator. If you use a lot of small group discussion you will lose less time than if you are predominantly reliant on lecture as a methodology.

Some accents are easier for translators than others. For example, translators generally find the American accent easier than other English accents due to their exposure to movies and television. Although people applaud an "Oxford accent," in point of fact it is not as readily understood as the American Midwest accent characterized by a fairly "flat" American tone but with the American articulation of the "r." You may like to enunciate the "r" at the ends of words even when this seems unnatural. The most difficult to translate are those for whom the translated language is not their native language. If you are being translated from a language other than your own it is important that you speak more slowly and enunciate as carefully as possible.

Listening to a lecture through translation becomes boring and tiring for the students much more quickly than it would without translation. And if your translator becomes bored you are unlikely to get a good translation! Consequently, you need to make a special effort to have interesting content when being translated – perhaps with lots of illustrations and stories. When you are being translated you should probably be more animated than you usually would be and give plenty of opportunity for student engagement. A good translator should seek to mirror your animation, and this will give life to the classroom dynamics. Animated presentation involves both physical expressiveness and a more varied tone in your speech.

Be aware that translation is an exhausting task for the translator. It is therefore important to ensure that translators have plenty of opportunities to rest. For example, if the teaching session is three hours, it is preferable to break it into three periods of fifty minutes rather than two periods of eighty minutes. You should also expect the quality of translation to be better at the beginning of the session than at the end. It is a good idea to plan for more engaged student activities and small group discussion towards the end of the session, when the translator is tired.

A tangential but important word of caution: you should be particularly cautious of students who have good fluency in your language. It will be natural for you to show these students a level of favouritism, giving them more of your time and attention, and even subconsciously viewing them as more intelligent or more effective in ministry. This is not usually the case. Consciously try to give time to those with little or no ability in your language, as these encounters hold great potential for significant mutual growth. You should also be aware that many students will see you as a potential target for funding. If they come from an HCC background these students will be very competent in flattery and in telling you what you are likely to want to hear. You will find yourself drawn in particular to those who can speak your language. Beware!

When Instruction Is in Your Language but Not the Students' Heart Language

In many parts of the world education is delivered in a global tongue such as English, French, or Spanish, but this is the second or third language of the students. Particularly in countries whose boundaries were set by colonial powers in the nineteenth century, there are multiple tribal or regional languages, but education continues to be delivered in the colonial language. Even when national languages have been established, higher education is often presented in the colonial language as it is perceived as more global in scope. For example, in India a person may have a local dialect within the state language, have completed elementary school largely in Hindi, then been introduced to English in high school, and finally be attempting tertiary studies in English medium, English being seen as the means for more global possibilities for employment.

When you teach in contexts such as these, most of the communication principles given in the section on teaching through translation apply, such as the need to speak slowly, articulate carefully, and avoid idiomatic speech. However, there are some unique concerns that you need to be aware of:

- Be aware that the language of instruction is not the students' heart language. If the school permits, you are more likely to generate quality discussion if you have students talk in their heart language in small groups and then report back in the instructional language.

- Students are often ashamed of their poor mastery of the language of instruction. In particular they are well aware that they make numerous errors in their written work. Consequently, the temptation to simply copy material in good-quality English is very high. Joanna will be discussing the issue of plagiarism in greater depth in chapter 5. Using oral rather than written assessment, and assessing conceptual insight rather than grammatical accuracy, will encourage students to distance themselves from practices of plagiarism.

- You need to be aware that it takes longer to read in a second or third language, particularly if the vocabulary and writing style are complicated. Consequently, you should shorten and simplify the class readings.

- Rather than requiring students to write essays in the language of instruction, a better learning task may be to have students work together on translating your outlines, PowerPoints, and study notes, and then share these with one another, or possibly in their ministry contexts. Equally you may better serve the students in their missional task by having them prepare ministry-relevant resources in their own native language and assessing their work by having them present their material orally in the instructional language.

Conclusion

As followers of Jesus the incarnate Word of God, communication is central to our calling and identity. "As the Father has sent me, so I send you" (John 20:21 NRSV) implies an invitation to communicate effectively across cultures. The principles and practices suggested in this chapter provide guidelines for that rich spiritual journey in the service of God's kingdom.

For Reflection and Discussion

1. Consider the story of George given in chapter 1. Give two or three ways in which misunderstanding emerged from the difference

between his LCC patterns of communication and the HCC patterns of communication of the students and administration of the school.

2. Describe at least one significant way in which your own rhetorical emphases may differ from those found elsewhere in the world. How might this difference be overcome in your cross-cultural teaching?

3. Make a list of at least three significant principles and practices that you personally consider important if you teach through translation.

5

Challenges of Doing Student Assessment in Cross-Cultural Contexts

Joanna Feliciano-Soberano

In one of the GATE[1] faculty development workshops held in the Philippines, a teacher shared with me his dilemma. One of his students had failed the Theology 1 course twice already, but when the teacher visited this student's church, the student was doing an outstanding work as a pastor and was very much loved by the faith community. The teacher asked me, "Why is this pastor failing in my course?" I challenged the teacher to consider reversing the question to "What is wrong with my assessment so that he keeps failing in my class?" To turn the question back to us and our approaches to assessment rather than directing it to the students makes us more responsible and opens the door for greater learning.

In what ways can we make our assessment more learning-focused? In its simplest definition assessment is a process of measuring the achievement of the intended learning outcomes. As one book title puts it, "How do they know they know?"[2] I would add a twist to this title: "How do we know they know?"

---

1. Global Associates for Transformational Education (GATE) is an organization of like-minded theological educators providing faculty development workshops in transformative learning. See www.gateglobal.org.

2. J. Vella, P. Berardinelli, and J. Burrow, *How Do They Know They Know?* (San Francisco: Jossey-Bass, 1998).

Assessment is "the umbrella term for the deliberate use of many methods of gathering evidence of meeting desired results."[3] We typically use exams, assignments, reports, and academic papers to come up with grades for our students, thinking that we have assessed fairly, but generally neither we nor our students genuinely know whether meaningful long-term learning has taken place.

Assessment has an often unfairly subjective dimension, in that the exclusive power of assessment is vested in the teacher: the verdict on whether a student will pass or fail a course depends solely on the teacher's personal judgment. Particularly when teaching cross-culturally, the problems associated with this subjectivity are magnified, as a cross-cultural teacher may be unaware of the extent to which personal subjectivity and learning measurements are culturally shaped. When our assessment practices are shaped by our own particular definition and standards of student evaluation, students in cross-cultural contexts frequently suffer, sometimes receiving an unfair culturally biased low or failing grade.

Many students sense the "oddity" or the awkwardness of some of our grading requirements, especially in cross-cultural contexts. In collective cultures, students talk about their experiences among themselves. For example, I once overheard a group of students complain that their professor in an online Theology 1 course had asked them to do something that could not be done in their context. Thankfully, the professor revised the requirement. Another group of students expressed in desperation how "one-sided" our assessments are, favouring only those who can actually satisfy the teachers, mostly the "bright" students. While in some cases the students find they can approach the teacher, in other cases the students' respect for the position of the teacher makes it difficult for them to speak up – but they will complain among themselves.

The primary thrust of this chapter is to provide a reorientation to assessment when teaching cross-culturally. Some cultural realities will be identified and brought to bear on our design of assessment rubrics. The chapter also aims to provide some helpful hints on the pedagogical and assessment tools available. On a more spiritual note, the essay endeavours to provide encouragement as

---

3. G. Wiggins and J. McTighe, *Understanding by Design* (Alexandria: ASCD, 2005), 6.

we take more personal responsibility for growth in our vocation as teachers.[4] There is much to learn.

What Is Assessment Really For?

Wiggins and McTighe's curriculum design framework *Understanding by Design* begins with the identification of the desired learning outcomes, and then places the determination of acceptable evidence of learning (assessment) as the second crucial phase in curriculum design, as shown in figure 5.1:[5]

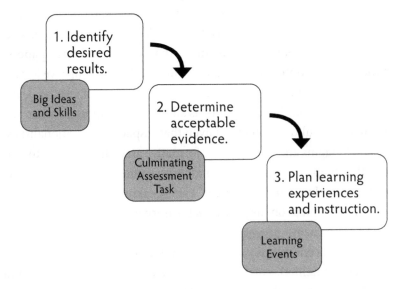

Figure 5.1

There are typically two forms of assessment that we apply in our courses. The first is *summative assessment,* or what Wiggins and McTighe refer to as *evaluation.*[6] This form of assessment is comprehensive and is done at the end of the course as we "sum up" the "score." This form is often used for credentialing.

---

4. For more on understanding our teaching vocation as an act of stewardship, see G. Jones and S. Paulsell, eds., *The Scope of Our Art: The Vocation of the Theological Teacher* (Grand Rapids: Eerdmans, 2002).

5. Wiggins and McTighe, *Understanding by Design*, 18.

6. Wiggins and McTighe, 6.

pointed to the connection between culture and learning.[12] When we are invited to teach in a cross-cultural context, we are often too rigid with the schedules we are used to, rather than beginning with a pause to take the sensitivity-to-context path which will help us enter into the often-unfamiliar context of students.

Culture is the backdrop against which teaching and learning actually happen. Culture is defined by Hofstede as "the collective programming of the mind which distinguishes members of one human group from another."[13] How do we picture the influence of culture on a human being? Consider, for example, the image in figure 5.2 of culture as an iceberg, only the tip of which is visible. Amorim posits that much of culture is hidden and yet "foundational to worldviews and personal epistemologies."[14] When thinking of students in another context we need to remember how different they are below the surface.

Nisbett and his team add their voice to the discussion of the "collective programming of the mind" and identify the specific influences of culture:

> the considerable social differences that exist among different cultures affect not only their beliefs about specific aspects of the world but also (a) their naïve metaphysical systems (from psychology, theories about the nature of the world) at a deep level; (b) their tacit epistemologies;[15] and (c) the nature of their cognitive processes – the ways by which they know the world.[16]

In other words, when we teach cross-culturally there is much that we do not know about the shaping of our students.

12. See, for example, G. Hofstede and G. Hofstede, *Cultures and Organizations: Software of the Mind*, 3rd ed. (New York: McGraw-Hill, 2010); R. Nisbett, *The Geography of Thought: How Asians and Westerners Think Differently . . . And Why* (New York: Free Press, 2003); and P. Shaw, "Culture, Gender, and Diversity in Advanced Theological Studies," chapter 5 in *Challenging Tradition: Innovation in Advanced Theological Education*, eds. P. Shaw and H. Dharamraj (Carlisle: Langham Global Library, 2018), 89–108.

13. Hofstede and Hofstede, *Cultures*, 5.

14. L. Amorim, "Intercultural Learning," Community Foundation Transatlantic Fellowship Orientation Session, European Foundation Centre, 2–4 June 2001, Washington, DC, http://www.angelfire.com/empire/sdebate/TCFF-Intercultural-Learning.pdf.

15. B. Hofer and L. Bendixen, "Personal Epistemology: Theory, Research, and Future Directions," chapter 9 in *Personal Epistemology: The Psychology of Beliefs about Knowledge and Knowing*, eds. B. Hofer and P. Pintrich (New York: Routledge, 2012), 227–56.

16. R. E. Nisbett, K. Peng, I. Choi, and A. Norenzayan, "Culture and Systems of Thought: Holistic versus Analytic Cognition," *Psychological Review* 108, no. 2 (Apr 2001): 291.

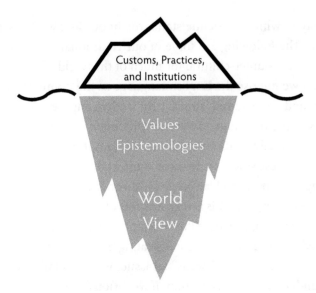

Figure 5.2

Ryan cautions against the preconceived notions of teachers about non-Western students being a homogeneous group, sharing the same learning preferences: as rote learners with a surface approach to learning; as unwilling to participate in class discussions; and as willing to interact only with others from similar backgrounds.[17] "Teaching is an art," says Eisner;[18] but it is also a complex cultural activity in which, as Lee puts it, "all the participants in the inquiry process bring their cultural and theological assumptions,"[19] and we commit "unintentional racism" when we fail to consider these cultural and theological assumptions.[20]

In what ways might we commit "unintentional racism" in student assessment? Which cultural factors vis-à-vis our assessment standards are worth probing? If the way students think is shaped by culture, then the traditional

---

17. J. Ryan, "Improving Teaching and Learning Practices for International Students: Implications for Curriculum, Pedagogy and Assessment," in *Teaching International Students: Improving Learning for All*, eds. J. Carroll and J. Ryan (Abingdon: Routledge, 2005), 92–93.

18. E. Eisner, *The Educational Imagination: On the Design and Evaluation of School Programs* (New York: Macmillan, 1985), 175–77.

19. K. Lee, "Teacher–Student in Multicultural Theological Education: Pedagogy of Collaborative Inquiry," *Journal of Supervision and Training in Ministry* 22 (2002): 82.

20. Lee, "Teacher–Student," 87.

Western way in which we define standards in our assessment schema may be disputed. The following are some of our traditional Western assessment schemes that are counter-cultural for much of the world:

1. When we impose the English language as the dominant language for instruction, and the required language for student engagement and academic work, we become oblivious to the fact that many students who can speak English do not really think in English, and do not use English in everyday conversations. These students are more comfortable and better versed in their first language. Thinking and language are directly connected (as discussed in the previous chapter), and this is why students of other cultures will often have difficulty in decoding a cross-cultural lecturer's expectations. They may also have reduced opportunities for demonstrating their learning and knowledge.[21] When we tell students to "discuss" an issue, we often fail to consider how they have understood the instruction. If we seriously think about this English language requirement when students do not generally use English in their ministry contexts, why do we strictly impose it?

2. When we define critical thinking based on the Western emphasis on formal logic and reasoning, and interpret thinking through Western rubrics for critical thinking (such as Bloom's Taxonomy), our approach to learning is imbalanced. This critique is plainly spelled out in the title of Egege and Kutieleh's article: "Critical Thinking: Teaching Foreign Notions to Foreign Students."[22] In this article the authors argue that international students think differently, and therefore how they perceive our instructions may not be as we intended. Our standard notions may be foreign to them. Nisbett and his team[23] differentiate between the Western practice of formal logic and the Asian practice of experiential knowledge. They contend that East Asians tend to be "holistic, attending to the entire field and assigning causality to it, making relatively little use of categories and formal logic, and relying on 'dialectical' reasoning." This stands in contrast to Westerners who tend to be more "analytic, paying attention primarily to the object and the categories to which it belongs

---

21. Ryan, "Improving Teaching and Learning Practices," 99.

22. S. Egege and S. Kutieleh, "Critical Thinking: Teaching Foreign Notions to Foreign Students," *International Education Journal* 4, no. 4 (2004): 1–11.

23. Nisbett et al., "Culture and Systems of Thought," 301.

and using rules, including formal logic, to understand its behavior."[24] We would do well to pay heed to Yung, who bemoaned that Western content and methodology of theology has been imposed in Asia, with categories that are incongruent with how Asians think about their faith.[25]

3. When we use Western understandings of "plagiarism" to strictly define the expectation for academic integrity, we may well be functioning in culturally inappropriate patterns. A typical Western definition of "plagiarism" is "To steal and pass off (the ideas or words of another) as one's own; use (another's production) without crediting the source; to commit literary theft: present as new and original an idea or product derived from an existing source."[26] However this Western definition is not universally understood or accepted.[27] If we ask our students why they "copy and paste" from sources, we will be surprised to find that our definition of plagiarism is incomprehensible to many non-Westerners! For example, many Asians would respond to a challenge of plagiarism in a way similar to one of my students: when asked why she copied from her source, she explained, without hesitation, that "the book says it better."

Why is the term "plagiarism" an inaccurate term to use cross-culturally? There are several factors. The first factor is the limited English vocabulary of non-English-speaking countries. They think in their language, not in English, and consequently phrasing original thoughts in English is more difficult for them. The second factor is the incomplete instruction provided about plagiarism. Teachers assume students understand, but there is not much foundational knowledge about this Western concept.[28] Third, if we strictly subscribe to the definition provided, we fail to understand the different ways in which other cultures and particularly emerging generations view an idea "borrowed" from an existing source. Emerging generations, influenced by such a barrage of information and content on Facebook and other social media

---

24. Nisbett et al., 291.

25. H. Yung, "Critical Issues Facing Theological Education in Asia," *Transformation* 12, no. 4 (1995): 1–6.

26. "Plagiarize," *Merriam-Webster* online, www.merriam-webster.com/dictionary/plagiarize.

27. M. Zahneis, "For International Students, Academic Dishonesty Numbers Don't Tell the Full Story," *The Miami Student*, 2 May 2017, https://www.miamistudent.net/article/2017/05/for-international-students-academic-dishonesty-numbers-dont-tell-the-full-story.

28. Zahneis, "International Students."

platforms, simply want to make already posted ideas their own. So reposting ideas with their own interpretation is seen as completely acceptable for their generation. For students in non-Western contexts there is additionally a desire to please the professor. "Many students will use outside resources, fearful that they will look bad to their professor if their words aren't good. They don't want to look bad on paper to their professor."[29]

In communal cultures, ideas are shared and owned by everyone. It is worth noting here that in many regions of the world, the practice of "plagiarism" is normal in the wider educational system. In the region of the Middle East and North Africa (MENA), for example, one college's policy on academic integrity begins with an acknowledgment that forms of "plagiarism" are assumed in the education system, and consequently the issue needs to be handled sensitively:

> In most parts of the MENA region the students' previous educational experiences have discouraged the development and expression of their own voices. From kindergarten to university success in the educational system comes from repeating the teacher's ideas and/or memorizing the content of texts. One of the great challenges is to help students develop a constructive voice in respectful community, and part of this is learning how to use resources with appropriate acknowledgement.[30]

4. There is a shared assumption that students from other cultures are "passive learners, quiet in class with an unquestioning acceptance of teachers' knowledge."[31] When this observation is equated with low-level thinking, the assessment is unfair. There is so much in the culture that influences the extent to which students may choose to be silent, particularly where authorities are regarded highly. As we have seen in chapter 3, many non-Western societies are predominantly what Hofstede and Hofstede describe as "high power-distance":[32] power operates vertically, with power from the top rendering the "subjects"

29. Carol Olausen, quoted by Zahneis.

30. Arab Baptist Theological Seminary, academic policy on Academic Integrity. Unpublished document, 2016.

31. C. Loh and T. Teo, "Understanding Asian Students Learning Styles, Cultural Influence and Learning Strategies," *Journal of Education and Social Policy* 7, no. 1 (2017): 194–210.

32. Hofstede and Hofstede, *Cultures*, 61.

passive recipients. Respect for elders is seen as all-important; questioning the teacher may be interpreted as disrespect and shaming to the elder. In this way power distance impacts communication.[33] Hofstede observes the differences in social positions of teachers and students in society and how this has impacted the "differences in profiles of cognitive abilities . . . [and] differences in expected patterns of teacher–students and student–student interaction."[34] It helps to remember that in other cultures, "silent waters run deep." The appearance of passivity does not mean thinking naively, and dependency on the teacher may simply be an expression of respect for the one in authority.

5. Related to "critical thinking" is the Western norm of requiring "academic" research papers for summative assessment, often an individual post-course assignment which constitutes the major portion of the final grade. We have already touched on the problem of subjectivity in assessment. But an emphasis on individual work, the teacher's topic preferences, and Western "academic" standards is often downright unfair for students of other cultures. When I was in my postgraduate program, another international student grumbled privately to me about a Western lecturer, "I have to strive hard to know what the lecturer wants written in my final paper, or I will fail." This comment speaks volumes of the bias of the Western lecturer, and the bias of many of us who were shaped by Western assessment standards. How many students have I failed because they failed a final paper built on distinctly Western expectations? How could the grade of a student become entirely dependent on passing a final Western-style paper when he or she was present in all classes and submitted all the other assignments?

The work of Hofstede, Nisbett, and Hofer and Bendixen[35] indicates the extent to which culture influences basic cognitive processes, including personal epistemologies. The tacit epistemologies of students' epistemic beliefs or beliefs about knowledge, knowing, and learning are like "filters of the mind"[36]

---

33. P. Goleman, "Communicating in the Intercultural Classroom," *IEEE Transactions on Professional Communication* 46, no. 3 (2003): 232.

34. Hofstede and Hofstede, *Cultures*, 302.

35. G. Hofstede, "Cultural Differences in Teaching and Learning," *International Journal of Intercultural Relations* 10, no. 3 (1986): 301–20; Nisbett, *Geography*; Nisbett et al., "Culture"; Hofer and Bendixen, "Personal Epistemology."

36. Hofer and Bendixen, "Personal Epistemology."

which students use in learning spaces. Because these cognitive processes are culturally shaped, as cross-cultural teachers we need to recognize that non-Western students do indeed think differently, not naively. These "filters of the mind" shape even the way in which students use reason and judgment,[37] raising questions about the common demand and standard of Western-style "critical thinking." When we use terms like "critical thinking," do we share the same definition or understanding of our students?

Other cultures thrive on community and orientation towards the other. But the students' natural inclination to work together has not been harnessed in our assessment schema. In many parts of the world, community and familial spirit is very strong, while competitiveness is seen as something foreign. In such situations it is educationally beneficial if we can bring some creativity, collaboration, and flexibility in the ways we ask our students to engage with the subject matter.

One final issue worth noting here is our overemphasis on grades, and our tendency to place a greater value on students' achieving high grades in the short term over students' actually learning at a deep level and becoming lifelong learners. Why have we become so obsessed with grades? Students often end up focusing on the grade and satisfying the lecturer rather than focusing on learning. For students of shame-based cultures, getting a low grade or failing in a course can cause intense shame and pain not only for the students but also for the family and the village that raised them. Looking back over my many years of teaching, this has been a nagging lesson: I have unfairly evaluated many of my students, and I can still see their faces. One way to honour them is to strive to be a better facilitator of learning and assessment.

There are many other cultural realities that impinge on our standard measurements for assessment, which traditionally have been shaped by Western rather than Majority World cultural understandings. All these culturally shaped issues are deep and interconnected. It will be beneficial for our growth as teachers if we begin to seriously rethink the way we do assessment.

---

37. Hofer and Bendixen.

Reframing Our Approach in Cross-Cultural Contexts

Many of us in the Majority World were either trained in the West or received training from Westerners in our own contexts. We have obviously imbibed Western assessment approaches in the way we apply these schemata in theological education in our own contexts. Consequently, exams, papers, and reports have become all too common as course requirements. We also bring our cultural assumptions, biases, and values when we do student assessment. Particularly as cross-cultural teachers we need to test these assumptions to determine whether they genuinely support learning, we have achieved the desired learning outcomes, and the students have learned something of significance to prepare them for ministry.

This is where the Backward "Understanding by Design" (UbD) framework of Wiggins and McTighe, referred to earlier in this chapter,[38] can be helpful in shaping our approach to teaching and learning, especially when applied in cross-cultural contexts. The UbD framework forces us to think of the intended learning outcomes appropriate for our students in light of the long-term needs of the students' future lives and ministries. When the intended learning outcomes have been determined, thinking of "evidences of assessment" brings us to think of pedagogies of engagement, tasks that students actually do to provide us with data for assessment. Our decisions in guiding student learning are informed by the data that we are gleaning from the performance of our students.

Curriculum, in its simplest definition, is the "course to be run, given a desired end point."[39] The proposed stages of the UbD approach to curriculum formation are as follows:

1. *Identify desired results (objectives and goals).* These are the intended learning outcomes for the course. Key questions and ideas in the content knowledge (content of the course) are determined, then skills, knowledge, and values to be acquired and developed are identified.

2. *Determine acceptable evidence (assessment).* These are the performance tasks, or what Vella calls "learning tasks,"[40] means by which students can demonstrate the extent to which they have attained the desired

---

38. Wiggins and McTighe, *Understanding by Design.*
39. Wiggins and McTighe, 6.
40. Vella, *Taking Learning to Task.*

learning outcomes for the course. The assessment methods chosen must be culturally sensitive and educationally efficacious to maximize the possibility for students to provide relevant evidence of the accomplishment of the desired outcomes.

3. *Plan learning experiences and instruction.* These are the ways in which the course content will be delivered by the teacher, and the learning activities or tasks students will engage with. The purpose of these learning experiences is to provide the resources which enable the students to reach the intended learning outcomes. Quality instructional design hooks the students' interest, provides space to rethink and evaluate ideas, and gives opportunities for students to reflect on their growing understanding and give expression to their learning.

The effective use of UbD begins with knowing our students. By gaining a clearer picture of the "who"[41] in their own context we are better placed to make decisions about appropriate learning outcomes and student assessment. The process of getting to know the "who" needs to take place prior to the actual curriculum design and assessment.

Using the steps of UbD, the following is an example of how understanding the "who" is particularly important when shaping course design and student assessment in a cross-cultural setting.

If I was to be assigned to teach a Theology 1 course for undergraduate students in a Bible school in South East Asia, I would begin by seeking to understand the students in their context and the ways faith is expressed in their churches. I would attend a local church. I would take the time to speak to some faculty and staff of the school to understand the uniqueness of the context and the students. I would take the time to get to know some of the students personally. Because of their shame-based culture, most of the students are likely to be reticent about speaking up in class. I would need to be clearly and authentically welcoming through my body language more than through my words. The students generally prefer to be met in groups rather than individually. It is likely that the students will appear accommodating at the outset, but this should not be interpreted as "earning their trust." The truth is that they will be accommodating because they will not want to shame the

---

41. Vella, 32–33.

teacher. At this point, trust has not yet been earned, so the conversation will likely be only at the level of surface knowledge, primarily given to please the teacher. Often the students will seek to say what they think the teacher wants to hear rather than what they actually think or feel, and so this initial interaction should be taken as more relational than informational.

The goal of my first meeting with the students is to get to know them better, and I would seek to ensure personal and relational introductions. My syllabus would still be in process at this time, a draft that has space to change as I get to know the "who" better. If possible, I would divide them into small groups and ask them to talk with one another about their ministries and their expectations of the course. I would have them discuss how the course might be meaningful for them. I would take time to change the groupings as an opportunity for further relationship-building in the class, and then ask them to explain their understanding of "theology." Have they encountered the term? What equivalent term (if any) exists in their own language? The purpose of this process is to explore the students' pre-understandings and the ways in which their cultural background may have shaped their understanding of the concept. In this way the lessons can be connected to and built upon what the students already know and understand.

My aim as a cross-cultural teacher is to make the learning and doing of theology meaningful and relevant to the students in their own context. My goal is to communicate more effectively and discover ways to measure the students' level of understanding. Through taking the time to understand the "who" I am in a better position to build the students' capacity to think deeply about how the Bible speaks to their own contextual issues and the ways faith might be better expressed and shared in their communities. This in turn enables me to make informed decisions in identifying the intended learning outcomes for the course and in determining appropriate evidences of assessment.

Based on the process of getting to know the students I learn the following: these South East Asian students use their own vernacular language as the ministry language in their local churches; they prefer working in groups; they understand content knowledge best through stories and cultural idioms, proverbs, and figurative language, and through examples from their own culture; in general there is no equivalent word for "theology" in their languages, and the concept is more like a learned story of their life with God than a series of propositional truths; their churches are not large, but more like family; and the students are primarily engaged in ministries of teaching and preaching.

With this knowledge about my students and their context, I am in a better position to identify meaningful learning outcomes for the course. As I identify the learning outcomes, I find it helpful to also include evidences of assessment and learning tasks.

Theology 1
Introduction to the Doctrines of Revelation, God, and Scripture
Undergraduate course

Intended Learning Outcomes
At the end of the course, students should have:
- Understood key concepts and questions about the doctrines of revelation, God, and Scripture;
- Identified issues in their own culture which are in conflict with biblical teaching about the doctrines of revelation, God, and Scripture.

Evidences of Student Assessment	
Basic Rubric for Assessment: a. Clarity b. Personal understanding with depth c. Uses Scripture for references when necessary d. Creativity e. Integrative of experiences	Demonstration of understanding of the doctrines of revelation, God, and the Bible by naming cultural issues that contradict biblical teaching. Demonstration of personal learning through feedback loop, debrief, and follow-through.

Instructional Activities
- Discussion on readings about doing theology in context.
- Discussion on a case study about doing theology in another country.
- Giving more specific examples of doing contextual theology.

Learning Task
To be given prior to the actual class presentation:
- Name two (2) beliefs and/or practices in your context that do not support biblical teaching. What are these?
- Choose any of the tasks below. In groups of four (4):
  - a.   Dialogue together, post a paper based on your discussions and share in class;
  - b.   Create a short play that depicts these beliefs or practices;
  - c.   Design a case study with reflection questions.

After each presentation, 2 students will share feedback.
Students will go through debrief and follow-through to discuss further what contextual theology is all about. This task will be presented in our meeting next week. This is a collaborative work. You are encouraged to source added information by talking to people. Each group is given 15 mins for presentation. If you have questions, you can talk to me.

In this example, assessment is used to empower students to think about the implications of theology for their day-to-day life experiences. Asking students to name cultural issues that conflict with clear biblical teaching will be a challenge, placing them on a significant learning curve. The learning task and corresponding evidences for assessment seek to measure the ability of the students to both think theologically and act theologically. The feedback loop, including a debrief and follow-through, provides opportunities for students to learn more about how to contextualize theology in a community of shared appreciation and personal learning.

You will also observe that the evidences for assessment are creative and flexible. Students are given different options for demonstrating understanding. I have asked the students to work in groups based on what I had learned previously: that students in cross-cultural contexts feel more comfortable and confident in expressing themselves when they meet in groups. I have applied three important principles of assessment design: (1) multiple means of representation – give learners multiple ways of sourcing information; (2) multiple means of expression – give learners alternative ways to demonstrate what they know; and (3) multiple means of engagement – give learners appropriate challenges and increase motivation for learning.[42]

An awareness of potential cultural barriers can sensitize us to better classroom practice: providing background knowledge, using scaffolding to build understanding, speaking slowly and clearly, giving local examples, providing a range of opportunities so students can demonstrate their abilities and succeed; and seeking inclusive pathways to assessment through providing different learning tasks and formats, or perhaps different time frames.[43] Note that in the example of the theology course, I did not opt for quizzes or exams, as the learning outcomes call for the students to be able to demonstrate deeper understanding in their own words. My goal is learning, not simply giving a grade. Especially in this cross-cultural context, I wanted to find a way to empower the students to demonstrate what they have learned, to reflect on

---

42. See G. Bass and M. Lawrence-Riddell, "UDL: A Powerful Framework," *Faculty Focus*, 6 January 2020, https://www.facultyfocus.com/articles/course-design-ideas/universal-design-for-learning.

43. Ryan, "Improving Teaching and Learning Practices," 93, 99.

how they are doing, and to plan what they will learn next in ways that are meaningful for them.

In high power-distance societies students are raised to look to authority figures as those who should be respected and followed. Even in these hierarchical contexts students can be guided to greater levels of reflection while remaining respectful of existing structures. Exploiting local leaders as knowledge sources alongside traditional library resources can be a rich means of navigating the complexities of more communal societies. For example, in a hermeneutics course, students might be asked to join a Bible study led by local elders. Given some guided questions, they would jot down their observations as to how a passage of Scripture was being interpreted. The students would also observe how members participated and responded. The observations gained from this field research can be brought to bear on the lessons and readings in class. In this way the intended learning outcome of growth in understanding approaches to biblical interpretation can be assessed through a form of field research that also provides quality training to students as they seek in future to understand and create knowledge.

The key to the whole process of culturally relevant assessment is knowing the "who" – our students. Through maintaining quality ongoing relationships with our students we will be in a better place to guide them in learning that is relevant and assessment that is meaningful. In the process we, as cross-cultural teachers, will also learn and grow.

Concluding Reflections

I wrote this article during the long weeks of community quarantine because of the COVID-19 pandemic. The crisis prompted so many questions, such as how a learning organization can survive and thrive, or what teaching and learning might look like in the aftermath. By the time you read this chapter the crisis may well have passed, but many of the questions will shape our practice for years to come. Over the past few months I have observed a number of seminaries in Asia scrambling to incorporate online learning into their programs. Will this default mode become the new norm? Probably not completely, but we are also likely to see an acceleration of already existing trends to greater use of virtual instruction. Will this chapter on assessment still apply for online and other forms of technology-heavy learning?[44]

Yes, I believe so, because classrooms will more than ever be multicultural. I am already seeing faculty begin to realize that assessment that focuses on student learning requires a lot of adjustments and creativity, and I hope this trend continues. A recent article from Duke University suggests that during situations of high uncertainty, we have the opportunity to view grades differently, including a move towards simple pass/fail strategies, or even developing a commitment to "ungrading."[45] In other words, we can consider assessment from a different standpoint, with increased flexibility. I am hoping that the current crisis will catalyse the re-evaluation of our grading schema, particularly in diverse and multicultural settings.

It is observed that students start doing wonderful things the moment we relax the rigidity of our assessment rubrics and let go of the emphasis on grades. This is particularly the case when you teach cross-culturally. In a hospitable learning space, students are more likely to take risks, collaborate, suggest creative formats and approaches, and reveal important pieces of themselves. There is much room for us to grow in our vocation as theological educators, and using innovative approaches when you teach cross-culturally is a great opportunity to grow as a teacher.

For Reflection and Discussion

1. Consider the story of George in chapter 1. Based on the material given in this chapter, what one or two suggestions might you give George for assessing students in the cross-cultural context where he is teaching?
2. As mentioned in this chapter, "plagiarism" is a distinctly Western concept, and yet the development of integrity is crucial to the formation

---

44. See C. Hodges, S. Moore, B. Lockee, T. Trust, and A. Bond, "The Difference between Emergency Remote Teaching and Online Learning," *Educause Review*, 27 March 2020, https://er.educause.edu/articles/2020/3/the-difference-between-emergency-remote-teaching-and-online-learning.

45. A. Rosenblatt, "Committing to Ungrading, in an Emergency and After," *The Chronicle*, Duke University, 27 March 2020, https://www.dukechronicle.com/article/2020/03/duke-university-gradin-coronavirus-covid-19-public-health-crisis-emergency-thinking-ungrading-pass-fail?

of Christian leaders. Give two or three key principles and practices for nurturing academic integrity in contexts where the copying of other people's work is seen as acceptable or even encouraged.

3. Consider a course that you teach regularly in your home country. If you were to teach this course in another cultural context, give two or three ways in which your assessment tasks and processes might function differently.

6

Gender Issues in Cross-Cultural Teaching

Joanna Feliciano-Soberano and Perry Shaw

All cultures have recognized customs regarding appropriate behaviour and expectations for boys and girls that influence gender role expectations in adulthood. While these customs clarify the proper ways to address and deal with both sexes, the social conditioning of children also includes a level of stereotyping that can devalue one gender in relation to the other. As with the rest of society, schools and teachers often wittingly or unwittingly promote gender bias. Cross-cultural teachers need to be aware of their own attitudes and sensitive to how local gender norms might impact the ways in which they should teach.

Joanna's Story

I grew up on a small island in the Philippines where respect[1] for elders, especially male elders, was a fundamental code of conduct, though mostly unspoken. Filipinos, like the people of many Asian countries, communicate much through proverbs and metaphors. I was oriented to contrasting images of a *Maria Clara*, a demure Filipina, and *ang babaeng mababa and lipad* (a woman like a bird flying low), a prostitute. A drizzle is *binabae*, a feminine rain, weak and slow. A very upset lady would be accused of behaving badly

---

1. More specifically, "respect" in our context meant you had no voice.

because she was having her period or was just *loka-loka*, or mentally deranged. I also witnessed mothers in my neighbourhood who worked hard to juggle household chores and the care of children, many of whom simply wept while silently trapped in abusive marriages. Two vivid memories from my childhood and youth are of my mother, who was herself denied schooling, telling me that she fought hard for her girls to be in school so they could earn a degree. That revelation later spoke volumes to me. I owe her much.

Stereotyping of gender roles was all too common in our local church with its white missionary pastor. I observed that only older men could preach and teach while women sat silently. During communion, men and women automatically sat separately. When some Filipino missionaries (from New Tribes Mission) visited our home, I observed that they were mostly women. They told stories of preaching, teaching, baptizing, and officiating at the Lord's Table up in the mountains, ministries that only men were allowed to do in our local church. These Filipina missionaries had to sit quietly in our church too.

Gender roles and expectations were likewise spelled out in school in many obvious ways. The expected behaviour in class was to "act appropriately as girls," that is, demurely and quietly. The kinds of school projects and chores we were assigned were shaped by gender expectations, with an emphasis on "home economics." Boys were pushed to excel academically over girls.

When I entered a Bible school in the city for my college degree, these gender stereotypes were reinforced with some additional flare, because this time the church and the school interfaced. Men and women were seated separately during weekly chapel time. That "women were to be silent" and woman's subservient role were repeated phrases in the chapel and classrooms with corresponding biblical support. I observed that most students and teachers were male. Male schoolmates often received commendation from male teachers for choosing to be pastors, and as a result I noticed that many male schoolmates tended to acquire a form of "pastor machismo," and that female students were drawn to dream of a pastor husband. I also saw that all student leaders were male; women were never nominated, even if the women were more capable.

I never fully understood the code of silence for women until one time I was asking questions in a theology class with a white male teacher. The teacher suddenly stopped and chided me, "I wish I could zip your mouth and cover it!" He said it with a half "joking" smile, and the whole class of mostly men got the cue and erupted in laughter. I sat there so ashamed and confused. From that time, I sat at the back of the class and chose to be silent. Thankfully, good at taking notes and memorization, I still came top in his exams, which was my other voice. At another time in the same Bible college, another white male teacher casually remarked outside the classroom that he felt led to tell me I would never learn to submit to men. I half smiled and remained quiet, out of respect, not out of agreement. I realized early on that the key to survival as a woman in a male-dominated and conservative Bible school was to be silent.

Clearly, I underestimated the power of social conditioning as a younger lady. The male leaders named and prescribed who we were as women in the world of theological education, church ministry, and marriage. It was not until my graduate studies that a relative who was a brilliant woman journalist and sociopolitically sensitive opened my ears to hear and my heart to feel the daily flagrant references that devalued the Filipina. Beginning from that time, something was awakened in me. I pursued academic training and later earned a leadership position without ever thinking that I could never achieve these because I was a woman.

Stories from Other Asian Women and Men

I (Joanna) am a graduate seminary teacher in Manila, and I have also had the privilege of visiting Bible schools in South East Asia and in other Majority World countries. I have found it fascinating to observe how the play of culturally and denominationally determined gender roles is acted out in these schools. In the process I have connected with many students and support staff. The stories of some women who are now leaders and of some male students provide an image of how these people have experienced gender bias. The themes emerging from their stories posit that there will still be hurdles in the future for both men and women students in theological education. These themes also show the different ways in which men and women have perceived and/or handled gender bias in their seminary education.

You Have No Place or Significant Role in the Bible School

I met two lovely Vietnamese ladies working as support staff in a Bible school in Vietnam. Listening to their stories and getting to know them better over lunch and coffee was a gift. Hanh is older than Lihn, but their stories and experiences were similar. Both of them had felt the call of God to ministry in their young lives.

Hanh told me that she knew God had intended her to receive training in her denomination's Bible school. However, she had to wait for her turn to be accepted because the priority was for male students. With only a small percentage of women being accepted, she had to keep applying until she was included. The moment she was in, she took every opportunity to excel academically, and her disciplined efforts paid off. But at graduation her male counterparts became the choice for ministries in her denomination, and there was no meaningful place for her. In spite of her dire predicament, Hanh persisted again and applied for a graduate program outside her country. It was a very challenging MA program and she struggled to keep up with the English. She finished her degree successfully and returned to Vietnam and to her denomination to serve. As we sat leisurely over our Vietnamese coffee, I felt her frustration. Because of her age, she was already resigned to the fact that her path was to provide support to teachers and students, but she herself could never be a teacher.

Lihn has an edge over Hanh as she's younger and learned to speak and understand English at an earlier age. But the Bible school she entered had limited space for women like her, as though "Men are the priority in this school" was printed at the gate. She recalled that because women students were only a small handful in classes, it was as though they were placed in a "frigid zone" in the classroom, where their names were not called and their voices were not heard. Male teachers, some of whom were white missionaries, dominated the major courses; female white missionaries taught English and writing. When Lihn finished her undergraduate degree, she knew that her ministry opportunities would be limited, and that she could end up teaching only English and writing. But she still dreamed of an MDiv degree and sought a way to study outside Vietnam. When she returned, she was treated as if her MDiv degree had no value, even though not many Vietnamese men had completed an MDiv in her denomination. Desperate for a paying job, she ended up as a member of the support staff. I told her that she was very well qualified to teach in the undergraduate program of a Bible school. In between far-away looks and bashful smiles, she expressed the hope for her gifts to be acknowledged.

You Cannot Preach over Men!

Women preaching can sometimes be a "painful" point of contention that theological education has to reckon with. When your institution subscribes to the "silencing of women," and you have women students in the MDiv program required to take the homiletics course, what will you do? There are gifted women in theological education who have gone through the "fire" because they were gifted preachers.

Anna, a Filipino Chinese now a New Testament professor at a seminary in Asia, shares her story of experiencing gender bias in her seminary education. In her Preaching New Testament course in the MDiv program, her professor was a white male. She did an excellent New Testament exegesis paper. After her actual preaching she recalled him saying, "I can see you have the gift of preaching, but I encourage you to preach among women at church." She pondered, "I can't remember the exact words any more. All I remember was that, while he was affirming my gift, he was also limiting the use of my gift."

This is all too common among women who share with me their experiences of seminary training. Some male professors can well accept the excellent exegetical papers of female students, but not their preaching!

You Are Not Worth Listening To

Another Filipina, Eva, has had to fight her way to be heard when teaching in some seminaries. She has had to explain to her young students why her ministry is preaching. She endeavours to encourage gifted women to preach! In one of our conversations she recalled preaching at an international gathering as an invited postgraduate student. An Orthodox priest "with an intimidating appearance" approached her later and commented: "Thank you for making me realize today that I can listen to a woman and learn too." At first, it seemed like a wonderful compliment for a woman preacher. But after much reflection, it dawned on her that she was actually being insulted. Eva understood how male leaders and teachers can devalue women without sounding like it. Eva laid bare her pain: "He was indirectly telling me that women generally are not worth his time to listen to because we (men) do not learn anything from them."

You Cannot Be a Woman Pastor Once You Get Married

I vividly remember a Korean lady, Yonhee, who studied in our seminary. She stood out to me because she was not the typical "quiet" Korean lady: she laughed loudly and spoke with great confidence, even in broken English. I found it interesting to have a Korean lady enrolled in the MDiv Pastoral Studies program. When I asked her why she chose MDiv, she did not hesitate to say that God had called her to be a pastor. She explained that in her Korean culture, if a woman got married, her primary responsibility would be to her husband. So leadership ministries would not be an option any more. She therefore decided to remain single and dedicate herself to God, because she wanted to be a pastor. She clarified that she could have chosen one of the many seminaries in Korea, but instead she chose a seminary in Manila that was interdenominational and had many women faculty, so she would not feel "different."

Women Teaching Bible and Theology?

The stories above are from women. The stories I heard from men were mostly about their disorienting experiences when they encountered women teachers in Bible school. They were brought up in cultures with strong patriarchal norms, and came from denominations and Bible schools with strong male leadership. If you come from a context where women are affirmed, you may be oblivious to the way male students in other cultures view women in leadership, which may be based on the students' personal beliefs about knowing and learning.

I have spoken with students from Myanmar, Nepal, Cambodia, and Nagaland who have struggled with women teachers, whether Western or Asian. Khine, a Burmese MDiv student, talked about being an A student in his undergraduate degree. But Khine's first year of MDiv study in another country did not go well. Aside from the challenge of learning English, he agonized at having female teachers of theology, homiletics, and Bible. He came from a Bible school and denomination with a strong male leadership ethos. For the whole year, he could not focus and could not perform with excellence in his courses; he was frustrated sitting in class and working on assignments. Thankfully, he reached out to the community of international students. These friends also shared their own challenges, and he felt very encouraged and supported, especially by those who decided to finally shift their thinking – to be open to women teachers. Later, he also learned to appreciate these teachers because these women took the time to talk to him and pray with him. Their kindness eventually meant more to him than their being women.

For another Burmese, Myat, the story took a different turn. He was also a bright student but was not able to cope with the huge disconnect he encountered – women teachers and the progressive teaching methods of some teachers. In spite of the support group of international students and teachers reaching out to him, Myat did not survive his many disorienting cross-cultural experiences. He returned to Myanmar very discouraged and depressed, without the needed degree.

Hartaj was a Nepalese student also in the MDiv program. The start of his story was heart-breaking, although it ended well. He enrolled in a seminary outside his country, but the seminary gave him only a year because his English was not good. He felt rejected and almost gave up. Another seminary in the same city accepted him, but he again struggled, in large part because it was women who were the ones supporting him. Aside from a generous scholarship from a woman, an added disorienting experience was that many of his teachers were women. "How to survive?" Hartaj asked himself. It was also the community of international students who became his companions in the journey. At the end of his program, he beamed at me and said, "I appreciate women."

Advice to Cross-Cultural Teachers

In order to gain a global perspective on key issues related to gender and teaching cross-culturally, Perry contacted women leaders in theological education from all over the Majority World with two simple questions:

- If a foreign male teacher came to your country to teach, what are one or two of the most important things that you would like to say to him about teaching women in your country?
- If a foreign female teacher came to your country to teach, what are one or two of the most important things that you would like to say to her about teaching men and women in your country?

We received thirty-three responses,[2] with many of these women leaders expressing thanks for being asked, and some commenting on how rare it is for their opinions to be taken seriously. The strength of feeling evident in the responses points to the concern and sometimes frustration women leaders around the globe feel at the level of insensitivity to women and women's issues.[3] Please pay attention!

It is important to note that some of the suggestions given below are regional rather than global. It is always important to talk to some women leaders in the context where you will be teaching. But be aware that some women who have been educated in the West may want to impress you as "modern" and tell you that the issues raised here are no longer relevant. Be cautious and err on the modest side, and you will likely be in a better place to enjoy both the men and the women you teach.

Advice for All Foreign Teachers

In many parts of the world women are trained from birth to defer to men. Women will consequently be reticent about sharing openly in class, particularly with a male teacher. It is crucial that you create safe spaces in the classroom so that women feel encouraged to voice their opinions in an open and honest way.[4] It can be very beneficial to have gender-based small groups in which women can discuss their ideas with other women. Rich learning takes place when the opportunity is given to let the class think together about women's opinions or experiences of the topic under discussion.[5] Be aware that women from more urbanized contexts are generally more willing to speak up than those from

---

2. In all of the references in this section, the material is from personal correspondence during early July 2020. For ease of reference the precise dates of the correspondence have not been given.

3. The astute reader will observe that the advice given below to foreign female teachers is more than twice as long as that given to foreign male teachers. Clearly it is more difficult to be a female teacher, and it may be that to survive in the male-dominated world of theological education women have needed to raise the bar on their own self-expectations. Perhaps also there have been foreign women who have damaged the advances which local women have made so carefully and at such great cost. Whatever the case, there is a particular plea to foreign women teachers to err on the side of caution – even if this at times may seem demeaning.

4. Sooi Ling Tan (Malaysia).

5. Atola Longkumer (India).

rural contexts, and older women might not be as shy as younger ones.[6] Avoid mixed-gender pair work. In much of the Majority World female students will be very uncomfortable doing pair work, however brief, with a man (unless he is her husband). Pair women with women and men with men. Even with small group work, it is often preferable to make groups of all women and all men.[7]

Broaden your teaching to include illustrations, examples, and historical characters and events that would be of particular interest to the female students. Assign female authors for reading and quote them in class. Provide female role models; don't give the impression that church history, theology, Bible translation, leadership, church planting, and pulpit ministry are the property of men alone. Local models of outstanding Christian women are valuable both for male and for female students. Do some research![8]

Be sensitive to the fact that in many parts of the world expectations of women continue to be high, and often women students are facing far more stress than men to balance marriage, career, and family life. These women thrive on the encouragement to press on.[9] Particularly be tolerant of student mothers when their occasional lateness or distractedness is directly connected with their domestic responsibilities. Many couples come from quite traditional settings, and regardless of what public claims are made, the woman will be expected by society, relatives, her husband, her children, and herself to carry the bulk of domestic and childrearing duties.[10]

In many parts of the world domestic violence is common, and violent husbands are not restrained by law or even social pressure. If you have a number of married students, assume that your class contains at least one abuser and at least one victim. Be aware that in many parts of Africa (including Egypt) female genital mutilation is still common, even in Christian communities. When talking about the issue in class, you should be sensitive to the possibility that some of your students may have undergone this procedure.[11]

---

6. Margit Schwemmle (Zambia).
7. Grace Al-Zoughbi (Palestine).
8. Karen Shaw (Lebanon).
9. Winnie Chan (Malaysia).
10. Karen Shaw (Lebanon).
11. Karen Shaw (Lebanon).

Advice for Foreign Male Teachers

Among those who responded, the most frequent comment was a call for male teachers to recognize women's intellectual qualities and to respect women as competent and capable. You should treat all students equally, regardless of gender, age, and social status. Let women know that they have a part in the kingdom, and you may even consider asking for forgiveness for the way they have been treated in the past, when so many in the church have undervalued their capacity, gifts, and intelligence.[12] Be aware that many women have experienced push-back if they have spoken up about unfair treatment from men. They will keep silent while being frustrated or even resentful inside.[13] Watch for non-verbals. Do not change your tone as if you have a more fragile human being in front of you, or be patronizing in the way you speak. You help women by treating them as equal disciples who should be learning what you teach and passing it on to others, just as men should.[14] When given the opportunity, many women students prove *not* to be the "weaker" gender.[15]

Your relationships with women students should be very circumspect. In most parts of the world you should not engage in any activity that may be perceived as having sexual overtones, even if these are "innocent" in your own country. Even when cities may practise such physical touch as formal handshakes, it is better to err on the conservative side. Such practices as kissing women on the cheek or giving them a hug would be deemed inappropriate in most of Asia and Africa. You should avoid touching, texting, calling, or meeting alone with members of the opposite sex.[16] In many parts of Asia, eye contact with female students should be avoided. Check with local women faculty as to what is appropriate. If a woman looks away when you give eye contact, do not take this as rejection of you or your teaching. Physical contact between the genders is more acceptable in Latin America; however, even in Latin America

---

12. Julie Bustamante (Philippines); May Ong Bee Teng (Malaysia); Sofía Quintanilla (Costa Rica).
13. Sooi Ling Tan (Malaysia).
14. Myrto Theocharous (Greece).
15. Chiu Eng Tan (Philippines).
16. Mano Emmanuel (Sri Lanka); Rosa Shao (Philippines); Agnes Ibanda (Madagascar).

you should ask local women leaders for guidelines regarding the appropriate boundaries. They will not be the same as in your home country.[17]

Avoid meeting alone with female students outside class time. If you must speak privately with a female student, always stay in full sight of other people; even better would be to have another trusted person join you.[18] Be aware that the #MeToo movement has spread around the world and many women are sensitized to issues of gender justice.[19]

In many parts of the world female students may find a foreign male teacher attractive and "flirt" with him, particularly if he is young and/or single, and from a wealthy country. You should seek to discourage this. If a female student frequently offers gifts or services you should politely decline her offers. Ask a local female teacher or staff member to talk with the student.[20] In much of the world women pay a lot of attention to make-up and how they dress. This is generally an issue of self-respect, not flirtation.[21] If you find certain female students physically attractive you should be particularly disciplined in keeping your distance.

While a level of friendliness with female students is expected, keeping an appropriate level of respectful emotional distance is important. A simple starting point is to give your full name and title, and not simply your first name only. Don't expect students to use your first name unless they can combine it with a title. In much of the world titles are important and they help to build respect for the lecturer and a healthy teacher–student relationship.[22]

Remember that you teach through the model of your life. Particularly as a visiting teacher you should strive to fulfil your role as a model to your students and preserve your testimony before the whole seminary community. Model for all your students masculine service through attentive listening and deeds of kindness. Students notice these as signs of godly humility.[23]

---

17. Orbelina Eguizabal Escobar (Guatemala); Sofía Quintanilla (Costa Rica).

18. Freda Carey (Pakistan); Jane Chuaunsu (Philippines).

19. Lisa Chang (South Korea).

20. Dwi Maria Handayani (Indonesia); Freda Carey (Pakistan).

21. Grace Al-Zoughbi (Palestine).

22. Margit Schwemmle (Zambia); Rima Nasrallah (Lebanon).

23. Chiu Eng Tan (Philippines); Karen Shaw (Lebanon).

Advice for Foreign Female Teachers

It is important at the outset to acknowledge that the role of women in theological education is changing. While there are still many who are uncomfortable with or even opposed to women teaching men, overall there is far less resistance than there was twenty to thirty years ago. A growing number of seminaries throughout the world have female presidents/principals or deans. However, be aware that in many countries the theological setting is more open and egalitarian than the wider culture,[24] and you may be surprised at the places you encounter patriarchal mindsets.

In much of the world both females and foreigners are looked at with suspicion, and when the two aspects are combined in a foreign female teacher the situation can become more difficult.[25] The key is excellence: the best way to silence doubters is through your mastery of the material and your creativity and competence as a teacher.[26] Respect is not automatically given, particularly to a woman teacher, but needs to be earned. This can take time and patience.[27] Part of this process may be gentle but firm confidence and the expectation that students give appropriate deference to you as an invited teacher.[28] Through your own firmness and confidence you will be in a better position to address any existing lack of respect for women students, and open a space in which there is no discrimination but equal treatment and opportunities for all.[29] Establishing authority by being serious and certain of your material is very important, particularly at the beginning. You may need to keep your private life rather hidden from the students, who may be waiting for you to make a "mistake" (such as dating or going for a run wearing shorts). Maintaining a professional look and relationship with all students is required, particularly if you are young.[30]

For some older male students, male students from conservative denominations, or students from less urbanized backgrounds, you may be

---

24. Jessy Jaison (India).
25. Rima Nasrallah (Lebanon).
26. Sooi Ling Tan (Malaysia).
27. Margit Schwemmle (Zambia).
28. Julie Bustamante (Philippines); Jeanie Shim (Singapore).
29. Dinorah Méndez (Mexico).
30. Rima Nasrallah (Lebanon).

the first female theological educator they have had. These students may not welcome being taught by a woman and will probably be sceptical about learning from a female teacher. You need to win them over with your capacity and content rather than trying to convince them with argument.[31]

If you are having particular difficulty with male students, have the humility to ask for help from local senior faculty. Rima Nasrallah in Lebanon tells the story of a number of students ganging up against a foreign female teacher to try to disprove whatever she was saying in class. Instead of listening and learning, they spent their time finding the gaps in her lectures (which, of course, were areas related to the local contextual situation and not related to her core material). Though she was an experienced and capable foreign teacher they made her doubt her own position and often drove her to tears. It took a local teacher to stand up for the foreign teacher and reprimand the students; once the students knew that the local teacher was aware of their behaviour, they stopped.

Someone may challenge you, "Why are you teaching?," so have a gentle and humble answer prepared. If someone quotes 1 Timothy 2:12 and tries to make you defend your right to teach, tell them their quarrel is not with you but with the administration that invited you to teach, and move on. Don't try to prove that you know better about the validity of women teaching, even if it seems obvious to you.[32] Be aware that every gender norm you break can create a barrier to learning for both male and female students. Make change slowly. While you should not tolerate disrespect, you should also be generous and patient, and do what you can to help your students adjust to the idea that a woman scholar/teacher is a normal human being and not a threat. Dressing modestly in distinctly feminine professional dress can help.[33]

Develop something of a "thick skin." Students, both male and female, generally find it easier to joke or make fun of a (foreign) female teacher outside class than a male or local teacher. Her dress code, her body language, her voice, and even her teaching style are often commented on and turned into jokes.[34]

---

31. Havilah Dharamraj (India); Danay Hernández Campillo (Cuba).
32. Sofía Quintanilla (Costa Rica); Karen Shaw (Lebanon); Margit Schwemmle (Zambia).
33. Karen Shaw (Lebanon).
34. Rima Nasrallah (Lebanon).

Be particularly sensitive to the fact that you are not merely a teacher but a role model to female students in your class. You will almost certainly find that the female students want to get to know you better. In your discussions with female students try not to be negative about men in the culture but rather encourage them to seek positive pathways to better use their gifts in the future. Be a role model specifically to women in scholarship, education, and leadership in the classroom.[35] At the same time, don't ever denigrate women who have chosen (or who have no choice but) to conform to traditional female roles.[36]

Be aware of fragile male egos and be careful not to embarrass a man in class. Use positive language; for example, "Your wife is a bright scholar – you must be very proud of her!" rather than, "That's the third quiz in which your wife got a higher grade than you did."[37]

In some parts of the world foreign women (particularly missionary women) have almost functioned like a third gender or as "honorary men." You should be sensitive to the fact that as a foreign woman coming to teach you may have certain advantages over local women.[38] If you are an older married woman, you may find that many male students want to see you as a "mother" figure, as in most cultures mothers are held in high regard, and are the only females many adult men honour and learn from.[39]

Don't expect local leaders to view you with respect. Even if you are highly qualified and respected in your home country it generally takes a long time for a woman to be invited to speak at public events in another country. Only when people see the consistency of your service and the value in what you do will more doors open and you will be trusted with more responsibilities, even ones that have previously been reserved only for men.[40]

In your relationships it is crucial that you remain conservative in how you interact with men. In most of the Majority World it is inappropriate for a woman instructor to greet male students or faculty members with a kiss or

---

35. Grace Al-Zoughbi (Palestine); Smyrna Khalaf (Lebanon).
36. Karen Shaw (Lebanon).
37. Grace Al-Zoughbi (Palestine); Theresa Roco Lua (Philippines); Karen Shaw (Lebanon).
38. Freda Carey (Pakistan).
39. Karen Shaw (Lebanon).
40. Dwi Maria Handayani (Indonesia); Myrto Theocharous (Greece).

hug, even if this is common in your home country. It may be acceptable for the female foreign lecturer to take the initiative to shake a younger male student's hand (since the student will regard her as a "senior"). However, if the man is older, then a nod will suffice unless the older man reaches out to shake hands.[41] In many parts of the world male students from conservative backgrounds are honouring you when they avoid eye contact or any form of touch.[42]

Avoid meeting alone with male students outside class time. If you must speak privately with a male student, always stay in full sight of other people; even better would be to have another trusted person join you.[43] You may find male students offering to carry your bags and books; while you might insult the students by refusing their help, don't let the same student do it all the time.[44]

If you are a single female teacher, avoid at all costs getting romantically involved with a local: there is a long history around the world of single female missionaries feeling lonely, becoming vulnerable to falling in love easily with a local man, getting married, and ending up living miserably. Be careful![45]

Find out from local women leaders what is appropriate dress in public – particularly while teaching. In some contexts you will be expected to dress in local fashion, while in other regions this will seem strange. In some regions it is inappropriate for women to wear slacks. Whatever the case, it is best to err on the side of modesty.[46] Get advice! Particularly in South Asia the norm is for Christian women to cover their heads when praying or reading the Bible in public, and it will normally be expected that foreign female faculty will observe this custom.[47] In most parts of the world tattoos, body piercings, unusual hair colours, or striking nails will probably not be well received and may undermine the credibility of a woman teacher.[48]

---

41. Davina Soh (Singapore).

42. Karen Shaw (Lebanon).

43. Jane Chuaunsu (Philippines); Freda Carey (Pakistan); Chiu Eng Tan (Philippines); Rosa Shao (Philippines).

44. Freda Carey (Pakistan).

45. Dwi Maria Handayani (Indonesia).

46. Jeanie Shim (Singapore); Mano Emmanuel (Sri Lanka); Theresa Roco Lua (Philippines); Havilah Dharamraj (India); Hanane Jabir (Morocco); Agnes Ibanda (Madagascar).

47. Freda Carey (Pakistan); Sajida Iqbal (Pakistan).

48. Danay Hernández Campillo (Cuba).

Above all, seek to be an outstanding model of Christian leadership to both men and women. The testimony of your life is all-important. Your command of the subject is only a part of the message you bring. Your life as a female faculty member must respect the local culture in etiquette, dress code, and relating to the opposite gender. Under no circumstances should you denigrate local cultural standards; rather than being a judge, be a student of the culture. As you listen and learn you will win the respect of local faculty and students, and be personally enriched by your cross-cultural teaching experience.[49]

Conclusion

The challenge of inclusivity in theological education is huge, now more than ever. More and more women in the Majority World feel empowered to receive training and proper credentialing for ministry, evidenced by increasing numbers of women students in many seminaries. To grow as teachers is to be aware of the power of culture and teaching. To be responsible teachers demands self-reflection as to how our lives and teaching are impacting both men and women. It can be challenging, and even angering, to begin to encounter our own biases. But, as teachers, we have a clear responsibility to respect both genders, and create equal opportunities for men and women. It is not your role to try to change the whole culture of those you teach, nor transform the ideas and worldview that are assumed in that culture. However, by understanding how those ideas influence our teaching practices, and perhaps gently addressing in word or deed problematic attitudes, you will be in a stronger place to create opportunities for both men and women to learn.

For Reflection and Discussion

1. Although not specifically mentioned in the story of George in chapter 1, based on what you read between the lines what might be one or two challenges that George might confront in the teaching of women in his cross-cultural class?

---

49. Chiu Eng Tan (Philippines); Danay Hernández Campillo (Cuba); Lisa Chang (South Korea).

2. Choose one of the women who are described in the first half of the chapter. Given the restrictions that have been placed upon her, what words of advice might you give her as she seeks to use her gifts in her local context? Keeping in mind the various cultural issues described in chapters 3 and 4, how might you encourage male leaders in the contexts of these women to better use the gifts and talents these women have to offer?

3. The second half of the chapter focuses on practical advice. If you knew someone who was planning to teach cross-culturally and you had only five minutes to advise that person on teaching women in that context, based on the material given here what would you say to him or her?

4. Try to envision a teaching situation where more traditional attitudes to women prevail. If you encountered a case of a male student belittling or silencing a female student in class, how would you seek to address this? Take into account the ideas and suggestions given in this chapter, and in particular keep in mind the damage that shaming a male student might do to your teaching in an honour-based society.

7

Emancipating Cross-Cultural Teaching

Nicolás Panotto[1] and César Lopes

One of the greatest dangers in teaching cross-culturally is the promotion of a level of "cultural imperialism" that dishonours Christ and undermines his mission in the world. A sensitization to the subtle but profound political nature of cross-cultural teaching opens the possibility for transformative mutual learning in a "third space" where both teacher and learners bring rich resources to the table. In this chapter we have sought to explain the challenge and suggest a pathway that can make the cross-cultural teaching encounter a context for emancipatory learning rather than coercive imposition.

This is probably the most complex chapter in the collection but it is crucial to a humble and empathetic engagement with those we teach. From experience we suspect that some very conservative readers, particularly those whose own particular brand of theology is perceived as "normative," may dismiss this chapter as simply "neo-Marxist rhetoric." We hope you will not do the same, as the issues discussed resonate so strongly with the material given in the country reflections in the second half of this book, and a whole-hearted embrace of the recommendations at the end of this chapter will empower your teaching and enrich your cross-cultural experience.

---

1. Nicolás Panotto works as Associate Researcher at the Universidad Arturo Prat (Chile). His studies include a doctorate in Social Sciences (FLACSO, Argentina), and degrees in Theology and in Social and Political Anthropology.

Between the Dark Places and the Splendours of Christian Faith

I (Nicolás) was once invited to share my experience as a theologian with a group of indigenous students in a seminary in a country in the South American Andes. They had previously heard me talk on the topic of public theology, but in this context I was specifically asked not to deliver more content. Rather I was asked to share something of my personal story regarding what led me as a theologian to link theology with political issues.

Among the various questions I was asked, one struck me powerfully and left me initially in a quandary as to how to respond: "How is it possible to share the good news of the gospel when Christian theology and the church itself have done so much damage to our peoples, especially our ancient traditions?" At a superficial level the question seemed almost to be a rejection of Christianity itself. But this was far from the student's intent. Rather, the question reflected a believer who was caught in the middle of the tension of recognizing himself not only as a Christian in terms of religious affiliation, but also as a person whose identity had been negatively impacted by the very Christian community to which he claimed allegiance. This identity included such diverse elements as indigenous belonging, spiritual tradition, family history, the conflicts of his country, and the sociocultural tensions between Christianity and his ancestral customs. Above all, the student's question reflected a struggle with the seeming contradiction of a faith that was, at the same time, both his framework of meaning and the representation of an open wound from his history.

Personal or communal identity is built at the intersection of diverse elements which are in constant overlap and tension. This is, in a way, what the student's question was intended to make clear. On the one hand, it reflected a critique of the Christian experience, situated in a set of historical, social, cultural, and political precedents which had their origin in the devastating role played by the church in the exclusion, exploitation, and marginalization of indigenous peoples in Latin America. On the other hand, it called for a reappropriation of that same Christian faith, through which it would become possible not only to critically question but also to provide space for rebuilding in light of the historical tensions of the church, with both its dark places and its splendours.

The student's question represents precisely what a cross-cultural teaching encounter should entail: there is an honest recognition of the historic damage done by Christianity and the church, but Christian faith is also seen as the place from which to go beyond the negative consequences. Creative and constructive intercultural encounters involve asking ourselves a number of questions regarding the intercultural experience of theological formation:

- Are we aware of the cultural foundations that inhabit our own personal religious and theological discourses and positions?
- In what ways might intercultural theological formation serve not only as an encounter between different people but also as a catalyst for promoting other possible readings that go beyond any of those involved in the intercultural encounter?
- Are we aware that intercultural theological formation intrinsically entails a political dialogue? And are we aware of the political background of our own theological presuppositions and the impact they have on the intercultural formative spaces that we create?

While the dilemma of interculturality is today an imperative for all types of teaching, it carries particular weight in the context of teaching cross-culturally. In the process of unpacking the cross-cultural teaching experience it is essential to address two fundamental issues:

- How do we understand the nature of "culture" and the impact of the crossing of borders?
- What might be the sociopolitical dynamics that emerge from the "cultural differences" that are born of our educational task?

How we understand these issues need not be seen as a "problem" but rather as an opportunity to promote spaces for dialogue and the construction of new approaches to theological imagination and engagement.

Culture and the Crossing of Borders

Traditional theoretical frameworks have tended to speak of "culture" as a homogeneous whole, based on a set of codes that are specific to a particular group. These perspectives have been found to be limiting and stereotyping, due to the too-close correspondence between territory, community, and identity, as though social dynamics are ruled by fixed general laws. Movement exists, but within the parameters of not very flexible borders.[2]

More recent work points to the need to understand *the cultural* in terms of *borders*, the interpretative spaces that emerge in the struggles generated by the *encounters* between people of different "cultures." Within this understanding "borders" are not seen as the delimitations of a homogeneous body, but rather as porous guidelines that help explain a plurality of people that move between them, and the diverse narratives and experiences that emerge from border encounters. The "border" is thus seen as more symbolic than material, more a basis for understanding the limits of cultural identity than a mere "customs line,"[3] in which identity and culture are constantly redefined.

These "borders" have a number of key characteristics that help us take a more nuanced approach to understanding culture: (1) they are fields of possibility; (2) they determine a logic of interaction between the parties; (3) they interweave symbolic plots; and (4) they demarcate shared cultural aspects. Immediately a tension can be seen with the institutional and geopolitical definition of "borders," in which tariff, migratory, and perceptive and classificatory barriers are practised, which are often at odds with the realities of cultural "borders."

In seeing culture through the lens of "borders" we are able to reclaim the notion of *tension* as an intrinsic dynamic in the constitution of "culture." In this sense, culture is not a homogeneous space delimited by a series of immovable rules or that almost by chance comes into being through invisible processes. Rather "culture" is seen as a space in constant transformation and intrinsically plural, emerging from the tension between the objective/structure and the subjective/particular.[4] Notions such as difference, hybridity, and otherness, among others, are no longer seen as descriptive terms in an attempt to explain evident diversity, but rather are seen as essential constituent logics of cultural spaces.

---

2. A. Kuper, *Cultura: La versión de los antropólogos* (Barcelona: Paidós, 2001), 20–38.

3. A. Grimson, *Cultura y Neoliberalism* (Buenos Aires: CLACSO, 2007), 130.

4. Kuper, *Cultura*, 261–83.

It is important to differentiate between *cultural boundaries* and *identity boundaries*. The cultural boundaries refer to the boundaries of meaning, which emerge from strongly sedimented practices, beliefs, and meanings, while identity boundaries are seen more in the feelings of belonging to a collective and groupings based on shared interests.[5] The borders of culture do not always coincide with the borders of identity,[6] and cultures are more hybrid than the identifications of the subjects themselves.[7] Cultural configurations hence tend to be heterogeneous spaces that come into being through the interaction of the parts that constitute them, in particular the elements of heterogeneity, conflict, inequality, historicity, and power.[8]

The Political Dimension of Culture

The creative tension that characterizes the "borders" of cultures is by nature a political tension. Politics is linked to the construction of meaning, the legitimization of one group's dominance in the determination of sociocultural dynamics, and the differentiation of others within that space. This aspirational antagonism of human societies is the essence of political realities.[9] Cultural "borders" are thus understood as a political space in that they both unite and distance, with different sectors seeking to appropriate cultural pre-eminence.[10]

These tensions of power rarely occur on an equal footing, but rather tend to emerge asymmetrically.[11] Not all the participants in the intercultural encounter possess the same status within the social process, and not all have the same possibility for manoeuvring, legitimization, and influence. Consequently, the sociocultural processes must always be understood within a framework of competences and power tensions.

---

5. Grimson, *Cultura y Neoliberalism*, 138.

6. Grimson, 113.

7. E. V. de Castro, *Metafísicas caníbales: Líneas de antropología posestructural* (Buenos Aires: Katz Ediciones, 2010), 40.

8. Grimson, *Cultura y Neoliberalism*, 189.

9. C. Mouffe, *En torno a lo político* (Buenos Aires: FCE, 2007).

10. Grimson, *Cultura y Neoliberalism*, 63.

11. D. Mato, *Crítica de la modernidad, globalización y construcción de identidades* (Caracas: Universidad Central de Venezuela, 2003), 41–44.

The application of power is subtle, particularly in postcolonial contexts in which the pre-existing imperial and colonial conditions continue to influence current processes towards the revision of norms and practices in line with the understandings of antecedent powers. In this way a form of imperial dominance continues in social and cultural spaces.[12] It is in this process of constant transformation of discourses, ideologies, symbolic objectifications, stories, memories, and narratives that the political dynamics of intercultural engagement are seen.[13]

Colonial dynamics remain particularly in the context of knowledge construction and definitions of social meanings, what is known as the *coloniality of knowledge.*[14] Three elements have been identified in the ongoing though often subtle imperial hegemony of knowledge construction:[15]

- The first is that "sciences" have always been associated with power dynamics. Particularly in Latin America, the construction of knowledge is historically related to the legitimization of situations of injustice and inequality.
- Second, the justification of such power dynamics has provided a way to legitimize and normalize existing patterns of relationships, dynamics, and social stratifications. An advocacy for cultural homogeneity and social hierarchy not only supports the installation of countries, groups, or ideologies in hegemonic positions, but also becomes the sociopolitical lens through which knowledge is constructed. This is seen most starkly in the dominance and assumed superiority of Western forms of education in both content and methodology.

---

12. J. K. de Alva, "La poscolonización de la experiencia (latino)americana: Una reconsideración de los términos 'colonialismo,' 'poscolonialismo' y 'mestizaje,'" in *Repensando la subalternidad,* ed. P. Sandoval (Lima: IEP, 2009), 109.

13. M. Jackson, *Minima Ethnographica: Intersubjectivity and the Anthropological Project* (Chicago: University of Chicago Press, 1998).

14. E. Lander, *La colonialidad del saber: Eurocentrismo y ciencias sociales* (Buenos Aires: CICCUS/CLACSO, 2011).

15. N. Panotto, "Rostros de lo divino y construcción del ethos socio-político: relación entre teología y antropología en el estudio del campo religioso; el caso del pentecostalismo en Argentina," *Debates do Ner, Porto Alegre* 16, no. 28 (2015): 69–97.

- The third holds a more positive potential. In the face of epistemological dominance alternative ways of resistance can generate new
constructions of sense and knowledge between the cracks of the
same "system" and a creative "border thinking"[16] can emerge that
holds potential for transformational understanding and mutuality.
In other words, educational processes are potentially contexts for
engaging tensions and conflicts, to the extent that they promote the
plurality of knowledge and know-how. When this "third space"[17] is
encouraged, new discourses, knowledge, and perspectives are born
from the encounter that allow us to build something innovative –
sometimes embracing what we bring as teachers, but at other times
challenging the framework of our assumed expertise.

Emancipating Cross-Cultural Teaching[18]

A recognition of the fundamentally political nature of teaching cross-culturally
challenges the cross-cultural teacher to seek pathways within the "third
space" towards creative and transformative mutual learning. A helpful way
of understanding potential pathways is through the notion of empowering
local emancipatory knowledges. As local indigenous content, methodologies,
or epistemologies are encouraged the doors are opened to gaining "insights
into relations of domination that may appear to express 'natural' laws, but can
potentially be changed."[19]

Each element takes us deeper into promoting contextually relevant and
significant learning: *local* sensitizes us to the anthropological dimension of
learning, *knowledges* points to the plurality of educational understandings
that need to be embraced, and *emancipatory* provides us with critical eyes
for the process. Although an emphasis is placed on the *critical*, both the

---

16. W. Mignolo, *Desobediencia epistémica* (Buenos Aires: Ediciones del Signo, 2010).

17. H. Bahbah, *Nuevas minorías, nuevos derechos* (Buenos Aires: Siglo XXI, 2010), 79–87.

18. This section includes material adapted from C. Lopes, "Nurturing Emancipatory Local
Knowledges," in *Challenging Tradition: Innovation in Advanced Theological Education*, eds. P.
Shaw and H. Dharamraj (Carlisle: Langham Global Library, 2018), 145–65.

19. R. A. Morrow and C. Alberto Torres, *Reading Freire and Habermas: Critical Pedagogy and
Transformative Social Change* (New York: Teachers College, 2002), 48.

anthropological and the educational components are crucial: *knowledges* will be actually *emancipatory* only if they are *local*. Let's explore each of these three dimensions.

Focusing on the Local: The Anthropological Approach

At the centre of this approach is the figure of the cross-cultural teacher. The aim is to enable a cleaner communication process in intercultural educational exchanges in order to maximize the potential of the "content" being taught. Key questions that are raised in this approach include the following: how can a teacher better communicate across cultural lines and "transcend cultural borders"?[20] What kinds of cultural adjustments can be made in order to maximize the retention of knowledge? What kinds of "cultural global competencies" are necessary for teachers?[21]

A deeper level of cross-cultural sensitivity delves into the extent to which rhetorical patterns relate to language.[22] Kaplan, among others, explores the idea that thought and grammar are related in a given language, and therefore an "academic sophistication" will not only sound and read differently in different languages, but will also be structured differently,[23] and will affect even a seemingly simple issue, such as the appropriate time a student should wait before taking his or her turn in classroom discussions, the role of silence, and the extent to which interrupting another speaker is accepted or even approved.[24]

However, if a teacher simply remains at an anthropological level at the expense of the other dimensions, there is a dangerous implicit assumption,

20. O. J. Jegede and G. S. Aikenhead, "Transcending Cultural Borders: Implications for Science Teaching," *Research in Science & Technological Education* 17, no. 1 (1999): 45–66.

21. R. Quezada and C. Alfaro, "Developing Biliteracy Teachers: Moving Toward Culture and Linguistic Global Competence in Teacher Education," in *Intercultural Student Teaching: A Bridge to Global Competence*, eds. K. Cushner and S. Brennan (Lanham: Rowman & Littlefield Education, 2007), 57–87; and G. Hofstede, "Cultural Differences in Teaching and Learning," *International Journal of Intercultural Relations* 10, no. 3 (1986): 301–20.

22. Stephanie Black deals in greater depth with this topic in "Scholarship in Our Own Words: Intercultural Rhetoric in Academic Writing and Reporting," in Shaw and Dharamraj, *Challenging Tradition*, 127–43. Also see Perry's discussion of this topic in chapter 4 of the current collection.

23. R. Kaplan, "Cultural Thought-Patterns in Inter-Cultural Education," in *Landmark Essays on ESL Writing*, eds. T. J. Silva and P. K. Matsuda (Mahwah: Lawrence Erlbaum Associates, 2001), 11–26.

24. I. Nakane, "Negotiating Silence and Speech in the Classroom," *Multilingua* 24, no. 1 (part 2) (2005): 77.

and that is the unconscious perception of theological knowledge as something that has already been *produced* and is somehow ready. The teacher's task would therefore be merely to "repack" it properly for the target cultural context, and the students' task would be simply to *reproduce* such knowledge. In the next sections we will discuss if this is really enough.

In summary, the anthropological approach focuses on the *local* aspects of cultural issues in a narrower sense, stresses the role of teachers in their dealings with students from a different cultural background, and has as its central concern the proper communication of the content.

Building Knowledges: The Educational Approach

The focus here is on creating educational experiences that not only reproduce, but actually *produce* knowledge. Particularly meaningful for our reflection on cross-cultural theological education is Amstutz's proposal of "adjustments" that are needed in order to provide meaningful learning experiences for learners coming from diverse cultural settings.[25] Such adjustments are not only in *teaching* but also in *learning*, through ideas such as helping students question theories according to their own cultural experiences, promoting non-dichotomous ways of knowing, seeking alternative forms of learning, and varying strategies regarding assignments.

Another rich example of an inquiry on the interplay between culture and education is Sharan Merriam's volume *Non-Western Perspectives on Learning and Knowing*.[26] The book includes contributors who address the manner in which some large cultural formations or worldviews approach learning. Merriam concludes the collection by summarizing key non-Western educational approaches that help learners build meaningful knowledges. These strategies (1) are more *holistic* in their approach to human beings, as opposed to the more *rationalistic* approach in the West; (2) evidence a concern for a deeper *integration* between knowledge and the real world, as opposed to the more *dualistic* view in the West; (3) are *collectivist*, concerned with the whole

---

25. D. D. Amstutz, "Adult Learning: Moving toward More Inclusive Theories and Practices," *New Directions for Adult & Continuing Education* 1999, no. 82 (1999): 19.

26. S. B. Merriam and Associates, *Non-Western Perspectives on Learning and Knowing* (Malabar: Krieger, 2007).

community, as opposed to Western *individualism*; and (4) consider people as a valuable *source* of knowledge, with a consequent narrative and oral approach to knowing, in a certain opposition to the more *descriptive and written* approach in the West.[27]

It is important to highlight that there is a deeper layer in this educational approach than what is found in a purely anthropological approach. In theological education settings, the educational approach assumes that the simple reproduction or contextualization of theological knowledge coming from the West is not enough. Rather, the educational approach stresses the role of students in building new local knowledges, in opposition to a practice which simply proposes the "localization" of established knowledges.

However, even this deeper level of the educational approach may be built on the assumption that knowledge and education are value-free, that they are sociologically neutral. Consequently, we need to wrestle at a deeper critical level to attain approaches that are genuinely emancipatory.

Local Knowledges That Are Emancipatory: The Critical Approach

The first two approaches described in this chapter tend to dialogue, respectively, with anthropology and educational theories. The emancipatory approach dialogues more with sociology and political science, especially from the perspective of critical theory and, more recently, postcolonial studies.[28]

---

27. For a variety of approaches that seek to promote creative and integrative approaches to theological education, see Shaw and Dharamraj, *Challenging Tradition*, and in particular P. Clark's chapter, "Pathways of Integration for Theological Knowledge," 189–207.

28. The word "critical" used to describe this third approach is an indication of the inputs this section receives from critical theory and critical pedagogy. The first is defined by N. Blake and J. Masschelein ("Critical Theory and Critical Pedagogy," in *The Blackwell Guide to the Philosophy of Education*, eds. N. Blake et al. [Malden: Blackwell, 2003], 38), when they examine the interface between critical theory and education "as the tradition of thought associated with the Frankfurt School of philosophy and social theory, which originated in the late 1920's," and focuses on issues such as liberation from false consciousness and ideology critique. Critical pedagogy, in its turn, "asserts that learning, like all other social interactions, is a political act with political purposes. It rests on a belief that it is in the very nature of pedagogy that it is a political, moral, and critical practice" (J. McArthur, "Time to Look Anew: Critical Pedagogy and Disciplines within Higher Education," *Studies in Higher Education* 35, no. 3 [2010]: 301–2).

Nicolás's discussion in the first sections of this chapter points to the subtle but powerful ways in which traditional intercultural approaches fall short in their efforts. As Gorski warns us,

> good intentions are not enough . . . The practice of intercultural education, when not committed first and foremost to equity and social justice . . . might, in the best case, result in heightened cross-group awareness at an individual level. But in many cases this practice is domination . . . [and] is a tool for the maintenance of marginalization.[29]

A starting point is often to include different ethnic and cultural perspectives in the curriculum. However, even these kinds of educational experience may be "little more than a way to promote self-esteem, or simply as a curriculum that substitutes one set of heroes for another."[30]

A *critical* approach to exchanges in cross-cultural theological education not only asks for a variety of content in the curricular menu and for cultural sensitivity in classroom exchanges. At a deeper level, genuinely emancipatory education reaches to more fundamental themes, such as fair access to education, matters of equality and inequality in terms of gender and ethnicity, social justice, achievement gaps, and especially reflection on subaltern knowledges and epistemologies. The challenge is thereby taken further than the issue of "content to be taught."

Advocating this critical dimension includes the assumption that the frontiers between producing and "consuming" theology should be dissolved. Learners are theologians, and it is crucial that the "content" of their learning involves not only static theological objects that should be somehow memorized, but rather critical reflection on *whose* theology ends up enshrined as orthodoxy, and training in *how to do theology*.

It is fair to say that the critical approach is more commonly adopted by those writing and teaching in contexts where participants see themselves as oppressed, as with the indigenous student who opened our chapter. In these

---

29. P. C. Gorski, "Good Intentions Are Not Enough: A Decolonizing Intercultural Education," *Intercultural Education* 19, no. 6 (2008): 519–20.

30. S. M. Nieto, "Profoundly Multicultural Questions," *Educational Leadership* 60, no. 4 (2002): 5.

contexts, expressions such as oppression, liberation, ideology, hegemony, and structure are seen as necessary language for expressing need and concern in striving after the emancipation of "subjugated knowledges."[31] Even while we say this, it is probable that for many evangelicals, even in Majority World contexts, such discussions will be dismissed as being situated in the field of radical theologies far away from evangelical orthodoxy – whatever that is! However, despite their co-optation by certain ideologies and radical theologies, categories such as oppression, liberation, and justice are simply biblical.[32]

A critical approach, therefore, encompasses the anthropological and educational, adding a concern that goes deeper into power relations by giving voice to the silenced. However, it is important to stress that a critical approach is not sufficient in itself. If it lacks the cultural sensitivity espoused by the anthropological dimension, a critical approach may paradoxically further a situation of oppression and hinder people from developing a free consciousness or from being "transformed by the renewing of your mind" (Rom 12:2). Similarly, if actions inspired by a critical approach lack an educational dimension in the terms we describe here, another paradoxical effect may take place: students may be simply invited to *uncritically* embrace ideas and formulations articulated by a professor in another context. For effective cross-cultural teaching to promote emancipatory learning, all of the anthropological, educational, and critical dimensions must be seen as complementary and mutually dependent.

Emancipatory Teaching Practices

How might committed cross-cultural teachers take seriously the political nature of the intercultural educational encounter, and promote within their

---

31. For Foucault, subjugated knowledges are "a whole set of knowledges that have been disqualified as inadequate to their task or insufficiently elaborated: naïve knowledges, located low down on the hierarchy, beneath the required level of cognition or scientificity . . . It is through the reappearance of this knowledge, of these local popular knowledges, these disqualified knowledges, that criticism performs its work" (M. Foucault, *Power/Knowledge: Selected Interviews and Other Writings, 1972–1977* [Brighton: Harvester, 1980], 81–82).

32. K. Higuera-Smith, J. Lalitha, and L. D. Hawk, *Evangelical Postcolonial Conversations* (Downers Grove: IVP, 2014), 26–27.

practice local emancipatory knowledges? As has been alluded to throughout this collection, the process will entail content, methodology, and right attitude.

Content Integration

The key to meaningful content in the cross-cultural educational encounter is integration – the recognition that while we as teachers bring a certain level of expertise, our students themselves bring a world of life and experience and knowledge. The integration of these diverse knowledges holds potential for discovering the "third space" where innovative and mutual transformative learning can take place.

Banks and Banks observe that

> content integration deals with the extent to which teachers use examples and content from a variety of cultures and groups to illustrate key concepts, principles, generalizations, and theories in their subject area or discipline. The infusion of ethnic and cultural content into the subject area should be logical, not contrived.[33]

Such wider context integration would mean that a cross-cultural teacher would look for local sources not only in terms of "illustrations," but also in terms of bibliographical sources and their theological formulations, biblical interpretation, missional practices, and so on. It means the intentional use of local poetry, music, and narratives[34] in dialogue with the professor's own sources, and stimulating the usage of these same forms for the students' production.

This sort of content integration is far from unproblematic. Even though many of the barriers in terms of access to information have been shattered by the electronic advancements of the last decades, there is still a real difficulty in terms of the availability of the "target context" literature for the professor to examine and integrate before the educational exchange happens. There is also the matter of micro-contextual theological tensions, so common in our evangelical settings: sometimes, quoting a certain local author may create more

---

33. J. Banks and C. McGee Banks, *Multicultural Education: Issues and Perspectives* (Hoboken: Wiley, 2010), 20.

34. See in particular H. Dharamraj, "Telling Tales: Stories That Embox Theology," in Shaw and Dharamraj, *Challenging Tradition*, 393–410; and X. Yang, "Poetry As Theology: A Creative Path," in Shaw and Dharamraj, *Challenging Tradition*, 425–45.

hindrances than pathways. However, it is possible to use "cultural brokers" who may guide the professor in this acquisition process, or even to propose pre-session learning tasks in which students themselves are invited to dive into their local literature.

As cross-cultural teachers we must also recognize our own tendency through our curriculum, textbooks, and bibliographies to establish an "official knowledge,"[35] or a sort of canon of approved texts in a certain subject area. An explicit inclusion of local sources that is "logical, not contrived" may strengthen the subjective value attributed to local sources by local students. However, such integration must happen beyond the mere inclusion of such materials in the bibliography of a course syllabus, as the lack of usage in classroom discussions may actually provoke a reverse effect.

Great wisdom is needed, for, while embracing local resources, it is also necessary to avoid a complacent attitude towards local formulations, as integration does not mean lack of critique. David Tracy accurately establishes a point of balance in declaring that "to hear those [local] voices is also to resist them when necessary . . . every response to their readings must be critical and active, not passively receptive."[36]

Student Production and a Safe Discussion Space

The literature on multicultural education envisions the ideal classroom as a place of minimal coercion and of free speech, with students and teachers voicing their informed opinions and sharing meaningful learning experiences that enrich and enlighten each other's cultural backgrounds. This is not a bad situation to idealize, and I believe our practice as teachers should aim towards that.

However, two important observations should be made. First, cross-cultural teachers need to adapt their teaching in their efforts to guarantee student participation in the classroom. The promotion of a safe discussion space will

---

35. M. W. Apple, *Official Knowledge: Democratic Education in a Conservative Age* (New York: Routledge, 2000).

36. D. Tracy, *Plurality and Ambiguity* (San Francisco: Harper & Row, 1987), 107.

emerge differently in high- and low-context cultures.[37] Second, within the world of theological education, mainstream theologies have had time and space to "colonize" their own context and organize themselves into a coordinated system. Those who come with these firmly established roots often see their systems as "normative," and to question some of these formulations – even if made in contextual terms – may be seen as questioning the faith itself.

In one of his very few personal essays, evangelical Puerto Rican theologian Orlando Costas narrated his "three conversions":[38] first, his conversion to Christ; second, when he started to unpeel some layers of his Christian experience while studying in an American university, and went through a sort of "cultural conversion" back to his own Latin American culture; and third, when he extended this reflection to his own way of thinking theologically, going through a final conversion to making theology from the perspective of the powerless. Many comparable stories can be found: a cycle involving an experience with Christ, a revision of our understanding based on the realization that other cultural experiences have shaped the theology we accept as orthodox, and finally a commitment to theologizing in a more culturally and contextually meaningful way.

Inviting students to reflect actively on the relationship between their Christian faith and their culture is not a guarantee that emancipatory local knowledges will flourish. In fact, opposite stories may also be found: when doing such reflection, people may take a step back and further reject local knowledges in favour of "orthodox" and "mainstream" forms of theology. Such voices are certainly welcome among others at the table of the kingdom. However, the kind of critical self-reflection in the "third space" being advocated here is crucial for the sort of transformative learning that appropriates and expands local knowledges.

The task of the cross-cultural teacher is therefore to try to establish an environment of trust and safety in which students are free to engage in new

---

37. L. Senanayake, "The Imperative of Cultural Integration in Advanced Theological Studies: Perspectives from the Majority World," in Shaw and Dharamraj, *Challenging Tradition*, 109–26; and P. Shaw, "Communication, Language, and Cross-Cultural Teaching" in the present volume.

38. O. Costas, "Conversion As a Complex Experience: A Hispanic Case Study," *Occasional Essays* 5, no. 1 (1980): 21–44. Orlando Costas was a prolific writer and practitioner until his early death in 1987 at the age of forty-five.

attempts at local or contextual theologizing that are by nature tentative. These attempts will mostly happen in classroom discussions and in class assignments done by students.

There will always be some hindrances to a free expression of tentative formulations whether done in oral or written form, due to culture, group dynamics, or learning styles. But more complex are potential coercive barriers to creative engagement. This coercion may be due to pressure, even if involuntary, from stakeholders and/or donors to embrace a particular epistemological framework, or institutional pressures on students that push them towards one line of thought, or a particular doctrinal stance.

There are a number of pathways for dealing with these various hindrances to meaningful discussion. Stephen Brookfield suggests "one minute [reaction] papers"[39] to be assigned to students after the discussion or exposition of crucial points. These may be collected by professors, revised, and addressed after a break or in the next session, without necessarily identifying the author. Hybrid classroom models can also be strategic in facilitating active student engagement. Wherever Internet access is readily available, it is possible to set up online environments to make resources available and to promote forums of asynchronous discussion, which provide safe spaces for engagement.

However, a great space for nurturing emancipatory local knowledges is in the assignments to be done by students. Joanna has already laid out the foundations of designing assessment instruments in her chapter on "Challenges of Doing Student Assessment in Cross-Cultural Contexts." On top of that, and in the light of what has been discussed in this chapter, teachers should ensure that assigned projects stimulate students to use their personal experience to describe and critique their theological assumptions in the light of their cultural beliefs, experiences, and practices.

In summary, the goal of a professor aiming to nurture emancipatory local knowledges should be to establish a safe classroom environment that enables students to make tentative formulations in this direction, either in classroom discussion (live or online) or in their assignments.

---

39. There are some interesting resources available on his website (www.stephenbrookfield. com), especially under the "Resources" tab. His book *Discussion As a Way of Teaching* (San Francisco: Jossey-Bass, 2005) brings together a comprehensive list of techniques to promote a healthy environment for an open classroom discussion.

An Attitude of Humility and Solidarity

Humility and solidarity are key elements in the work of Paulo Freire. While Freire did not necessarily have a cross-cultural educational situation in mind, he points towards a path that may serve as a starting point for nurturing emancipatory local knowledges:

> If in fact the dream that inspires us is democratic and grounded in solidarity, it will not be by talking to others from on high as if we were inventors of the truth that we will learn to speak with them. Only the person who listens patiently and critically is able to speak *with* the other, even if at times it should be necessary to speak *to* him or her. Even when, of necessity, she/he must speak against ideas and convictions of the other person, it is still possible to speak as if the other were a subject who is being invited to listen critically and not an object submerged by an avalanche of unfeeling, abstract words.[40]

Throughout the current collection, both in the opening chapters and in the country reflections, humility and solidarity are repeatedly mentioned as essential elements of quality cross-cultural teaching. Where humility and solidarity are embraced and teachers eschew talking to students "from on high" or as "inventors of the truth," the transformative "third space" is opened for nurturing and promoting local emancipatory knowledges.

Final Remarks

The serious cross-cultural teacher will be sensitive to the extent to which many students live between the dark places and the splendours of the Christian faith. All educational encounters carry political elements, and even more so cross-cultural teaching. It is in providing a safe space for border thinking that new pathways for understanding and engagement can take place. As we affirm the rich resources of the global evangelical community through nurturing emancipatory local knowledges the cross-cultural teaching experience can

---

40. P. Freire, *Pedagogy of Freedom: Ethics, Democracy, and Civic Courage*, Critical Perspectives Series (Lanham: Rowman & Littlefield, 1998), 110–11.

genuinely become a context for promoting the mission of Christ to the whole world.

For Reflection and Discussion

1. Consider the story of George in chapter 1. What were some of the power issues he needed to address before he was able to win the respect and appreciation of the students? What specific actions facilitated George's eventual success?
2. What are some of your favoured rhetorical patterns in teaching? For example, do you tend to a linear rationalist approach, or do you prefer communicating through stories, or do you tend to talk around a subject? In light of what has been discussed in this chapter, suggest one or two ways in which you might adapt your approach to local learning patterns when teaching cross-culturally.
3. How comfortable are you with words such as "oppression," "liberation," and "justice"? Give two or three specific actions you could take when teaching cross-culturally to empower your students to engage meaningfully as Christians with the political and social context in which they live. In particular, consider ways in which you might create safe spaces for your students.

8

Theological Humility in Cross-Cultural Teaching

César Lopes

In my early days as a theology student in Brazil I participated with some colleagues in a conference for pastors and leaders on world evangelization, hosted by a Brazilian evangelical press. As members of the Latin American Theological Fraternity, we knew that the main speaker, an ascending lecturer coming from the United States, would not get even close to the integral mission approach we shared among ourselves, but we were eager to participate and learn anyway.

Halfway through the second session, when talking about the main obstacles for preaching the gospel in the world, the lecturer started to address some items that really did not sound like challenges to world evangelization for us – which some years later I found were part of the agenda that was very present in the cultural wars being waged in his country. Then he moved on to address what he generally described as "groups that call themselves Christian, but lose their focus by placing a high value on social justice." My colleagues and I started to exchange puzzled looks among ourselves, wondering: is he talking about us? Are we obstacles for the advancement of the gospel in the world?

After many years, I realize that, although I do not share some of the theological perspectives of that lecturer, we do have many things in common, which you probably share as well: we all tend to have a sense of theological superiority. This is a complex issue in that when we are being invited to teach theologically in another cultural context it implicitly means we are to share our point of view, to "bring content" from abroad. However, the guest teacher or lecturer must realize that his or her selection of topics, approach, and sources (even of "enemies") has a validating effect and tends to establish a sort of canon.

In this context, theological humility invites us to ask some questions: how can we contribute effectively to the growth and theological autonomy of the students attending our classes or sessions? How do we pay proper respect to local theologies and theologians while we come from another context to teach? How do we create opportunities for students to engage meaningfully with their local theological frameworks in a critical dialogue with other global and local theologies? How do we avoid bringing our own personal agendas into a context that has its own specific challenges and needs?

I address these challenges and write this chapter with considerable dread. Some of the points presented here may be read as bearing some sort of resentment or grudge. As I read it myself, it sounds to me that a person who is asking others to be humble needs to be a bit more humble him- or herself! But I invite you to read this chapter as a frank conversation that aims to sensitize you to important aspects of your eventual incoming cross-cultural experience that you will not likely hear otherwise, for two notable reasons. First, your peers in the Majority World generally prefer to be indirect and perhaps even apologetic about matters that are felt deeply. Second, your host institution will probably not address these issues with you in pre-visit interactions because its focus is so much on just getting the job done. However, although you may not hear the issue of theological humility talked about, it is a key to fruitful cross-cultural teaching.

Humility about Theology Itself

The most immediate challenge theological humility presents us with is to think of our theology as "a" theology and not as "the" theology. We should ask ourselves: whose theology is our theology? What labels are attached to the theological system we adhere to? Do we think of our theology just as systematic, orthodox theology – or even as simply "theology"?

There has been extensive discussion about the implications of having a sort of hegemonic, adjective-free theology in contrast to "genitive" theologies – those theologies that have a qualifier in front of their name: Asian, African,

Latin American, liberation, feminist, womanist, black theologies, and so on. In other words, there is an underlying assumption that the classic "systematic theology" developed though centuries in Western contexts, although certainly not monolithic, is somehow "perspective-free."[1] Crossing boundaries to teach means to be inserted into an exchange with other rationalities and epistemologies which translate themselves into other theologies. In other words, crossing boundaries to teach challenges the hegemony of Western theologies.

That pure objectivity is a myth has been recognized in many academic circles, but there is still some strong resistance in evangelical contexts, usually based on a fear of pluralism or subjectivism. However, theological humility does require, according to Ellen Ott Marshall, "a posture that admits limitations of knowledge and partiality of perspective." It is not a matter of relativism, but of an attitude that should be present even without cross-cultural interactions, acknowledging that "the partiality of our perspective means that we no longer equate our interpretation of God's will with God's will."[2]

In many local contexts you will find a highly suspicious attitude towards doctrinal affirmations claiming to be uninfluenced by their contexts, value-free, or politically neutral, and any attempt to formulate a universal, de-contextual, and apolitical theology may be seen as something that further alienates Christians from their environments. Local perspectives not only see the task of theological reflection as a means of providing tools for understanding, evaluating, and/or applying doctrines, but are also concerned to make sure that these tools are not sponsoring further injustices.

---

1. See, for example, L. W. Caldwell, "How Asian Is Asian Theological Education?," in *Tending the Seedbeds: Educational Perspectives on Theological Education in Asia*, ed. A. Harkness (Quezon City: Asia Theological Association, 2010), 23–45; N. Kang, "Envisioning Postcolonial Theological Education: Dilemmas and Possibilities," in *Handbook of Theological Education in World Christianity: Theological Perspectives, Regional Surveys, Ecumenical Trends*, eds. D. Werner, D. Esterline, N. Kang, and J. Raja (Eugene: Wipf and Stock, 2010), 30–41; V. Ramachandra, *Subverting Global Myths: Theology and the Public Issues Shaping Our World* (Downers Grove: IVP, 2008), 258–59; T. C. Tennent, "New Paradigm for Twenty-First-Century Mission: Missiological Reflections in Honor of George K. Chavanikamannil," in *Remapping Mission Discourse*, eds. S. Samuel and P. V. Joseph (Delhi: ISPCK, 2008), 185–203; G. Hill, *Global Church: Reshaping Our Conversations, Renewing Our Mission, Revitalizing Our Churches* (Downers Grove: IVP, 2016), 422.

2. E. O. Marshall, *Christians in the Public Square* (Eugene: Wipf and Stock, 2008), 75–78.

Humility by Doing Theology from the Periphery and from Below

A fundamental aspect of theological humility is the realization that teaching cross-culturally implies a change not just in geographical location, but also in the *locus* of our theological reasoning.

We generally welcome "light" theological differences generated by our diverse cultural backgrounds. For instance, most Christians today, especially those who have cross-cultural experience, readily accept that liturgy and worship in a local church in South East Asia will look very different from its counterpart in a Western country. Theologically, we grasp that a Western concept of sin as transgression may differ from the idea of sin as shame found, for example, in some African cultures. Such differences may puzzle, but rarely cause major dissent among us as evangelicals.

However, discussions about issues that involve social, political, economic, or power variables are more complicated. Topics such as ethnicity, gender, power, privilege, and economics more often than not cause divisions and polarize. In many circles these are viewed as less than orthodox, or "too political" for the church. Particularly where hegemonic forms of theology are embraced, there has been a tendency to stay above these issues, or to come "from above" in approaching them.

For instance, for the last couple of years, the popular Pope Francis faced unusual waves of criticism for his harsh critique of the effects of capitalism on the underprivileged populations in our global society. In the United States, minority and female theologians sometimes struggle to have their voices heard beyond their own "ghettos" – or to be heard as more than just token representatives of their groups. Closer to home for me, for the last half century Latin American evangelical theologians have sought a seat at the global theological table while advocating that the mission of the church must also include concrete actions of solidarity with the poor and disenfranchised, and the promotion of human dignity.

In many circles in the Majority World, we take contextual realties quite seriously. With an approach to theology that is "from below" we bring the questions of society to the truth of Scripture. When our Christian life is viewed from perspectives that are not located at the "centres" but at the "periphery," ones that are not developed in spaces of money and power but of poverty and powerlessness, theology looks and sounds fundamentally different.

Although the idea of doing theology from below has found fruitful ground in recent contextual theologies coming from the Majority World, this concept – and the ongoing tension with theology from above – is not new. Historically, this tension is evident in how we think of Christ, as exemplified in the traditions of Alexandria and Antioch – the tension found between Jesus as the almighty, transcendent God and as the immanent Christ, "who, being in very nature God . . . made himself nothing, by taking the very nature of a servant, being made in human likeness" (Phil 2:6–7).

The creative tension between a theology from above and one from below is found in a full array of biblical texts and traditions: the Psalms emphasize the importance of the rituals in the temple; Isaiah and many other prophets boldly challenge the traditional contemplative and liturgical life, stressing that the sacrifice God actually requires should focus on the lower orders of society:

> Stop bringing meaningless offerings! . . .
> Learn to do right; seek justice.
> > Defend the oppressed.
> Take up the cause of the fatherless;
> > plead the case of the widow.
> (Isa 1:13, 17)

Theological humility calls us, when teaching cross-culturally, to bear in mind this biblical creative tension and seek the necessary balance. I do not claim that theology should always be done from below. However, if a teacher is coming from a Western into a Majority World context, that teacher must realize that he or she is not in the "centre" any more. Theological humility is necessary in realizing that the conclusions drawn "from above" may not be fully compatible with the realities from below.

Humility about Theologizing

What does theology look like? Although a blatant generalization, standard Western systematic theology tends to be done individually, "objectively," in an impersonal tone, within an Aristotelian, dialectical framework, valuing strict and abstract categories. The advancements made with this kind of reasoning are vast and invaluable, and both in the West and in the Majority World we all benefit from the contributions left by great theologians thinking exactly within this pattern. However, it is not the only way of doing theology or of reflecting theologically.

Rather than dive into the specificities of different theological methods, we will explore general aspects that demand theological humility from cross-cultural teachers and lecturers.

Doing Theology with Different Categories

Theological humility means to realize theology may be done with different categories. I remember a dialogue with a dear professor at Trinity Evangelical Divinity School about the categories "reform" and "revolution." In his opinion, the only valid category from a truly Christian worldview was "reform." He understood that we live in a fallen world, and we, as believers, should act in our societies in order to reform it and gradually implement changes and get them closer to the values of the kingdom. His starting point was consistent with his context and the social space he occupied. For him personally, the established social order basically worked well, although he definitely had plenty of sensibility regarding its flaws and problems. Thus, it was only a matter of adjusting some issues.

My argument with him was that the "revolution" category is valued in Latin America, for the problems of our societies are too evident and harder to circumvent. It is not a matter of tweaking or adjusting, but of fundamentally reconstructing relations and structures. Those who make contextual theology in Latin America share the image of Christ as a revolutionary, a subversive element, a radical.

When we are crossing borders to teach theologically, we are bound to meet people who will use different categories from ours. When offering contributions to their theological growth and reflection, theological humility demands that we evaluate how much of the difference we see between our theologizing and theirs is related to using such different categories.

Doing Theology from Different Starting Points

Theological humility implies there are different, equally viable starting points when doing theology. Such a perception was already pointed out earlier in this chapter, but it needs to be highlighted and clarified here. In much of the Majority World the way we read Scripture while doing contextual theology is to come to the Bible as the "second act." This expression conveys the idea that what the people of God encounter first is not the biblical text, but their own concrete life, with all its problems, struggles, and beauties. Reflection on the word of God in light of these life experiences and circumstances follows and gives clarity and meaning to these experiences. In most Majority World contexts, life experiences and circumstances are marked by the omnipresence of human misery due to such things as violence, poverty, inhuman living conditions, hunger, homelessness, and political corruption. While these are an overt and overwhelming reality in the Majority World, it is also true that not even the world's richest nations are able to eradicate these conditions from their own contexts. If you are open to listening to local voices when you teach cross-culturally, there is so much to be learned.

There are numerous other starting points you may encounter – not necessarily common in Western theology, but significant to many Majority World theologians: living in a disputed land; the relationship with ancestors; being a religious minority, often with the experience of discrimination or persecution; and others.

Theological humility is necessary to realize that attempts to make sense of the Bible "before" making sense of these realities may eventually lead into a kind of preaching that is dogmatic but disconnected from life. Accurate propositions may be constructed, but they almost unavoidably stand hanging in the air. This way of doing theology may even stimulate an aspiration pointing exclusively towards a future salvation at the end of time with personal disconnection from the world in which we live.

Doing Theology in Community

In other sections of this book you will find discussions about collectivism and individualism.[3] Such a cultural parameter is not just valid for how people

---

3. P. Shaw, "Three Key Cultural Parameters," in this volume.

organize their relationships, but is also true for their theological concerns and processes. Theological humility calls us to realize that community is more than a mere affective or superficial aspect of doing theology in the Majority World. Rather, in many contexts doing theology is in and of itself not an individual enterprise but a community one, in which collective and community categories are incorporated into the theologizing processes and theoretical references are used that are coherent with such an approach.

For example, the idea of structural sin is among the many issues that cause estrangement between North Atlantic and Latin American theologians. The former accuse the latter of not paying enough attention to individual sin and the need for personal redemption; Latin Americans, in their turn, charge their North Atlantic colleagues with developing an individualizing and privatizing theology that overlooks the building of the kingdom of God and focuses only on an other-worldly and future salvation.

We may also think of other contexts in which Christians are a minority, in which doing theology is not just an abstraction but a fundamental exercise of collectively building an identity, of making sense of ethical decisions to be taken on a daily basis. The conclusions drawn by one member of the community are not simply an academic exercise, but deeply affect the lives of the other members of that community.

If doing theology encompasses critical reflection and redemptive praxis at the community level, proper tools are required to analyse the current situation or context – hence the importance of incorporating a robust social theory in the theological method itself. It is not surprising that many local evangelical theologies developed in the Majority World have a strong dialogue with social sciences, and not just with philosophy. Theological humility recognizes the richness of these approaches.

Doing Theology in an Emotional and Personal Way

It took me some time while I was studying in the United States to realize that when somebody says "you are emotional" in a discussion it is actually a dismissive or derisive comment. In my own Brazilian context, using language with an affective dimension was considered normal and healthy. In fact, from my experience, one of the most important aspects in interacting with Latin

American theology is to realize that there is a level of passion involved in our theological formulations.

Connected to this idea is the manifest self-awareness when making theology in the Global South. Theological ideas and formulations are seen to stem from personal experiences and trajectories, which in turn are affected and transformed by new discoveries from biblical and theological texts. Such experiences actually make sense of our encounters with God – the recognition that these encounters are not simply shaped along confessional lines, but are also heavily influenced by context and culture.

In other words, theology is often made, written, and spoken in the first person, many times using a subjective language that challenges not just our ideas, but also our emotions. Theological humility means to embrace a broader understanding of how different people experience God in their lives, to value theological formulations made in the first person, and not to dismiss these approaches as a lower category of "emotional," or to reduce them to a testimonial value.

Humility in Respecting and Acknowledging the Work That Has Already Been Done

Although there could be more dimensions to explore, an overarching aspect of theological humility is the realization that people have been doing theology in your host context before you arrive. It sounds obvious, but sometimes, in order to justify the investment of getting a professor from overseas, individuals or organizations may be tempted to paint a dire picture. Allow me to illustrate.

In the last few months of research for my doctorate at Trinity Evangelical Divinity School I was frantically evaluating a vast bibliography on Latin American theology and relating it to curriculum theories in order to finish writing my dissertation. With books and articles written by men and women from our subcontinent surrounding my computer, I came across a blog post from a US organization inviting their readers to help them fight what they called the "theological famine in Latin America." The strategy proposed for addressing this supposed "famine" was to translate a specific set of books written by North American authors into Spanish and Portuguese.

What struck me most was the image they chose to illustrate the post: a deserted and desolated landscape, with dead trees in the foreground. It left me wondering if all my colleagues and I, struggling, living, preaching, and thinking theologically within the Latin American context, were just . . . dead trees, absolutely dry, bearing no fruit.

The issue that organization was addressing was clearly not the absence of quality locally written theological materials in Latin America. Rather the organization had a specific agenda in making the materials written by their particular favoured North American authors available in other languages. I do not question the sincerity of their efforts. I certainly do not question the fact that there are profound needs in terms of theological literature in Latin America – and in so many Majority World contexts. However, my point here is that in order to go ahead with their agenda, the organization resorted to disrespecting and disregarding the hard work done by local theologians and presenting themselves as the proverbial Western "saviours."

Theological humility demands that we avoid such an attitude in our cross-cultural exchanges. The seminary inviting you to teach may not have as many PhDs in its faculty as in your home school, but you will find colleagues engaged in trying to articulate profound biblical and theological principles for the challenges of their contexts. Even if you are only dropping in for a short conference, you need to be aware that local theologians have been dealing with the challenges of their societies before you arrive, and there will be others after you leave. It is unhelpful, and will undermine your credibility, if you arrive in a different context considering it to be a deserted land in which you are the only source of life.

There is a balance to be reached here. It is not a matter of adopting a complacent attitude towards your peers in the host college – theological humility does not mean an absence of critique! However, you should honestly ask yourself how much of this critique is due to your own agenda, whether intentional or not.

Teaching with Theological Humility

There are many ways to translate the observations I have given on theological humility into practice when you teach cross-culturally. While some of the broader issues discussed here can be addressed only in the long term, there is much that can be done even in shorter cross-cultural engagements.

1. Honour the Work Your Colleagues Are Doing in the Host Country or Organization

Please allow me to stress this point. To enter a cross-cultural exchange with theological humility means understanding that you are not moving into a desert landscape or a place absent of theological reflection. The table may not be as abundant as in your home institution, but your hosts have been working hard to provide some solid food for their students.

The general attitude of honouring your colleagues translates into several concrete possibilities. For example, you would do well to try to engage in conversation with your colleagues as much as possible. Demonstrating interest in their lives and challenges is a polite act, but you will be enriched far more if you go beyond and explore their theological ideas and their unique answers to the issues they are confronting in their context. Bring to them your own unanswered questions, or even situations that may have happened in the classroom. You may well find their responses insightful and transformative.

Take the time to learn local theologies and insights. Do not look just for local versions or translations of your own theology to validate your agenda. You will certainly find local circles that attempt to emulate Western theologizing in *almost every* Majority World context. But you will help neither yourself nor your students by doing so. Rather ask yourself what unique perspectives are present in this context that may offer you a broader understanding of theology. And do not look only for some exotic seasonings that may give a different flavour to your existing theological platter, but also for unique ingredients that may substantially change and challenge your whole menu!

2. Incorporate Local Theological Sources in Your Material

In the introduction to this chapter I mentioned in brief that your selection of sources has a validating effect and creates a sort of canon – "official knowledge" as opposed to other "heterodox" or "marginal" knowledge.

In other chapters of this collection, you have been challenged to think about the examples and illustrations you use in a cross-cultural classroom.[4] But a component of theological humility goes beyond illustrations to the incorporation of local or regional sources of theological knowledge in your course material, not simply as additional sources but as a part of your basic, mandatory bibliography. You show great respect to your host country when you identify local or regional authors who address similar issues to those you are discussing. The school librarian or local faculty who teach in comparable areas of study may help in this task, especially for finding sources in languages you have not mastered.

Accessing local sources is not without its problems. Many times there are local tensions that an outsider may not be aware of; hence the importance of having somebody from the host institution help you sort through these issues.

3. Look for Feedback in Informal Settings

In any meaningful teaching context you are likely to get pushed back in the ideas you present, and responding to this resistance is a central educational task – and not only when you are crossing borders to teach. However, the nature of a cross-cultural classroom creates particular challenges. As you have already read in previous chapters and is documented repeatedly in the country pieces of part 2 of this book, students in many contexts are not comfortable expressing disagreement or criticism in public, or even voicing their personal perspectives. The same will likely be true of your colleagues also. Although they may disagree they will not openly confront you; the resistance will become passive and unspoken.

However, if you make yourself available in informal settings, sharing a cup of coffee or tea, you are more likely to open the space for honest disagreement, which is key to better cross-cultural engagement. Even if you are in a short-term engagement, you will find students discussing theological ideas more freely during the break than in the classroom setting.

---

4. B. Heaton, "Teaching Cross-Culturally . . . Did I Learn More Than My Students?"; and P. Shaw, "Three Key Cultural Parameters," in this collection.

4. Speak about What You Were Invited to Speak About

In the 1990s discussions on urban missions were popular in Brazil. My school launched a specialization program on this subject, and our program design included, among other things, a class on the biblical bases for urban missions from both the Old and the New Testament.

We invited a renowned scholar to talk about this topic. Our intention overtly was both to cover that area of our curriculum, and also somehow to advertise our new program by bringing in an international lecturer with name recognition. We gathered resources from partners to fund the travel expenses, relied on his willingness to receive a compensation that was largely symbolic by Western standards, and hosted him. In the first session he went on about how the *real centre* of the biblical theology of urban mission is in Luke–Acts, and then he spoke the whole week about Luke–Acts. He barely mentioned the Old Testament or other books in the New Testament. We later found out that his next book was going to be on Luke–Acts and urban mission.

The students were happy to have had a great week of brilliant teaching and challenging content. Our school did get the attention of prospective students. But we were disappointed that the design we had planned for the program as a whole ended up with a major gap.

When you teach cross-culturally with theological humility, you would do well to realize that you are filling a gap in the local school's curriculum, and you are coming to serve the school's needs and agendas – not your own. You bring your "baggage" to address a specific need, but this is fruitful only when done in a respectful dialogue with your hosts.

Being a Theologically Humble Learner

Throughout this collection a repeated theme is the importance of a humble learning attitude when you teach cross-culturally. It is from this posture that you can open a "third space" for mutual transformative growth. Coming with theological humility is an essential element of this posture. You may be surprised what you discover about God, yourself, and his people on this journey.

For Reflection and Discussion

1. Of the various issues raised in this chapter, which did you find most challenging? Why? Give at least one specific action you hope to take to express theological humility in practice when you teach cross-culturally.

2. To what extent do you see your own theology as a perspective-free or normative theology? Considering the discussions of this chapter, list two or three elements that may contribute to the "partiality of the perspective" you carry.

3. In what ways does the characterization of how "Western theology" is done presented in this chapter differ from your own understanding and experience of it? What elements of the characterization given in this chapter do you feel are fair and perhaps challenging to your experience of teaching cross-culturally?

4. We all have theological convictions. In light of the issues raised in this chapter, talk about one of your theological convictions that potentially might be a barrier to teaching cross-culturally. Describe one or two ways in which you might be able to both retain this theological conviction and yet allow your time teaching cross-culturally to be a quality learning experience for both you and your students.

Part Two

Listening to Local Voices

L ocals know best. In the first half of this book we have tried to sketch
some of the key general issues that will confront you when you teach in
a different cultural context. However, the realities on the ground vary from
region to region, and even locally within countries. The second half of the
book is therefore devoted to listening to the voices of local leaders. While it
was not possible to have a piece from every country, we have tried to collect a
diverse sample that is representative of a large portion of the Majority World.

Through our network of friends around the world we asked individuals and
groups of national faculty to respond to the basic question: "If a visiting faculty
member comes from another part of the world to our region to teach, what must
he or she be aware of and sensitive to?" We suggested that these national voices
speak to cultural, educational, historical, religious, political, and postcolonial
issues, as well as provide practical suggestions and recommendations. In
trying to get to the heart feelings of local leaders, we specifically asked that
these reflections be predominantly conversational in style, rather than formal

academic pieces. In this process we have provided some basic guidelines but have intentionally given freedom to develop the material in different patterns.

Generally, the design of the responses reflects something of local patterns of leadership and communication. Regions that are more direct in speech have tended to be more confrontational in style than the reflections coming from cultures that value a greater level of circumlocution in speech. Throughout we have added headings for ease of reading, but due to the different emphases of each piece these headings have been intentionally left somewhat inconsistent. To gain a deeper understanding of each region you would do well to go beyond the content of the reflection to the style and emphases that are evident.

You should constantly bear in mind that the comments given in these regional pieces are helpful generalizations, but that significant diversity exists within the countries represented. On the other hand, in some cases you may discover more information in the pieces presented here than you will ever receive in calls and conversations you have with representatives of your host institution before you travel to teach! It is best for you to use these pieces as conversation starters with representatives of your host organization, rather than as the sole source of information.

We have never seen a collection quite like this. Even though there are certain common themes that resonate strongly with the first half of the book, the richness of insight in the responses we received is a great gift to the global church. You will probably begin by reading the local voices of the place where you are planning to teach. However, a more comprehensive reading of this collection will make your stint of cross-cultural teaching more valuable to the recipients, while you yourself are enriched in the process.

Teaching Cross-Culturally in Aotearoa New Zealand

A Maori Tangata Whenua Perspective

Collated by Rev. Hone Te Rire on
12 March 2019 on behalf of the group

Social and Cultural

- Greetings and relationship-enhancing: it is acceptable for men to *hongi* (press noses with) other men. It is acceptable for women to *hongi* other women. This is a normal way of greeting for Maori. In the modern era where handshaking is the norm this may be used as well as the *hongi*. It is acceptable to kiss females on the cheek only if they motion to you that they are fine with a kiss on the cheek. If not invited then it is a "no go" to kiss on the cheek. On the other hand, it is the height of rudeness to not greet either with a *hongi*, handshake, and if a female, a peck on the cheek. Relationships can be ruined from the outset if any of the above principles are deliberately or mistakenly missed. Ignorance is not accepted – you must know the protocols.

- *Whanau* (family) relationships are very important in Maori communities. Outsiders must be aware not to insult a *whanau* member. If you insult one *whanau* member you are at risk of insulting the entire *whanau* even if the other *whanau* members are not present or in direct contact with the teacher/foreigner/*manuhiri* (visitor). *Tangata whenua* (local people of the land) are also mindful that their utmost priority is to *manaaki* (care for) their *manuhiri* (visitors). For the *tangata whenua* not to do so is also the height of rudeness and an insult. As *manuhiri* (visitors), be courteous and accepting of being spoilt with care by the hosts (*tangata whenua*, locals).

Hospitality and respect are strong values. For example, never turn down an offer of a good meal or an opportunity to sit and have a cup of tea, cordial, or drink of water. Please receive hospitable gestures graciously, and with humility.

- Maori culture and ways of doing things are different from region to region in New Zealand. Never expect all Maori from different *iwi* (peoples) to be the same. Each has their own specific and unique *tikanga* (protocols). It helps to find out about your hosts first before entering their domain. To do something wrong in terms of *tikanga* (protocol) is seen as the height of rudeness and offence. For example, Maori from the far north of the North Island ensure their esteemed visitors are never kept waiting. Other tribes expect visitors to wait for the more formal aspects of welcoming visitors, such as speech-making, to be done first, as these are seen to be of foremost importance. Only then will a meal or sorting accommodation take place.

Religious

- Maori are very spiritual people and have taken to accepting mainstream churches. Maori also have their own specific Maori-centric religions. It pays to know what those religious beliefs are. Some tribes have taken to their traditional religious forms. It is important to be sensitive to and affirming of these practices. All *karakia* (prayers) are done in the *Te Reo* (Maori language) and are invariably led by a minister or *Tohunga* (religious expert in traditional prayers and incantations). In many Maori facilities such as *Marae* or churches, shoes are taken off and left outside the front entrance. Shoes are considered unclean because of the dirt under them.
- Maori have prayers for the beginning of gatherings and before eating meals. At the end of the day prayers are said in thanks to *Atua* (God) for keeping them safe during the day and before going to sleep at night.
- The *Paipera Tapu* (Holy Bible) is not just any book – it is a special book. Never put the Bible on the floor, and never sit on top of the Bible. Never put the Bible on the dinner table or on a place where food is consumed. Most but not all Maori *iwi* treat the Bible with the utmost respect. Maori

priests or ministers of all religious denominations have a special status among their communities; you should treat them with utmost respect.

Educational

- Maori are predominantly kinaesthetic and oral learners. Generally, teachers need to embrace these two learning styles to engage with their Maori students. For the majority of Maori literacy is low. Most Maori students have come through a very traditional education system that uses a lot of rote learning. Particularly at the beginning it is best to give information to students, either orally or in notes, rather than expecting them to find out for themselves or develop independent ideas. Keep in mind that for most Maori their previous experience of education has been traumatic.

- Know your audience. In some classes you will have a wide range of age groups, from youth to adults, to elderly (*kuia* and *koroua*). They may vary substantially in their educational qualifications, church backgrounds, and social backgrounds. Please note that Maori males think differently from Maori females. Be patient with the males and don't treat them with disrespect.

- Maori students, especially the youth, generally respond well to creative teaching methods. They respond more readily to hands-on, creative learning than to lectures. Sitting and listening to a lecturer in a traditional classroom environment bores them, and you will likely find little attentiveness and probably distractive behaviour such as doodling. Interactive learning occurs best for most Maori students in a natural setting. For example, if you hold your class in the forest or gardens you will likely get much better attention and better-quality learning: happy students, heaps of learning, and a happy teacher.

- Do not publicly criticize or shame a student, as this student will likely shut down and cease engaging, or perhaps even leave the classroom or learning group. The public critique may also have a knock-on effect and other students who are close *whanau* (friends) may leave in solidarity with the student.

- Family is a strong connection for all Maori. Be careful not to offend a student's friend, as this friend may be a close relative.

- Quietness from a Maori student must not be construed as stupidity or not understanding. In fact, quietness can mean exactly the opposite. Maori are good readers of body language: your expressions and mood can give away your views if you are critiquing a person's response. Please be aware.

Language

- It is good if you can attain a basic-to-average understanding of *Te Reo Maori* (Maori language) and can speak comfortably, even if only a few basic greetings. Your attempts will be well received and applauded as you show respect to your students by trying to speak in their native cultural language of Aotearoa New Zealand. But don't try to do more than you are able in the language: it is better to get the language speaking correct than embarrass yourself.

- Keep in mind that the Maori language differs in dialect from one tribe to another. Words will be different as well as *tikanga* protocols around greetings – both formal and informal. Don't fall into the trap of thinking that all Maori use the exact same words while speaking the same language. It can be embarrassing if you use a word that is acceptable to one *iwi* (tribe) but is seen as offensive by another. Please learn beforehand. As a general rule, if you don't know, ask someone who has expert knowledge.

- Be aware that for many if not all students their first language might be English, and their second language might be Maori. However, their thinking patterns and perspective on the world will most likely be Maori, not English. Even when English is their first language most will understand the *Te Reo Maori* but might not necessarily be comfortable speaking it. That said, the majority of Maori can speak and understand *Te Reo Maori*.

- Maori language encompasses a holistic worldview. Spirituality, family, health, and thought are all seen as belonging together and not viewed separately. When addressing spiritual matters it is important to be aware that most have come from strong religious and spiritual upbringings.

Practical

- For Maori, eye-to-eye contact is generally very offensive. It is safer not to do this. In particular, avoid eye contact when talking to older Maori persons. Talk to them but with your eyes looking down and not directly at the other. This particular behaviour is especially important when talking to males and elderly males. The eye-to-eye contact of a male with younger females can be construed as being sexually flirtatious and should be avoided. With females you will get a harsh rebuke if making eye-to-eye contact that is not welcomed.

- While Maori are known as the *Tangata Whenua* of Aotearoa New Zealand – the original indigenous inhabitants and people of the land – they have been marginalized since the arrival of European culture in their lands. Since the 1860s the Maori have been treated unequally by the dominant (population-wise) *Pakeha* (English-speaking) cultures. Most Maori have been driven off their lands and into poverty. Be careful to treat the *Tangata Whenua* with the utmost respect, even though they may live in poverty. Avoid flashy dressing or an "I am greater than thou" attitude, as it will most likely not be received well. Be moderate but respectful in choosing your dress code, keeping in mind that as the teacher you will be viewed as the *Rangatira* (the leader of the group).

- In general, Maori are a happy-go-lucky people who like to enjoy what they are doing and who they are with, regardless of cultural difference. They like to laugh and have fun, and share jokes with each other. Don't be afraid to join in. They enjoy a hearty meal, and you should always join in with a *kai* (meal). To refuse is seen as of the utmost rudeness. The meal and the joining in is all about *whanaungatanga* (relationship-building). Building good relationships always comes before business. It is about building connections and trust. Once you have the latter, you have a Maori friend for life, a friendship which will never be severed.

Teaching Cross-Culturally in Singapore

East Asia School of Theology, ACTS College (ACTS), and Singapore Bible College

Political and Economic

- Singaporeans are very proud of their culture, education system, history, and religious traditions (including respect for ancestors for Chinese Singaporeans). Avoid insulting any of these aspects of culture. Singaporeans are an amazing group of people who have changed a small country into one of the economic powerhouses of Asia with a rich culture and diversity.

- Singapore places a strong emphasis on racial and religious harmony and the government takes this very seriously. With the Religious Harmony Act citizens and residents are to show respect to all religions and not give offence in personal or social media. Speaking negatively about another race or religion can be a criminal offence. For example, while theologically we must deny idols, for many religious groups idols are a normal part of their religious life and attacking idols can be seen as offensive. Visiting faculty should never write or post on the Internet any negative statement about other races or religions. It is also not wise to comment jokingly or in jest about another culture, either in person or online, as these comments may offend.

- In many Western countries a free exchange of political opinion is encouraged; in Singapore you need to be more circumspect about political issues. Singapore views political freedom from a collectivist rather than an individualistic perspective, with communal harmony as a central value. Are my words going to be beneficial to communal harmony or are they going to be divisive? For those coming to Singapore from outside, it is best to stay away from politics as you probably won't understand the issues. Focus on the gospel.

- Unlike most equatorial countries, Singapore is fast-paced and punctual, and Singaporeans are quick to complain when things don't run efficiently. Singaporean society is rooted in meritocracy and is urgent and competitive, with a strong fear of failure. On the whole, Singaporeans tend to be better educated and more affluent than other Asians. However, despite the relative wealth of the city, many Singaporeans struggle financially. People fight for an existence. As a small country there is something of a sense of inferiority, and we see a need to work diligently to establish ourselves in the world.

- If you teach in a theological college in Singapore it is not enough just to see Singapore, as many of your students will be coming from other parts of South East Asia. You need to know the region. For example, poverty is not "in your face" in Singapore, but it is an evident reality in much of South East Asia. Reading broadly can help enormously.

Social and Cultural

- Singapore is a very modern city greatly influenced by globalization. Consequently, at first sight it can appear that in spite of different ethnic backgrounds people "think" and "act" alike. But as you dig deeper you soon realize that there is a plethora of subtle yet important differences between peoples of different origins, in particular with regard to philosophy of life, priorities, and educational choices. You cannot assume a single cultural framework in Singapore. In the multiracial and multi-ethnic contexts of countries such as the USA and Australia there may actually be a more common culture than in Singapore. Even though Singapore is multi-ethnic, people from different backgrounds do not see things the same way. In Singapore there are television stations in totally different languages, and Singaporeans do not generally watch the same thing. Patriotism is probably the major common denominator that holds the country together. Because of the diversity of students you are likely to encounter, you need to take time to "double-confirm" your assumptions about how the students learn.

- Singapore is world-connected, modern, and globally mobile, but, at heart, it is an Asian society, both tolerant and conservative. The majority of Singaporeans may receive Western education all their lives, but their values are still very much Asian. We may be English-speaking, widely travelled, and exposed to world culture, but we are fiercely loyal to home and country. It is important to come to Singapore with an open mind. We may have our world-class Michelin-rated restaurants in the sprawling malls, but people still prefer their *pratas* or rice porridge for breakfast and use chopsticks and bowls (the Chinese) or hands (Malays and Indians) for meals at home. Just because the context here is multicultural, the subcultural enclaves remain; it is not a hot-pot blend. In particular, it is important to realize that while the country is predominantly Chinese, Singapore is very different from China, Hong Kong, or Taiwan. Do not let previous experiences in other Asian settings mislead you into thinking that you understand – or can understand quickly – Singapore and its people. Singaporeans appreciate outsiders who appreciate the diversity of food, music, accents, and festivals!

- Do not assume that everyone speaking with a Singaporean accent is a Singaporean. The person may be a citizen of a neighbouring country who has lived in Singapore for some time.

- As a visiting instructor coming to teach at theological schools in Singapore you must realize that while you may teach classes that are intercultural and multinational, the way things are done at the school remains very Singaporean. For example, while office staff are generally very friendly people, they may not make the first friendly move when they meet a visiting faculty member. They are not proud or intimidated, just cautious – even shy. They know Singapore is no longer a colony, but they are not sure if you know.

- In working with your Singaporean teaching colleagues, you will notice very quickly that they come in different shapes, sizes, and subcultures. Some may be comfortably expressive while others withhold their comments. This, no doubt, is in part a result of their temperament, but equally it emerges from their understanding of what they consider to be appropriate or inappropriate because of their background and upbringing. Don't jump to quick decisions and conclusions based on what people say; be aware of both the verbal and the non-verbal communication.

- Despite the number of women in the business and political arenas, gender continues to be an issue, particularly for students coming from elsewhere in Asia. Some students may have difficulty with female leadership or teachers. For example, one female dean found that many male students would go to her male colleague and ask him to talk to her instead of talking with her directly. However, as a visiting faculty member it is crucial that you view male and female students equally.

Educational

- In general, Singaporean students do not complain about a heavy workload. They are eager to study, eager to read, and ready to write long papers. Among East Asians there is a historic competitive approach to education, somewhat patterned on the ancient Confucian imperial system in China, in which there is one major entrance exam to university with little opportunity for other pathways. This leads to a mindset where I need to get rid of my competitors to get into my desired study program. The broader education system trains Singaporeans to be competitive, and so students generally prefer to work individually and can be overly concerned about their grades. East Asian students often have difficulty with collaborative learning, preferring individual competitive learning – which from a Christian perspective is a less-than-desired approach. It takes intent to help students learn the benefits of collaborative learning. Have students work together on translating the resources (PPTs, study notes, etc.) and then sharing their resources with one another. Look for ways in which the students' work is a mutual resource for one another. Faculty members should have clear rubrics and follow these carefully.

- Some theological schools in Singapore have a primarily Singaporean student body while others are very multicultural. It will be very helpful for you to learn ahead of time the ratio of Singaporeans to international students in the class, and then do some research to find out the issues of some of the countries from which the students come. In this way you are more likely to teach with an understanding of student needs. If your class has international students, their mastery of English may not be strong. It is advisable to slow down and speak clearly.

- Those who come from the Singapore education system are more accustomed to reading and asking hard questions. Those who come from other educational backgrounds may be reluctant to speak up and may feel somewhat intimidated learning in Singapore. Some students come from an educational system that emphasizes critical thinking; others come from a context that primarily uses rote learning right through to university; the latter would not even dare to challenge what is being taught to them. You will need to sensitize some students to be humble in their "critical thinking" while encouraging others to develop their voice.

- There are several systems within Singapore – the Chinese system, the English system, the Malay system – and they do not all emphasize the same content or methodologies. You will find different backgrounds and academic levels even among Singaporean students. You will find a much broader range of students in your theology classrooms than you would in the West.

- When you teach, demonstration (show them) is valued more than explanation (tell them). In general, Westerners are trained to go from theory to practice, using Western "logic" by organizing, structuring, and sequencing content. In Singapore, students generally prefer to see how something is done without necessarily having to first understand the logic behind it.

- In the East, the emphasis seems to be on preserving time-tested truth as passed on by "the master" – but adapting these truths to changing circumstances. In the West, the education system seems to promote the creation and discovery of new ideas.

- Traditional Asian respect for the teacher remains, particularly among those influenced by a Confucianist heritage. Students will find it difficult to relate to faculty as friends or to address them by their first name, and questioning the teacher is generally seen as a sign of disrespect. Accept the students' "title" and designation for you. If they call you "Dr. _____," accept that.

You can say, "I prefer to be called [given name]," but do not insist. Students are very respectful and generous and may bring gifts to teachers.

- It is important to realize that a lack of questions from students does not imply they understand; in fact, the opposite is often true! Hence, a teacher cannot simply ask, "Does anyone have a question?" as the means to determine if students truly understand, since students will most likely remain silent. A much better way to check for retention is by asking students specific questions that demand a response from them. Students expect this.

- Many Singaporeans, along with others from East and South East Asia, hesitate to speak up in class for fear of giving the wrong answers and losing face. It does not mean that they are not thinking or do not have opinions or thoughts on the issues raised. A helpful way to address this is to use discussion groups (two to four persons) and appoint spokespersons to present the answers on behalf of each group. This approach helps overcome the shame factor and allows the quiet ones an opportunity to speak up. It is good to have different members of the group take turns to present on behalf of the group.

- In many fields of study articles and books from the West have minimal or no relevance in East Asia – particularly in counselling and ministry-related topics. For example, while "millennials" in Singapore superficially look a lot like "millennials" in the West, in reality they are very different. Accessing local studies from Singapore or East Asia will give a clearer picture of the issues at stake. You need to minimize your use of Western cultural references (including television programs and popular Western movies), many of which will not be understood by most of your students in Singapore.

- There is still something of a subconscious "colonial deference" which causes Asian students to be fearful of approaching a teacher from the West. It is particularly crucial for Western teachers to go out of their way to be approachable to students.

- Singaporean English is not the same as British or American English. So what you say may not be heard as you intended.

Practical

- In Singapore the weather outside is hot, while the use of air-conditioning keeps the inside of buildings cold. As a result, it is easy to become sick if you are not prepared for the temperature changes.

- The cost of living in Singapore is high, even for people coming from wealthy nations. If you are coming long-term make sure that you raise the expected backing of support before coming and be willing to make major adjustments to what you perceive as a "normal" lifestyle.

- For longer-term foreign teachers, the biggest challenges are housing, transport, and visa renewal. If you come prepared to downsize and live in a high-rise apartment yet trusting God to supply above and beyond out of his abundance, you will be off to a good start. If you are ready to get going on public transport, it will spare you the major disappointments of not owning your own car – among the most expensive in the world because of taxes and government levies. If you come with the knowledge that your visa renewal may suddenly be rejected – which happens a lot because of the local–foreign workers quota – your time here will be more wisely used and treasured.

Teaching Cross-Culturally in Indonesia

Bandung Theological Seminary

Social and Cultural

- Indonesia has many ethnicities and cultures. Each culture has a different way of doing things, and there are several ethnicities that are very proud of their culture. Lecturers must be prepared to face these differences. Don't offend or demean one particular tribe or culture.

- On the whole, gender is not a big issue in Indonesia. However, in many traditional evangelical churches, and especially those with a Chinese background, more traditional gender roles are still strongly held, and this can affect the theological campuses belonging to those particular churches.

- Most theology students come from outside Java. Usually when they register for theological school, they have the goal of returning to their area and serving there. However, after getting an education in a large city and on an extensive campus, many students end up remaining in the cities to serve. Therefore, as a lecturer it is good to continually remind the students of their calling.

- Most theology students come from underprivileged families, so they need to get a scholarship. This affects their confidence, especially when they have to do weekend ministries or internships in big cities whose congregations are middle to upper class.

Religious

- Expect a wide range of denominational backgrounds among your students.

- Because many theology students come from areas where the Christian faith is syncretic with local beliefs, don't be surprised if there are theology students who are still involved with occultism.
- Religious radicalism and fundamentalism are being widely discussed in Indonesia. This makes a very sharp separation between Muslims and non-Muslims. Theological schools therefore very rarely interact with the Muslim community. It is very helpful if the lecturer can help students see beyond their own Christian communities to the wider world around them.
- Blasphemy law is applied in Indonesia, so be careful when discussing other religions. Open critiques of Islam may be perceived as illegal.

Educational

- Theological education in Indonesia is usually very Western-oriented. The curriculum, materials, and teaching methods are generally imported from the West. This is in contrast to Islamic education which strongly emphasizes local culture. Bringing local cultural elements into your teaching will be very beneficial to the students.
- Because theology lecturers usually do not get a large income compared to pastors who serve in the church, often lecturers are underappreciated, and some have problems with self-confidence. Theological schools which are quite rich usually employ lecturers from abroad with a salary far greater than the salary received by local lecturers. This can cause jealousy.
- Indonesian people tend to be oral and do not like to read, so teachers need to be creative in developing appropriate learning methods. Usually students are not ready for too many assignments.
- Because of the traditional educational model they received in school, theology students from rural areas tend to be quiet and don't dare to ask questions. Students from the city are more confident and may dominate discussions in the classroom. You need to find ways to bring out the voices of rural students as against urban students, perhaps through small-group work.
- Due to government regulations, all theological institutions must meet the requirements for accreditation, including qualifications for lecturers from

both within and outside the country. So make sure the degree you have comes from an accredited school.

Language

- Most theology students in Indonesia do not speak English, so lecturers from abroad are often translated.

- There are not many theology books in Bahasa Indonesian. Teachers must be prepared with material that can be easily accessed by students. You should contact the school librarian in advance to see if the school has any relevant resources in Bahasa Indonesian.

- Teachers from abroad who come to teach intensive classes are usually translated while foreign lecturers who live in Indonesia are expected to learn Bahasa Indonesian. Indonesian is one of the easiest languages in the world, so usually within one year of study missionaries are able to preach or teach – even though it may not be perfect.

- When teaching in English, use short, simple sentences. Speak clearly and slowly.

Security and Visas

- For teaching in a short module a tourist visa is acceptable, but where possible it is better to get a social-cultural visa or an educational visa.

Practical

- Indonesia is a tropical country with a lot of rain. We have many good hiking tracks and beautiful mountains.

- Many foods are spicy. If you cannot take spicy foods you will need to be careful with the food your hosts offer.

- Although we have the largest Muslim population in the world, by constitution Indonesia is not an Islamic country, and you don't need to wear Muslim styles of clothing.

Teaching Cross-Culturally in the Philippines

Asian Theological Seminary, International Graduate School of Leadership, Biblical Seminary of the Philippines

Social and Cultural

- The Philippines is often referred to in history books as the "pearl of the Orient seas" because of its shape and its many islands. It is also referred to as "the only Christian nation in the Far East," with a predominance of adherents to the Roman Catholic faith. The country was a Spanish colony for three hundred years, followed by the Americans for a hundred years. These Western influences have shaped the political, social, and religious life of Filipinos.

- The Philippines is slightly less than 50 percent urbanized, although 25 percent of the population lives in the Metro Manila area. The character and quality of life is very different in the provinces, which are much more "laid back," embrace more traditional values, and evidence fewer social extremes. The vast majority of Filipinos have deep links to the provinces and define their culture and heritage by the province that bred them.

- Group harmony: Filipinos place a very high value on *pakikisama* or getting along well with others. Harmony in the group is very important, and friendliness among classmates is expected. Everyone works together to create a sense of unity and belongingness, and students may give way during a disagreement to avoid tension in the group. Students who appear haughty or impolite are not appreciated by other students.

- Family ties are very important, and there are generally deep extended family relationships, with special obligations and financial support expected for family events such as weddings and funerals. Cross-cultural marriages to non-Filipinos are seen as a social bonus, as outsiders are generally viewed as wealthy, with obligations to help the Filipino extended families.

- Respect for authority: Filipinos show respect to parents, teachers, and those in authority. You never argue openly with a key leader. In an educational setting, students show honour and esteem to their professors by addressing them politely and obeying their instructions. While this is true for all Asian cultures, it may be seen more strongly among East Asian students, to the point of bowing and stepping off the sidewalk when a teacher passes by. In a Christian seminary, students will greatly appreciate a teacher who can treat them with respect, friendliness, and care – but wise teachers learn to do this while not setting aside their authority and leadership. It is important to cultivate a biblical emphasis on servant leadership among the faculty, modelling the fruit of the Spirit while strongly leading the students towards God-given goals.

- In meetings (including faculty meetings), generally newer and/or younger members (whether Filipino or non-Filipino) would be expected to listen to and respect the older and more experienced members of the group, even when they disagree. Never walk out of a meeting if you disagree.

- You also need to learn to read non-verbal cues. Filipinos will ask questions indirectly to pursue issues rather than arguing openly. Likewise, a student may hesitate before agreeing to a special project that the teacher has asked him or her to join. Sensitive follow-up questions may help the teacher discover that the student does not have the resources (time, money, or other assets) to do the job. The student would not disrespect the teacher by saying "no," but that momentary hesitation is a clue that the teacher should be aware of. Other cues include the student saying "I'll try" (rather than a strong "yes"), or suggesting another student to do the assignment instead.

- Honour and shame: finding honour and avoiding shame are important cultural values in all of Asia, and can be seen in everyday interactions in a school setting in the Philippines. Entire books have been written on the topic, but suffice it to say that one of the important responsibilities of a teacher is to protect every student from public humiliation. Asking a question directly to a student puts the student in a very awkward position if he or she doesn't know the answer. Giving an example that makes a person or his or her country or local culture look foolish will not easily be forgiven or forgotten. A teacher should filter each interaction through the grid of protecting the honour of the students. If there are important issues that need to be addressed (even though they are shameful), it should be done privately, taking time to assure the student of the teacher's love and acceptance.

- The Philippines has many poor people, and you can expect that some of your students will come from economically challenging situations. You may also encounter quite wealthy students. Keep economic realities in mind as you teach. In particular, be very careful about how you present yourself and what illustrations you use, so as not to create a barrier between yourself and your students.

- Over 10 percent of Filipinos seek to earn money through migrant work in richer nations, especially the Middle East and wealthier Asian nations. These Filipinos hope to earn triple or quadruple the amount they might earn within their home country, allowing them to send home "remittances," but always with the goal of returning. Sadly, many testify to abuse in the countries where they work, and family division and chaos at home.

- Recognize that Filipinos are an amalgam of cultures. Many are of Chinese derivation, and many have been deeply influenced by South Korea or other Asian countries. Be careful about denigrating other nations or cultures.

Political

- The Philippines is a developing nation where most Filipinos are quite nationalistic and proud of their country. Filipinos can be very critical of their own governance, but very defensive if a foreigner criticizes their country. You should not be critical of the Philippines, but rather speak with respect for what has been accomplished despite the challenges. Whatever you do, don't look down on Filipinos or treat them in a condescending way.

- Presidential elections are held every six years. The president can serve only one term. Recent presidential transitions have been peaceful. There are dozens of political parties, so all kinds of deals and negotiations take place to jockey for power. In general, Filipinos are cynical about their leaders and their motives, but support them anyway. Elections are occasions for national holidays.

- It is important not to take sides publicly on political issues, whether in church or in school. Rather you should show respect to people on all sides of a political debate. It is inappropriate to insult political leaders; talk about issues, not personalities.

- You should model praying for those in authority and obeying the government.

Religious

- The Philippines is a very Catholic country with over 80 percent of the population being Catholic adherents. Catholic values are deeply imbedded in the culture. Religious festivals and walking pilgrimages are common. There has been no clear separation between the church and state in the Philippines, and the power of the Roman Catholic Church to dictate political decisions has been evident. The Catholic influence is prominent throughout the country, reflected in such things as the prohibition of divorce and abortion. Particularly as a foreign teacher you should treat the Catholic Church with respect.

- Despite the Catholic heritage, animistic beliefs in spirits, ghosts, and the like remain widespread. Many Filipinos continue to engage in folk practices that may appear to be "superstitious" to non-Filipinos. It is important to approach this common Filipino worldview with a non-condescending attitude. It needs great wisdom to help local Christians better understand what a genuine biblical worldview looks like.

- Evangelicals in the Philippines tend to be conservative and hold to denominational perspectives on theology. Before teaching in the Philippines you should ensure that you are comfortable with the school's theological stance. You should not criticize the position of the school where you teach. Most schools, however, encourage a level of open discussion through the fair presentation of the pros and cons of different perspectives. Talk to your leadership about what is and is not acceptable.

Educational

- Many schools are international, with students from different Asian cultures. Generally, other South East Asians have similar values to the Filipinos' *pakikisama*. Students from South Asia are often more assertive and do not give way so easily, and South East Asians may be tempted to view them as contentious and rude. It's important to take time at the beginning of the school year to orient students and professors to each other's cultures and values.

- You need to be aware that the majority of students, particularly in graduate learning, are already professionals. Bi-vocational study is common. Knowing key life issues will play a significant role in motivating the students.

- Navigating the teaching environment: try to understand the students' life circumstances. For example, if the school does not provide housing, students may spend many hours commuting to attend classes, and lateness may be due to heavy traffic. Filipino time is not fixed or clearly defined, so give room for gracious extensions, or be very clear about deadlines for academic requirements.

- Make sure your assignments are relevant to the students' contexts. When critiquing student work, offer more positives than negatives, and be soft in the critique. Filipinos are very sensitive, even if they don't show it.

- Dealing with shame: you need to avoid shaming students in class discussions, especially if the students' answers do not hit the mark. Accept when students use "go-betweens" to express requests or appeals. Ask if students are ready to openly share their views. Minimize direct comments or assessment of learning.

- Learning preferences of Filipinos: place less emphasis on readings and lectures, and more emphasis on immersed activities and engaged pedagogies.

- Students of any age express respect for teachers, regardless of the teacher's age or gender. "Sir" and "Ma'am" are common designations even when outside the campus, with an added "*po*" or "*opo*" at the end of the sentence to express agreement and respect.

- Building trust is important before teaching. Teaching is seen as a personal gesture, and the first question students will ask is, "Can I trust you?" Students generally have their "small groups of trust" or peer groups and prefer to learn in community. Be aware that what happens in your class will be known by everyone; how you are as a teacher will be known by everyone.

- Generally, Filipinos do not immediately interact or answer a question in a large class. Dividing them into small groups with open-ended questions is very effective. You will suddenly find that everyone is speaking and interacting in the small group. You can encourage quality critical thinking without intimidating students by having groups discuss questions among themselves, reflect on the issues, and report back.

Language

- English is taught in the early grades but then required as the operative language in high school and beyond. Because of the prevalence of the English language in entertainment and on social media, most middle-class and urban Filipinos have a working knowledge of English, but generally less verbal practice. In the provinces and among the poorer populations English is far less used or known.

- Students may have difficulties with English as the language of instruction. Also, their first language may not be Tagalog (Filipino), because there are many dialects in the Philippines.

- Non-verbal cues: get to know the culture of conversation, as it is quite varied and complex.

Practical

- Filipinos ordinarily dress in relaxed mode, and simple, light clothes are prominent. In casual settings shorts are often worn by both men and women. Sandals are common. However, for major cultural events, Filipino women dress in elegant, long flowing gowns of rich colour and ornamentation. Men will dress normally in their "*barong*," a light, starched traditional shirt. Teaching is seen as a significant activity for which more conservative dress is appropriate. Men should wear long trousers and a pair of good-quality shoes when teaching. Women should wear modest clothes, not showing too much skin; trousers paired with a long-sleeved blouse is considered appropriate.

- The rainy season is from June to December, and the dry season from January to May. However, it is best to have an umbrella available in all seasons.

Teaching Cross-Culturally in Taiwan

China Evangelical Seminary

Taiwanese Students

Politics

- Avoid speaking about Taiwanese politics or Taiwan–China cross-straits geopolitics, even if you have studied the issues. Chinese history is too complicated for foreigners to understand. Do not pretend to know. Rather, for contextualization purposes, make an effort to know the latest social issues as they relate to the class discussions.

- Unlike Mainland China, which is a unitary-socialist country, Taiwan is a unitary multiparty democratic country. Human rights are highly valued (including LGBT rights, and the rights of aboriginal minority groups and foreigners). Taiwan is the first country in Asia to legalize homosexual marriage. The Taiwanese highly value health and well-being, as reflected in their National Universal Health Care Service and Insurance. Thus, when combating the COVID-19 pandemic, Taiwanese citizens were united in prioritizing the health and well-being of the community over individual rights. They policed each other in maintaining precautionary measures. Resistance to social consensus on matters of health is negligible.

Culture

- Family is front and centre in Taiwanese culture, although this is being increasingly challenged by modern Western influences.

- The Taiwanese are generally very friendly and polite. There is great respect given to the elderly, evidenced by the reserved priority seats on public transport and priority service in public places.
- The Taiwanese share a social consciousness of rule and order, evident in the low crime rate. Attention to well-ordered behaviour is also seen in such things as lining up and priority numbers when taking buses or receiving public services. To "jump the queue" is frowned upon in Taiwanese society.
- Gender boundaries: observe male–female boundaries. There should be no physical contact. Shaking hands is generally permissible.

Religion

- The majority of the Taiwanese are highly religious and spiritual, with Buddhism, Taoism, and local folk religion (including ancestral worship) widespread. Islam and Christianity are considered minority religions. There is freedom of religion in Taiwan such that social religious persecution is not readily evident. That said, there have been instances of family ostracism when people have converted to Christianity.
- Taiwan churches: people respect megachurches because they have more resources and an organized structure.

Education

- Teaching: pay attention to the speed and to students' reactions or facial responses to see whether they understand or not. Make sure there are almost complete handouts and PowerPoint slides to receive in advance before class.
- Teacher's image: avoid debatable behavioural practices, such as going to bars, smoking, and drinking. The Chinese have a great respect for teachers; they see them as life models. Chinese students admire humble teachers. They do not like teachers who possess a superiority complex, particularly those with an arrogant "colonial" mentality. For example, a comment like "Don't you even know this?" would be received poorly.

- Critiques: the Chinese cannot bear to lose face publicly. They easily get hurt when criticized harshly. The Chinese have a "glass heart" – they break easily. You should therefore correct students in private and with grace, to save the students' face.

- Grade-consciousness: the Chinese care about the final grade they will get. Their abilities and knowledge are measured in terms of grades. Therefore, teachers should provide a clear set of grading standards and expectations. Students are nurtured to compete with one another. They compare grades. They dread this competitive culture but can't avoid it.

- Learning: the Chinese are trained to be passive learners. They are reared in a "banking" culture in which information is delivered by the teachers. They are not used to asking or answering questions for fear of giving wrong answers or asking wrong questions. They are afraid to lose face! Students think there should be a standard answer to each question and are not comfortable with ambiguities and grey areas. However, if teachers can guide them to become active learners, most Chinese students appreciate the more creative way of learning. Use small groups to encourage students to speak up among themselves.

- Teacher–student relationship: this relationship matters, as it allows students to feel comfortable and at ease in learning. Use ice breakers or warm-up activities to start class. However, the teacher–student relationship is still seen within the traditional hierarchical structure, the boundary of which has to be maintained. In order to maintain this boundary, the students may appear cold and unresponsive, but it is their way of showing respect.

- New information: Chinese students expect teachers to give new and recent information and resources. They are more practice-oriented than theoretical.

Practical

- Before coming to Taiwan you should check Taiwan's National Immigration Agency for the latest information on Taiwan's bilateral relations with other countries. Generally, Taiwan is friendly towards foreigners and other nationalities, with little in the way of xenophobia. Red tape, corruption, and bribery are not readily observable in frontline public government offices and institutions.

- Technology: Taiwan is a technologically "smart" country with many services and processes modernized and digitized. This is seen in the public transportation system, the banking system, the postal service, digital payment systems, food and restaurant services, and in many other areas of society.

- Food: no chopsticks, no food. Learn how to use chopsticks. Learn local food culture. If you have particular food preferences, it is best to make these known in advance; do not wait until the food is already offered to you. The Chinese are very hospitable and warm, and like to share good food. Inform the host directly if you are already full. Try to accommodate whatever is offered.

- Clothing: you should dress decently and respectfully, particularly as a teacher.

Mainland Chinese Students

You may encounter students from Mainland China when you teach in Taiwan, and there are a few particular guidelines that you should respect with regard to these students:

- Politics: do not address political issues, even if you know a lot. Just listen.

- History: after decades of national isolation, Mainland China has opened up to all sorts of information, ideas, and beliefs, only to find out that these need to be critically filtered. As a result, Mainland Chinese students have learned to be cautious and defensive about what they hear and read. And because now as a nation they have become a superpower, they are less likely to accept whatever is given to them.

- Learning: self-directed study is not the norm for Mainland Chinese students. They expect direction from the teacher.

Teaching Cross-Culturally in Korea

Torch Trinity Graduate University, Seoul, Korea

Cultural

- A visiting instructor to Korea should be aware of the pervasive influence of Confucianism, which was the national ideology of Korea's pre-modern kingdom (Chosun) for nearly five hundred years. Korean students will generally be age-sensitive and hierarchy-sensitive, showing respect to seniors and authority figures, including professors.

- Greetings: traditionally, when men meet men or when women meet women, they bow to one another when greeting and departing. The younger person should bow lower than the older. This is most typical of the first meeting; subsequent meetings usually involve more of a slow, polite nod. It is always a good idea to initiate the greeting when you meet an elderly person, but *not* to initiate a handshake. When men and women meet, a slight nod or bow of acknowledgment is appropriate. Handshaking is becoming more common in official and professional contexts, particularly when a foreigner is present. The hug is still a rare way of greeting unless the two people are very familiar with each other.

- Korean cultural pride is quite strong. When people ask you whether you like Korea or Korean food or culture, they want to hear you praise Korea, not give a critical analysis of an ancient culture. If you cannot say something positive (and truthful), you are probably not ready to teach in Korea. It would be unwise for someone who knows little about Korea or about the Korean church to criticize the Korean church, its pastors, its music, and so on. Students may criticize, but an international teacher should not be drawn in by the critical comments and offer hasty generalizations. While everyone enjoys the sharing of amusing experiences, you should avoid sharing anything that could be perceived as a negative commentary on some unique aspect of Korea or Koreans. This will usually offend the host. Respect! Respect! Respect! Don't leave home without it!

- Korean culture is changing rapidly, and this is reflected in changing classroom culture. Emerging generations (what have been termed Generations Y and Z) are very different from their parents' generations, although Korean young people continue to be sensitive to the age of others, in part because the Korean language itself differs depending on age: the language Koreans speak to people younger than themselves is different from the language they speak to people older than themselves.

- Korean young people are high tech, fashion conscious, pragmatic, and industrious. They thrive on fast-paced activities, including learning and information-gathering. "What do we have to know for the test?" may be a common question. Similar to other Asian cultures, there's a mix of acceptance and rejection of foreign (Western) ideas and cultural characteristics, probably from a strong sense of cultural identity. The movie industry is a good example in that domestic movies outperform Hollywood releases in box offices across the nation.

- Time: for appointments it is considered polite to arrive on time or just a few minutes early. Arriving late may be viewed as rude by your host. If traffic or other problems delay you, call ahead to inform your host that you are running late. At an initial meeting, be prepared to begin with some small talk, including discussion on whether you are making your first visit to Korea, your impressions of the country, as well as your family, favourite sports, and other interests.

- In Korea, people rarely thank one another for gestures of courtesy (e.g. holding open doors), nor do they generally apologize if they bump into someone on the street. Foreigners may interpret this as being rude or disrespectful, but Koreans consider such minor incidents or manners to be actions that one should anticipate and expect in life. Therefore, they generally do not require a profuse apology, a "thank you," or even an acknowledgment. Respect is exhibited in other ways.

- You should remove your hat when indoors and remove your shoes before entering a Korean home. Blowing your nose at mealtimes is seen by many Koreans as offensive.

Political and Historical

- Please name the country as "Korea," not "South Korea," unless you are specifically contrasting the South and the North. In our daily conversation, we rarely name the South as South Korea, but as Korea.

- Korean history dates back over five thousand years, and many of the older traditions still influence Koreans today. National pride is strong. It is hard to pin down what historically is influencing Korean identity and culture because the impact of the twentieth century is overwhelming: Japanese imperialist domination, a catastrophic civil war between North and South, fast-paced modernization, industrialization, and democratization have all left Koreans somewhat traumatized – but also resilient and determined. Koreans feel proud that they have passed through many painful historical events but have overcome these hardships. It is good to remind your Korean students of their historic identity and national achievements.

- Please do not talk about Korean politics or the relationship between Seoul and Pyongyang. Korean society is polarized, ideologically and regionally, and it is best to distance yourself from these political tangles. You should never openly criticize any of the Korean politicians or political parties. Even regarding international politics it is best to remain circumspect. Be particularly sensitive about people's feelings towards Japan.

- The political history of the twentieth century has left a deep impression and often scars on Koreans. Political partisanship and overall fervour are quite strong, and it is not uncommon to see demonstrations and protests, name calling, and even, on occasion, fist fights based on political partisanship. Korean Protestant Christians tend to be quite conservative politically, which means they are generally pro-American and anti-communist, and relatively more favourable towards normal relations with Japan. Koreans were never colonized by a Western power, so views of the West and globalization are generally more positive than is the case in countries that have been directly subject to Western imperialism.

- As political polarization has grown within Korean society, the same has been seen in the Korean churches and seminaries. Although there is some space for diverse perspectives on various social and religious issues, other issues (such as views on homosexuality or attitudes towards Islam) are viewed through dichotomistic lenses, with divergent views being rejected. Professors from other cultural backgrounds should approach these topics cautiously, carefully and clearly conveying the reasons why they hold their own perspectives on such issues. You best serve the students by helping them see multiple perspectives and come to reasoned decisions based on careful analysis. On occasion it can be appropriate to challenge more partisan or polarized perspectives held by students – but this is best accomplished when done with grace and mercy rather than judgment.

- It might be helpful to encourage students to get involved with international organizations such as the UN, ILO, WTO, and so on. While Korea is contributing a lot of money towards these organizations, actual Korean representation is far less.

Language

- Korean is a phonetic language, and Korea has a near-100 percent literacy rate. Many international words (esp. English) have found their way into the Korean language, but these words may carry slightly different meanings from the original.

- Where English or some other language is the medium, you will gain respect from your students by trying to use some basic Korean language, such as in greetings, self-introduction, or expressing some of your first impressions of Korea.

- English learning is highly prized and children are taught English from an early age. Thus, educated Koreans can read and understand written English fairly well. However, many Korean students are shy about speaking English and also find listening difficult. Koreans feel pressured to speak English without an accent, and there are many after-school academies that look to hire "native speakers" as teachers.

- Korean names consist of a family name, usually of one syllable, plus a given name, usually of two syllables. The family name comes first (Shin Sook-Goo, for example). Until one gets to be on very good terms with a counterpart, it is best to use the family name preceded by an honorific such as Mr., Mrs. or Miss, or Dr. (where relevant), whether speaking directly to the person or speaking about him or her to another Korean. If you are able to do so, learn how to address each student by name in his or her own dialect.

Religious

- Korean Christianity has undoubtedly been influenced by Confucianism. As a result, one may discover a version of Confucian hierarchy in many Protestant churches in Korea.

- In many Korean churches there is a very strong emphasis on the canonical texts, often with a near-literalist interpretation of the Scriptures. This is partly due to the influence of North American fundamentalist missionaries who came to Korea at the early stage of Protestant mission, but it may also be due to the large number of early converts who had been Confucian scholars, who tended to emphasize the close reading of classical texts. The high view of Scripture has played a key role in shaping Korean Christianity's unique spirituality.

- Within Korean Christianity there is great diversity. You should not assume that all Korean churches have the same convictions or structures. The largest denominations of Protestant churches are Presbyterian, although these have become very splintered. Other common denominations are Full Gospel, Methodist, and Baptist.

- Statistically, secularity is now the largest group in Korea, and significant numbers of Koreans claim that they are non-religious. The next largest "religion" is Protestant Christianity, followed by Buddhism and Catholicism. Other groups are negligible in number. While Protestant Christianity is strong in terms of numbers, church size, and influence in society (business, education, government), the media and society at large do not generally look with favour on Protestant churches. Inter-religious relations are generally peaceful and non-violent.

Educational

- Due to the Confucian background, the relationship between teacher and students is usually vertical; regardless of what students think of their teachers inwardly, they usually demonstrate polite and submissive manners to their teachers. Professors occupy a respected role and are generally seen as sages from whom to receive wisdom rather than discussion partners with whom to disagree. Consequently, Korean students will rarely raise questions or bring discussions to the class which may disagree with the teacher's ideas or opinions; instead, students will listen to and accept what teachers say – even if they personally have different ideas or opinions. You will need to be diligent and creative to draw students out and enable them to express their own opinions. It can be very helpful to employ small-group work in which each group has a spokesperson who presents the group's ideas, not any particular individual's ideas.

- Due to the Confucian influence, Koreans intuitively establish hierarchical relationships based on the age, position, status, and educational background of other people relative to themselves. Do not be surprised to be asked questions about your age, marital status, or educational background – even when these questions are considered by many foreigners to be personal in nature. Koreans have been trained that humility is a virtue that a mature man or woman should possess, and that self-exaggeration is arrogant and contemptible. Your students will therefore tend to underestimate their abilities, or at least be reticent about acknowledging them. However, even when a student appears not to be confident about him- or herself, that does not mean he or she is not competitive!

- Korea is a shame-based culture, and students will be reticent about taking any action that might be perceived as shameful. Consequently, you may encounter many students (particularly female students) who are quite silent, even during discussion or question-and-answer times.

Student reticence to speak may be due to (1) limited English fluency and a desire not to reveal their lack of English conversation skills; or (2) lack of confidence with respect to the lesson content; they don't want to be perceived as not-smart students. In each case a desire not to be "shamed" in front of their peers is a motivating factor. Rather than speaking in public you may find that students will approach you individually to ask questions. Sometimes students may speak in a direct and straightforward way that seems out of place; be aware that this is almost certainly due to a lack of English rather than aggression or dissatisfaction.

- Koreans will rarely show heated displays of negative emotions or openly criticize anyone, as such behaviour may be considered impolite. In classroom settings, students rarely raise their voice or aggressively insist on their opinions, even though they might not agree with the opinions of their classmates or instructors. In order to save face, Koreans will seldom give a flat negative response to proposals you make, even when they do not agree with them. Therefore, focus on hints of hesitation and pay close attention to what they may imply. Double-check your understanding by asking open-ended questions.

- Like most Asians, Koreans are collectivistic. They respond well to group work and projects, or when the whole class does something together, rather than individual work. They also share assignments and are ready to help others. Smart students who keep to themselves or don't share their "smarts" are not liked.

- Koreans, especially Korean Christians, normally achieve a high level of education. Korean families spend a higher proportion of their income on children's education than families in most other countries. Graduate theological education is quite saturated, and student numbers are high compared to other countries. Professors will generally find an eagerness to learn among students, especially with foreign instructors. Korean students value handouts and PowerPoint slides. They may also ask to record the lecture for personal review. This is probably due to both language limitation (if teaching in English) and their eagerness to learn.

- Korean students are goal-oriented and interested in what grades they will be rated. While this may serve as a motivational factor with some students, you should also remind students of the internal rewards of learning without grades, if you want to see them continue in self-motivated lifelong learning even when there is no external reward.

- Be careful to minimize the amount of cultural baggage you bring with you. Illustrations and applications that are relevant in your own context may well be irrelevant or even offensive in Korea. Take time to get to know the students outside class. Listen to their struggles and life circumstances. You will then be better able to relate your teaching to the students' world. Even then, be aware that the general setting of Korea finds multiple expressions as students come from different parts of Korea. Seek to choose texts that are more international in approach, rather than texts that reflect Western culture and values. As a foreign professor you should listen and ask more than you speak and tell. You should avoid passing judgment based on your preconceptions.

- Because of language issues you should speak slowly and clearly and repeat your points. Using a clear PowerPoint presentation can help students follow the lesson. If you do not understand the students' questions or comments, be patient and ask politely for clarification. Do not openly express your frustration.

- Do not expect the students to address you by your first name, which would be unthinkable in Korea. In your first session clarify how you want to be addressed; for example, Dr. [first name] or Dr. [last name].

- Avoid terms such as "Third World," "developing world," or "Global South," which can be seen as pejorative. "Majority World" is an acceptable alternative. Even this term should not be used to refer to Korea, which is an economic powerhouse in Asia.

- Time: Korean students like their classes to begin and end punctually on time. You should respond quickly to emails or text messages.

- Be aware that student solicitation is against the law. In Korea, college professors need to take seriously the Improper Solicitation and Graft Act.[1]

---

1. The English version of the Act is found on the Korean government website, http://www.acrc. go.kr/en/data/3.0.Improper%20Solicitation%20and%20Graft%20Act.pdf.

Teaching Cross-Culturally in India

Indian Theological Educators Forum (Beacon Baptist
Theological College and Seminary), South Asia
Nazarene Bible College (Bangalore), and Centre
for Global Leadership Development (Bangalore),
with Additional Material from Dr. Jessy Jaison

History and Politics

- Be aware that India may be one nation, but it represents a wide variety
  of languages, peoples, and cultures. The country has people of enormous
  wealth and abject poverty, as well as a substantial middle class. Urban and
  rural contexts differ dramatically. You can often gain a good understanding
  of your students by discussing in advance with the administration and
  faculty at the school where you are teaching.

- In the postcolonial period, the government of India made efforts to
  promote a universal education system as a way to develop the nation.
  Since 1949 successive Indian governments have sought to achieve universal
  primary education, to eradicate illiteracy, and to establish higher levels of
  education through several planning commissions. In 2009 the Right to
  Education Act was passed to give free education to children aged between
  six and fourteen. The level of education in India is developing across the
  board, but particularly in the fields of information science and technology.

- The socio-religious and political situation is shifting dramatically in
  India, with numerous implications for those who come to the country
  and those who host them. The dominance of the current Hindu nationalist
  party (Bharatiya Janata Party) in India is largely a reaction to historic
  grievances, in particular the centuries of Mughal and British rule. The

BJP are particularly sensitive about anything that would appear to be anti-Hindu – including evangelism and conversions. It is important for visiting instructors to understand these historical-political issues.

Social and Cultural

- Dress code: the visiting instructor must follow a decent dress code that is acceptable in the national context. Students and faculty come from diverse cultures and a modest dress code is a sign of respect for the nationals whom you are planning to serve. Men should wear trousers and a long-sleeved shirt, and women should wear a sari, *chudidhar*, long skirt, or formal dress pants with long top, falling to just above the knee. You should take off your footwear when you visit homes, a church, temple, or mosque, or any other religious place.

- Gender relationships: proximity and interactions between the genders often follow set limits. This might vary from place to place. In certain parts of India women are not allowed to look directly into the eyes of a man or sit alongside or eat together with men. It is disrespectful for a man to ask the age of a woman or the salary of her husband. The norm throughout much of India in church and in the classroom is for women and men to sit separately. It is best to first consult with the school leadership if you wish to have students engage in mixed small-group discussions or assignments. That said, it is common for two men or two women to hold hands while walking in the streets or market. They are not gay or lesbian; it is a gesture of friendliness and closeness of heart.

- Greeting people: shaking hands with a person of the opposite gender is generally inappropriate. One should never greet someone with the left hand. Particularly in rural areas, the preferred greeting and leave-taking is the *namaste*: a slight bow, with hands pressed together, palms touching and fingers pointing upwards, thumbs close to the chest.

- Respecting elders is highly valued throughout India. Indians do not address elders by name as is done in the West. Even Indian professors do not call by name students who are older than they are. Older students are addressed either as "brother" or "sister" or "pastor" (if a male student has been a pastor).

- Hospitality: hospitality is highly valued throughout India, but the practice varies from region to region. In much of India friends and guests are happily welcomed in homes, even without prior appointment. The host expresses his or her welcome by offering you a cup of tea if you arrive at odd times, and dinner or lunch if you happen to arrive at a mealtime. If a person invites others for tea or for a meal in a restaurant, the expectation is for that person to pay for all. You should check what is appropriate to the local context, to understand preferred protocols for inviting and being invited by local Indians. You may also need to watch what is served: you may enjoy the hospitality but end up in a hospital. Do not be the victim of hospitality! In church or inaugural services, guests are often welcomed and appreciated by having a flower garland placed around their necks.
- Indians love to hear visitors trying to learn and speak the local language.

Religious

- Be aware of the range of denominational backgrounds of the students and show respect to all.
- Be aware of other religious faiths, especially the predominant faiths in a given locality. Avoid denigrating other religions. Religion is considered an essential part of every sphere of life. Indians are very sensitive to their traditions and beliefs and feel pride in belonging to their particular religion. There is freedom in India to speak about other religious beliefs along with your own beliefs in Indian classrooms, but ridiculing other religious beliefs in public is not acceptable.
- Treat the Bible with respect. Out of respect for the text Indian students generally prefer professors to use printed copies of the Bible rather than digital versions. You should check to see if there is a preferred translation at the school and/or among the churches represented by your students.
- It is very important to remember that Indians respect sacred texts. Consequently, you should avoid placing the Bible on your legs or on the chair next to you, and never place the Bible on the floor.

Educational

- In India there is a traditional distance of respect between teacher and students. Consequently, you need to accept honorifics such as "Dr." Since Indian culture is a shame-based culture it is inappropriate to criticize anyone publicly. Even Indian teachers can be insensitive to the unspoken feelings of their students. In light of the general social value of hospitality, it can be valuable to see yourself as a host for your students. You may be asked personal and family questions in class. While these may be seen as intrusive in another culture, in India matters relating to family are shared to strengthen relational rapport. However, be careful about sharing negative personal stories. While in some cultural contexts sharing a personal testimony of brokenness or family problems can be a powerful means of being transparent and transformative, in India students may internally perceive these stories as evidence of moral or spiritual decline. Great wisdom is needed to find the balance between vulnerability and authority in the classroom.

- India is largely an oral society, and students generally prefer oral learning patterns such as storytelling and practical life experiences. Having students relate personal experiences helps make your teaching live, but you will need to be prepared to moderate: many students take a lot of time to tell their stories. Often it can be better to have the students tell their stories in small groups, but even then the process needs to be supervised.

- Even when the medium of teaching is English, for most students English is not their native language. Consequently, you should use simple and plain language, and avoid slang or idiomatic expressions, as students will likely not understand what you are saying. If you do choose to use an idiomatic expression, make sure to explain its meaning and significance. Humour is particularly shaped by culture, and a joke in one country will likely fall flat in another. It can be valuable to practise a few expressions in the local dialect for use in class.

- South Asian non-verbal communication is unique and there are different patterns throughout India. For example, the nodding of the head is often confusing to a Westerner in terms of determining whether the response is positive or negative. A slight variation in nodding can change the meaning to the exact opposite of what is meant. A quiet smile can sometimes signal the learner's shyness or graceful withdrawal from an active conversation.

Avoid winking, whistling, pointing your fingers, or shaking your legs, as these carry negative cultural meaning in some localities in India.

- Be aware that rote learning is still the norm in much of India, and students may not have experience in Western approaches to "critical thinking." It is important to plan your classes carefully with lecture notes and thought-provoking questions in order to promote analytical thinking among your students. It is often helpful to begin with rote-learning elements and move on from there.

- Due to the high cultural regard for sacred texts in general, critical analysis of scriptural passages or theological topics should be engaged with great caution and discretion. If you feel it crucial to challenge a loved local belief, then do it pastorally, with plenty of space for students to express their feelings and concerns, and discussion of how the students can continue to show due respect to existing church leadership.

- Under no circumstances should you make promises to students (e.g. of any sort of financial assistance, travelling abroad, or future collaboration). You should keep in mind the goal of training the students to live in their own cultural contexts and avoid making other contexts seem attractive.

- Helping students see similarities between their own cultural background and the cultural background of the Bible can contribute to the students' appreciation of their heritage.

- Teaching students coming from village settings will require more adaptation skills on the part of the teacher. Keep in mind that many learners are facing multiple challenges simply for daily survival. Most village students have not been trained in how to approach a formal education. Often these students are highly intelligent and insightful, but their thinking processes are different.

- You may encounter strikingly different concepts about time. Indians sometimes joke that "Indian Standard Time" (IST) is actually "Indian Stretchable Time." You may need to put aside much of your planned curriculum, seeking rather to engage students through a process of learning from observation and continual feedback.

- Be an active participant in the community life of the college, walking around the campus and chatting with the people you meet. India is a highly communal society and your community engagement will mean a lot to students.

- Do not attempt to give personal or professional counsel to students. If a student raises issues with you, contact the student dean or counselling department of the school. It is probable that you will not understand all the cultural factors at stake, and it is best to leave these discussions to local professionals.

Security and Visas

- There is some uncertainty about what visas are appropriate for those coming from overseas to teach in India. With the current Hindu nationalist government, long-term missionary-teacher visas are now virtually impossible to secure. There have been cases of missionaries being deported. If you come on a tourist visa, it is wise to do some tourism as a part of your visit, and you should avoid any sort of public ministry beyond the college where you teach.

- From an ethical point of view, it is preferable that you do not come on a tourist visa, but rather get advice from the school as to what sorts of visas might be legal and possible. If you seek to come for any extended time on a tourist visa you will likely lose your credibility among the staff and students of the college, and eventually among the Christian community. Imagine the hypocrisy of a visiting faculty member teaching ethics, but not following proper visa rules!

- Submission of a Form-C to the local police is mandatory for foreign nationals even when they are staying in a hotel, homestay, serviced apartment, or with an Indian family. Having a trusted local contact address is vitally important. Most importantly, avoid terms like "ministry," "mission," "preaching," and so on, particularly in more sensitive regions of the country.

- In the past there was not much concern about having international faculty teaching Christian communities in Christian churches or conference centres, but the situation is changing in many parts of the country. Be particularly aware that teaching or preaching in public places can be interpreted as an attempt to proselytize.

Teaching Cross-Culturally in North-East India

Shalom Bible Seminary and Oriental Theological Seminary, Nagaland, India

Cultural

- The north-east can be very culturally diverse and quite different from the rest of India in terms of culture, ethnicity, food habits, and perspectives.
- North-eastern peoples of India have very strong allegiance to their traditions, cultural mores, belief systems, and village polities.
- Respect of elders is seen as a tribal virtue. High respect is given to elders at every level of society. This can sometimes inhibit leadership development as the elderly continue to be in responsible positions without proper educational qualifications. However, it is crucial to be respectful of elders in every situation.
- Hospitality is valued extremely highly. Embrace hospitality generously; your hosts may be offended if you are not open.
- Food habits can seem a little strange at times; try to be accommodative. Some people joke that north-easterners eat anything that moves!
- Technology is still limited even though outwardly the north-east is globally connected.

Political and Postcolonial

- Generally, the north-east of India is a politically restive region, characterized by a people's movement towards autonomy and a desire for freedom from mainstream Indian domination.

- Militarization by the Indian government in the north-eastern states has led to many conflicts which have remained unresolved. For this reason the entry of foreigners in north-eastern states is sometimes restricted. Advance planning is crucial to ensure that special permits are secured as necessary. These permits are in addition to the usual visa requirements.
- Human rights violations and issues related to the imposition of draconian laws by the Indian armed forces in the north-east have brought associated problems to the region.
- Because of the diversity of the region, state politics in the respective north-eastern states are driven by linguistic, tribal, and geographical loyalty.
- Politically, India is a multiparty, constitutional democratic and secular country. It is of value to be aware of the local dominant party and its policies, and how these may differ from prevailing politics in the rest of India.
- Because of problematic politics, especially an electioneering system in which money power decides the fate of a political party, the quality of infrastructure in some north-eastern states (particularly Nagaland) is poor.
- Throughout India (including the north-east) people tend to mix politics with religion and religion with politics.

Historical

- India was a British colony until it gained independence in 1947. The colonial era brought much good alongside many negative side effects.
- Historically, most of the north-eastern people were formerly independent tribal communities. Nagaland declared its independence from India on 14 August 1947 but was nonetheless incorporated into India. Many current tensions have deep historic bases.

Religious

- Many of the north-eastern states of India are majority Christian. However, tribal religious beliefs and practices (animism) remain dominant in north-east India, such as the importance of dreams, fortune telling, the use of seers and healers, belief in lycanthropy, witchcraft, and fetish objects. A level of syncretism that involves these traditional practices is prevalent in north-east India, even among Christians and especially among the older generation. Such practices appear to be in decline among younger generations of Nagas.

- Unlike the dominant secular belief structure of the West, in north-east India belief in supernatural beings and realities is still very strong.

- The north-eastern people of India have their own church traditions which are grounded in their denominational backgrounds and traditional village polities.

- Oral tradition remains strong, and people (including students) respond well to narrative teaching and preaching.

- There is often a dichotomy between faith and action among many professing Christians.

- In church worship, especially in the villages, men and women are seated separately, and a broader level of segregation is common.

- In village settings, as well as in other formal settings, both men and women dress conservatively, particularly in church services. On the other hand, in many urban churches, going to church is like a "fashion show." Most visitors experience an urban setting first before going to rural areas, and it is important that you be aware of the differences.

Educational

- Teacher-centred: the teacher is viewed as the main source of learning. This is culturally conditioned in that elders are highly respected and listened to.

- In many secular schools and universities students are still expected to be passive recipients in the classroom setting. They will not generally stop the teacher to ask questions, clarify doubts, or engage in the discussion voluntarily unless they are specifically asked. Students are dependent on the teacher for receiving information and are not disposed towards critical thinking. This traditional approach is changing with new curricular patterns, and most seminaries are moving to more interactive approaches to learning. However, many students are still not used to articulating their personal ideas and perspectives and may prefer the teacher to provide ready-made notes and direct answers.

- Generally, the broader educational system is centred more on quantity than on quality of learning. There is a strong emphasis placed on the power of memory, with rote learning being a standard learning methodology. Within secular colleges and universities a "banking system" of education prevails, with grades based largely or exclusively on exams which test memorization. While many theological colleges are developing more varied learning and assessment practices, the dominant memorization and assessment-by-exams pattern remains a challenge.

- Nagas in general prefer more practically oriented learning to theoretical learning. However, in some schooling contexts it can be the reverse, because education in Nagaland by and large depends on how much you know rather than how much you can apply. The large number of "educated unemployed" is indicative of this problem. Theological education that focuses on practice will generally be valued and can counter wider negative patterns in education.

- North-east India is a "degree-oriented society" in which a strong emphasis is placed on educational qualifications attained, and self-esteem is related to the qualifications held.

- For cross-cultural teaching, one needs to be open-minded, flexible, willing to learn, and not rigid with presupposed theological, political, or religious opinions, notions, and ideas.

Teaching Cross-Culturally in Sri Lanka

Lanka Bible College and Seminary

Political, Geographic, and Historical

- Sri Lanka is a unique island, and its shape and location (a mere 48 km from India) have led some to call it "the teardrop of India." The land measures 435 kilometres in length and 225 kilometres in width.

- The current constitution stipulates the political system as a republic and a unitary state governed by a semi-presidential system.

- Sri Lanka's documented history spans three thousand years, with evidence of prehistoric human settlements dating back at least 125,000 years. Because of its colonial past Sri Lanka has a love–hate relationship with the West. After its independence in 1948 Sri Lanka was marred by a thirty-year civil war which ended in 2009.

- Most Tamil students do not trust the early history of Sri Lanka as given in the book of *Mahavamsa*, as the *Mahavamsa* was written by Buddhist monks from Buddhist perspectives. Most Tamils believe that the account is highly exaggerated and has been made to conform to the writer's religious assumptions. Also, they think these are so improbable that they cannot be accepted as historical facts. Therefore, we cannot mention the book of *Mahavamsa* to Tamil students as a source for the history of Sri Lanka. If you do so, Tamil students will almost certainly be offended.

- Sri Lankan history in general has been interpreted from a majority Buddhist perspective, with an anti-white and anti-colonial perspective. A foreigner who comes to Sri Lanka needs to remember that the country was colonized three times, by the Portuguese, Dutch, and English, and much pain is still felt as a result of the foreign exploitation of the Sri Lankan community that took place during this period of history. Many Sri Lankans see Christianity as simply another form of colonization. Therefore, any sort of prominent white presence among Sri Lankan Christians must be avoided.

Cultural and Religious

- Sri Lanka is the home to many cultures, languages, and ethnicities. The majority of the population is ethnically Sinhalese, with a significant minority of Tamils. Moors, Burghers, Malays, Chinese, and the indigenous Vedda are also notable minority ethnicities on the island.

- Sri Lanka is also a religiously diverse country. While Buddhists comprise a majority at about 70 percent of the population, there are sizeable minorities of Hindus and Muslims. These three religions are officially affirmed in the Sri Lankan flag, with the golden lion in the Buddhist yellow field, and orange and green stripes recognizing the Hindu and Muslim minorities. Christianity entered Sri Lanka during the period of Western colonialism from the early sixteenth through to the twentieth century. Around 8 percent of the Sri Lankan population is Christian, the majority of whom trace their religious heritage directly to the period of Portuguese influence.

- Most of your students will come from Buddhist or Hindu backgrounds. In order to engage meaningfully with these students, it will be valuable for you to have a working knowledge of these religions – particularly the Sri Lankan expressions of Buddhism and Hinduism. On the other hand, you may find that a significant number of Tamil students come from several generations of Christian background, and although their deep background may be Hindu, many of these students know little or nothing about Hinduism.

- Many Sri Lankan schools are interdenominational, with students coming from various denominations. Consequently, some students will be very sensitive about certain topics, and you need to be particularly careful when you are speaking about the Holy Spirit, spiritual gifts, views on the end times, marital issues such as divorce, and other topics where there are differences among evangelical believers. If you approach these topics critically your students may feel that you are attacking their church and/ or their pastor. You need to show grace and patience when dealing with these sensitive topics.

- In some parts of Sri Lanka, watching movies is seen as inappropriate for Christians. Consequently, you need to be careful about making references to movies in class; for many Sri Lankans the illustrations won't make sense, and the students may not understand why you know about movies. If you want to discuss recent movies to highlight social issues or help students engage with contemporary society, you should first consult the leadership of the host school to see if there is any issue. It may be best to be circumspect and leave local teachers to address legalisms in the church.

- Be aware that activities that may be acceptable among Christians in your home country might be misunderstood or frowned upon in Sri Lanka. In particular, while you are in Sri Lanka it is best to refrain from drinking, smoking, visiting pubs or nightclubs, or spending time alone in private with someone of the opposite sex.

- Learning religion is compulsory in the Sri Lankan education system.

Educational

- The Sri Lankan education system is top-down and memory-centred. Success comes through memorizing and then repeating the material in exams. Sri Lankan students are used to learning very passively. Consequently, you should not expect students to know how to engage creatively in class. They will need a lot of guidance and help in independent thinking. You may need to play a stronger role in stimulating thinking and interaction than you would in your home country.

- Given that school education is done primarily on the basis of the teacher supplying information, most students are reluctant to ask questions of a teacher. In fact, in Sri Lanka, to question a teacher is often considered an act of disrespect towards a higher authority. Most students will take without question what the teacher says on a certain topic rather than developing their own thinking and perspectives.

- Plagiarism is normal in Sri Lankan culture. Since students make use of teachers' material for their exams without any reference to the original sources, some guidelines must be given to them regarding plagiarism. Great care, patience, and clarity must be exercised in handling this issue.

- Many who come to theological education in Sri Lanka may be from poor backgrounds and may not have had higher educational qualifications prior to their theological education. This needs to be taken into consideration when you set your expectations as a teacher.

- Students will not call a lecturer by his or her first name because it is considered disrespectful. The normal way to address those who teach is "sir" if you are male and "teacher" or "madam" if you are female.

- Students enjoy integrative educational approaches, in which theory and practice are interwoven with stories, but they often struggle with linear "systematic" Western approaches.

- Students appreciate creative learning methods which resonate with traditional Sri Lankan culture – such as writing poems, developing dramas, composing songs, and drawing.

Language

- Remember that English is a second or even third language for students. Even when class sessions are delivered in English, many students will have limited fluency in English, and consequently may find it difficult to understand your accent and grasp what you're trying to communicate. You should speak slowly and clearly. Avoid complex vocabulary, and try to communicate things in a simple way.

- Avoid using Western jokes. Students probably will not understand the joke. And if the joke is to be translated, the translator will find it difficult if not impossible to put the joke into the Sinhala or Tamil language.

- Very few theological books are available in the Sinhala and Tamil languages. If students are asked to read texts in English, many will have difficulty with complex ("heavy") vocabulary, so make sure that your assigned readings use simple and clear language. You should be realistic in the amount of reading you ask from students.

- Be practical. Students will respond best when the courses are beneficial and relevant to their lives and ministry contexts. Assigning practical work alongside the academic materials is helpful. Seek to integrate theory and practice.

Teaching Cross-Culturally in Pakistan

Pakistan Theological Educators' Forum

Social and Cultural

- Dress codes: women should dress modestly. Women are usually expected to wear a head covering in church and whenever praying or reading the Bible. Men should also be well covered and should not wear shorts. Naked flesh is generally frowned upon. For preaching or teaching a jacket and tie is seen as appropriate. Your appearance matters.

- Gender relationships: be aware of what is appropriate and inappropriate behaviour between members of the opposite sex, and what is appropriate and inappropriate behaviour between members of the same sex. For example, shaking hands with a person of the opposite sex is often inappropriate, but embracing or hugging a person of the same sex is appropriate. Men holding hands is normal and does not have sexual overtones. Do not use the East Asian/Indian "praying hands" (*namaste*) for greetings or thanks; it is seen as "Hindu" and is disliked by the Muslim majority.

- Family relationships are very important in Pakistan and in a clash with work responsibilities, family responsibilities will usually take precedence. This may be a problem for a teacher with a strong "Protestant work ethic." Hospitality is also very important, and a Pakistani teacher may give priority to guests over students (which may also cause conflict).

- Hospitality and respect are strong values. For example, expect to be greeted with the traditional garland. Please receive hospitable gestures graciously.

- Pakistan varies by region, and you should have an idea of the ethnic background of the city in which you are teaching. For example, Lahore is a Punjabi city while Karachi is more ethnically diverse. Regional historical and ethnic backgrounds shape every aspect of your listeners.

Religious

- Expect a wide range of denominational backgrounds among your students. Please do not try to press your own theological beliefs too much. In general, the Pakistani church is theologically conservative.
- In many churches, shoes are taken off and left outside. Shoes (and feet) are considered unclean.
- The Bible is not just any book – it is a *holy* book. Never put the Bible on the floor, and never sit on top of the Bible. Treat the physical book with respect, preferably keeping it on a stand or in a high place. The Bible and preaching are viewed as having great authority deserving of respect. Please be careful not to be critical of either.
- For many Pakistani Christians, much Christian practice is influenced by Muslim practice. For example, common popular beliefs include the following: reading the Bible is a meritorious thing to do even if you do not understand it; fasting between sunrise and sunset for forty days in Lent earns merit in God's eyes; menstruating women should not read the Bible, pray, fast, or attend church.
- Be aware of the other faiths around, especially the majority faith, and be aware of its complexity. Not all Muslims are the same. There is a strong element of folk Islam in Pakistan. Be aware of the tensions between the religious communities and the reasons for them, especially the blasphemy law, extra-judicial killings, and mob violence on the pretext of blasphemy.
- Please speak graciously and politely about Islam. While the teacher can return to his or her country, the locals have to live with the consequences if a teacher makes derogatory remarks about Islam.

Educational

- Understand the lower level of education of most Pakistani students compared with that of students in your home country. Pakistan is a predominantly oral society, and even at Bible schools and seminaries students prefer the oral over the written. Literacy levels are quite low throughout society. Most students have come through a very traditional education system that relies on rote learning. Don't set unrealistic assignments. Students' expectations may be different from what you are used to. Most notably they may expect to be given information rather than being made to think or find out for themselves, because that has been their previous experience of education.

- Know your target audience – their age range, educational qualifications, church backgrounds, social backgrounds, and so on. Be aware that, historically, the majority of the Pakistani Christian community came from a low-caste Hindu background, and any Pakistani Christian can face discrimination on the grounds of caste ("untouchability") whatever his or her background.

- Students will not be familiar with Western educational approaches, but generally respond well to creative teaching methods. They may have more difficulty being creative themselves. Giving very detailed step-by-step guidelines helps students be more comfortable with approaches they may not have encountered previously.

- Do not publicly critique students. Expect students to talk around a sensitive issue rather than addressing it directly. For example, if students differ from one another in their faith perspective, they may be reticent to argue about it in class.

Language

- Expect to be interpreted. Most students will not be comfortable with English and will prefer translation into Urdu. Assume that you will cover less than half of your normal content because of time needed for translation. If possible, provide the text of your teaching notes in advance for the translator so that he or she can be prepared. It is good to prepare supplemental teaching aids (PowerPoints etc.) to ensure the message is clear.

- Try to avoid very idiomatic language. The structure of Urdu grammar makes it difficult to translate complex sentences. In particular, keep in mind that in Urdu the main verb comes at the end of the sentence, unlike in English where it is towards the beginning.

- Be aware that for many if not all students, their first language is a local dialect, their second language is Urdu, and (if at all) their third language is English. Whether you teach in English or through translation into Urdu, keep your vocabulary as simple as possible and speak slowly and clearly. Speak in short, simple sentences. Use complete sentences as far as possible. Avoid using excessive sub-clauses.

- Be extremely circumspect in the use of animals in illustrations. Animals are generally seen as dirty and offensive.

Practical

- Avoid talking about politics.
- Be aware that there is an element of risk in coming to Pakistan, but don't exaggerate it. In most places life continues peacefully most of the time. Expect to enjoy your visit.
- When travelling to Pakistan, avoid having an Indian visa or stamps in your passport, and certainly not Israeli stamps. Don't travel via Delhi or Mumbai. Be aware that India and Pakistan have a seventy-year history of bad relationships. A Bangladeshi visa might also be a problem. Be aware that the reverse is also true: you may be refused entry to India or Bangladesh with a Pakistani visa in your passport! Some international guests use two passports to enable them to travel more freely.
- It is preferable (if possible) to get a religious or educational visa rather than a tourist visa. Please consult well in advance to see if the school can arrange this. Schools are regularly interviewed by the police after a visitor comes and the school needs to be able to give an honest response to their questions. Remember that it can take weeks and even months to get a visa approval.
- Determine what the weather will be like at the time of year you are visiting and be aware of the diversity of climates in Pakistan. Bring appropriate clothing for the season and the region: warm clothes and waterproofs for winter, light cotton clothes for summer.

Teaching Cross-Culturally in Bangladesh

College of Christian Theology Bangladesh

Social, Religious, and Cultural

- It is very important for a teacher who comes from a different country to know the religious context and background, because these shape the behaviour and attitudes of the people. Try not to apply your own religious context and culture, which the students or the local people may find hard to accept. Wisdom and patience are needed to determine what change is possible and appropriate, and what is not.

- Even within our country there are different religious understandings in different contexts. For example, for some people, using "Allah" for God is acceptable but others will not like it. A newcomer should be respectful in dealing with the religious context and background as he or she communicates with people. Be careful not to show disrespect towards other religious perspectives, as this will cause you to lose acceptance.

- Bangladeshis value hospitality highly and greatly appreciate the time taken to eat together or chat over a cup of tea. However, you need to be aware that food is a big issue in Bangladeshi culture because there are different foods that are allowed or forbidden depending on the religion and culture. For example, in most of the tribal culture wine is acceptable, but not among other groups; in Hindu culture beef is forbidden; and in Muslim culture pork and alcohol are prohibited. Some of these religious taboos have found their way into the church; most notably the drinking of alcohol is seen as inappropriate among many Christians. Be cautious about offering the sort of food you would eat in your home country. Equally, if someone offers you food that you do not eat, you are free to refuse, but do so gently and graciously, so as not to cause offence. The bottom line is to respect one another's eating restrictions.

- Bangladesh is a profoundly hierarchical society. You are either further up or further down, and as a teacher you will be disrespected if perceived as lower in the hierarchy. Patron–client relationships put great pressure on the leader to meet the high expectations of the people. As a possible "patron" you may be expected to provide funds or at least access to donor organizations, and you will need wisdom in knowing how to discourage these expectations. Keep in mind that Bangladeshis do not say "no" to a superior, but simply don't fulfil the request, or explain that they did not understand it.

- Personal honour is very important, and consequently Bangladeshis will seldom admit their mistakes or apologize, instead seeking to put the blame on others who are absent or have a lower position in the hierarchy. At all costs you need to avoid shaming a student.

- In seeking to honour a guest, Bangladeshis will try to say what they think the guest wants to hear. Consequently, you should take compliments lightly. Sometimes Bangladeshis will flatter a foreigner in the hope of obtaining something from him or her – perhaps a higher grade or financial help.

- Clothing is a very important issue in Bangladesh. The national dress is *panjabi*, which some leaders display proudly. Women should dress modestly. Traditionally it has not been acceptable for them to wear T-shirts, shorts, or sleeveless outfits publicly, although this is changing – particularly given that the Bangladeshi garment industry produces T-shirts and jeans for much of the world. If possible, follow the dress code of our country and wear similar clothes to those worn by national women leaders. Men should wear trousers (not shorts) and quality shirts. For special programs *panjabi* or a suit and tie is often expected. However, accepted dress codes are changing. Come prepared, ask your host in advance, and observe local leaders.

- Usually people in Bangladesh arrive for visits a little late. When you invite someone to your home or you get an invitation from others, keep this in mind so that there is no misunderstanding. The people of Bangladesh are highly relational, and they may visit you and your family without any notice. You should accept this as normal and respond positively with acceptance and respect.

- Weather is an important issue to keep in mind. In Bangladesh we have six seasons and weather changes frequently: heat, heavy rains, and floods are all normal. Those who come to Bangladesh should be prepared to cope with all kinds of weather.

- Bangladesh is one of the most populous countries in the world and Bangladeshis feel comfortable in crowds and large groups of people. You will particularly notice the dense population if you stay in one of the two largest cities, Dhaka or Chittagong, where you need to be prepared for extremely crowded streets, heavy traffic jams, and pollution. Particularly in the cities, Bangladeshis, in their fight for survival, can become very "me-first"-oriented, with little care for other people's opinions and needs.

- The people of Bangladesh are very sensitive about political issues. As a visitor you should not discuss or try to influence others about politics.

- We suggest that every visiting faculty member finds a local accountability partner or mentor to help him or her understand the culture, context, language, and so forth. If you stay longer, having a local mentor with whom you share life will be crucial in case you are in a crisis and need assistance.

Teaching

- The educational system in Bangladesh traditionally relied on memorization. Some students even memorize mathematics! An essay-type exam may cause fear, although students will recognize it as an important part of their study. Often students will feel that if there is no final exam their learning is inadequate. Teachers should provide some lectures in their teaching. Keep in mind that Bangladeshi students are often afraid to ask questions of the teacher.

- It is recognized among many in Bangladesh that higher education (including theological education) needs to go beyond memorization to the development of more complex forms of thinking and behavioural competencies. But many teachers have received inadequate training, and you will need patience in helping both your students and your colleagues to adapt to new approaches to instruction and assessment.

- Students in Bangladesh strive to please their teachers in the hope of getting good grades. Keep in mind that many Bangladeshis have had the experience of receiving poor or failing grades when they expressed their personal opinions – largely because they did not simply repeat the teacher's opinion. It will take time and creativity to open a space for your students to develop their own voices in class and written work.

- There is a great need for practical resources in Bangladesh. You will do a great service if you can train students in designing materials that can be used more widely in the church, such as resources for Sunday school teachers, pastors, and lay preachers.

- Language is a common obstacle for both visiting teachers and local students. Even where English is the medium of instruction, most students have difficulty communicating in English because their experience in the use of the English language is very limited. When someone speaks quickly or teaches in "high" English the students might not fully understand the teaching and instructions. Try to avoid making complex sentences or using idiomatic expressions or colloquialisms. A hard copy of lecture notes with very simple sentences is helpful. It is very much appreciated if visiting teachers learn something of our language. Even a basic knowledge of the vernacular can help you to understand student misinterpretations, weird grammar, and inappropriate choice of words.

Teaching Cross-Culturally in Lebanon

Arab Baptist Theological Seminary

Social and Cultural

- There are multiple cultures in the Arab world. Defining "Arab" is very difficult, if not impossible. Many who study in Arabic do not consider themselves to be Arab – and may even have a tribal communal hatred towards the Arabs. For some students, Arabic is their second or even third language. Students are generally very proud of their country and can often be easily insulted if their country is denigrated.

- While some parts of the Middle East and North Africa (MENA) region are renowned for how expressive the people are, other regions encourage quiet deference to teachers. In particular, Sudanese students come from deeply tribal contexts in which the questioning or criticizing of authority figures is seen as shameful. Some visiting instructors are taken aback by the reluctance of students to participate and/or the tendency of a small handful to dominate discussions. You should plan ahead of time to develop strategies for promoting the quieter voices and laying down boundaries for students who seek to monopolize class discussions.

- Many parts of the MENA region are still quite traditional in terms of gender role expectations – although this is definitely changing, particularly in urban contexts. It is still a common expectation in many parts of the MENA region for women to defer to men in the classroom, and you may need to be intentional in giving space for quieter women to speak. Some instructors use gender-specific small groups in the classroom to ensure the women's voices are heard. Female instructors occasionally face challenges from men coming from more traditional contexts. However, as a counterpoint, be aware that throughout the MENA region more women graduate from university than men.

- Racism towards Africans and Asians is widespread in the MENA region. In particular, be aware that Sudanese students may experience racist comments or attitudes – certainly in the wider community, but even at times in local churches or within the theological community. You should feel free to address such racism.

- A dominant question for many students in the MENA region is, "Who is the pharaoh?" Students come from contexts with the assumption of patron–client relationships, and many students will seek to ingratiate themselves with those they perceive as having power, including visiting instructors. You should therefore be extremely cautious of flattery, and view students' affirmations of your teaching circumspectly.

- Students who are stronger in English will sometimes talk up a foreign teacher as a potential patron for emigration or ongoing financing. This practice is generally very destructive and most schools discourage it.

- Poverty shapes identity in many parts of the MENA region. Irrespective of how you view yourself, students will see you as wealthy. You should be very cautious about flaunting your comparative wealth, as this can be very damaging to student morale, discouraging them from returning to more impoverished ministry contexts.

- There are many "taboo" topics in the region which should be avoided or at least treated circumspectly. For example, MENA societies approach issues such as homosexuality and transgenderism much more conservatively than they are treated in the West.

Political

- Politics are a very sensitive issue in the MENA region, especially questions regarding Zionism, Israel, and Palestine. You should avoid linking modern-day Israel and Palestine with the Old Testament. You should avoid the use of Hebrew words (such as "shalom") in social situations. Under no circumstances should you arrive in Lebanon with any evidence that you have been in Israel. This includes exit/re-entry stamps from Jordan with a space of days between; even though you may not have an Israeli stamp in your passport, the immigration official will assume you have been in Israel and you will likely be refused entry.

- The international portrayal of organizations such as Hezbollah and Hamas is often something of a caricature, while the reality is much more mixed. For example, Hezbollah represents a large proportion of the Shi'ite population in Lebanon, is a significant political party, and has a charitable arm that runs schools and clinics. Also, situations of conflict such as Syria, Yemen, Iraq, Libya, and Sudan are often approached simplistically in the Western press. In all MENA politics there is a lot of complexity and nuance.

Religious

- Islam dominates the MENA (Middle East and North Africa) region. Be careful not to speak in a derogatory fashion about Islam or Muslims. Students who come from a Muslim background generally have a deep love for their families and can be hurt by insensitivity or ignorance. On the other hand, it can be quite surprising to hear highly polemic and hostile comments about Islam and Muslims from other students, particularly from those with a Christian background. Be aware that these comments can be reflective of deep pain from long-term discrimination and sometimes persecution.

- Visiting instructors need to be aware of the history of the Palestinian–Israeli conflict, and perhaps the history of the Armenian–Turk situation. They should also be aware of the deep wounds carried by students coming out of civil war – Lebanon, Iraq, Syria, Sudan, Yemen, and Libya. In many regions people need to "fight" to exist, and may bring a certain belligerence to the classroom.

Educational

- Plagiarism is normal in this part of the world and needs to be handled sensitively. In most parts of the MENA region the students' previous educational experiences have discouraged the development and expression of their own voices. From kindergarten to university, success in the educational system comes from repeating the teacher's ideas and/or memorizing the content of texts. One of the great challenges is to help students develop a constructive voice in respectful community, and part of this is learning how to use resources with appropriate acknowledgment.

Language

- Be aware of some of the basic features of the Arabic language – especially if your teaching is being translated. For example, the verb is the first word in the sentence in Arabic, and consequently you should try to put your verb early in your sentence for the translators.
- There are severely limited resources in the Arabic language, and most students can't read English. Research whether there are suitable Arabic resources available. Ask for help from the school librarian several months in advance. If you need written materials translated into Arabic, be aware that translation is costly and time-consuming. Consequently, you should be highly selective in the resources for which you request translation.

Practical

- There are critical shortages of both electricity and water; please use these extremely sparingly. Never drink water from the tap. Never flush toilet paper; always use the garbage bin provided.
- Do not bring fruit or vegetables in your luggage; these are now strictly prohibited.
- Check with locals whether you need a visa. Even though many websites claim you need to purchase a visa in advance, in reality citizens of an increasing number of countries are granted thirty-day visas gratis at the airport.

Teaching Cross-Culturally in Africa

Rev. Dr. David Tarus, Executive Director, Association for Christian Theological Education in Africa (ACTEA)

African Culture and Diversity

- Africa is a diverse continent. Sub-Saharan Africa alone has over 3,000 distinct ethnic societies that speak over 2,100 languages.

- There are four major racial categories in Africa: Bantu, Hamites, Semites, and the Nilotes. We also have many immigrant communities from various parts of the world who are now residents of Africa.

African Spirituality

- Africans have a strong belief in God. Africans take belief in God for granted.[1] African philosophy (ethno-philosophy), aesthetics, art, music, and politics are intimately linked to religion because African people are by nature "notoriously religious."[2]

- African traditional life embraces the holistic nature of life. Because the African traditional cosmology values the interconnectedness of life, it opposes a dualism or dichotomization of life into the sacred and the secular. For the African, the sacred and the secular, the supernatural and the natural, are inextricably linked and cannot be separated.

- Space is considered sacred, holy, and symbolic. Everything – objects, nature, events, and actions – is viewed from a religious perspective.

---

1. J. S. Mbiti, *African Religions and Philosophy*, 2nd ed. (London: Heinemann, 1989), 29.
2. Mbiti, *African Religions*, 1.

- Traditional religious officials and leaders view their task of leadership as mediating between God and the people. Their lives are bound up with the whole life of the community, not simply with religious meetings.

- Since Africans value community, faith is not private. For Africans, religion is in their whole system of being.[3] Mbiti writes, "African peoples have no creeds to recite: their creeds are within them, in their blood and in their hearts. They have a body of beliefs about God, but this is not formulated into single creeds that can be recited. Their beliefs are expressed through concepts of God, attitudes towards him, and the various acts of worship. Furthermore, they are collective, communal, or corporate beliefs, held by groups or communities. The individual 'believes' what other members of the corporate society 'believe,' and he 'believes' because others 'believe.'"[4]

- Africans turn to God for help in everything they do. Prayer saturates everything an African does. Prayers are conducted in schools, parliament, public transport, vehicles, and so on. In moments of desperation, God is the answer. "When everything else within man's abilities fails to cope with misfortune, the people say, 'Leave it to God.'"[5]

- Ancestors and the recently deceased (the "living dead") are implored to assist in overcoming the complexities of life.[6]

- African spiritual, cultural, and social ways of life have been severely and negatively disrupted by forms of political, educational, cultural, and spiritual conquest and dominance, as opposed to persuasion – what Benjamin Musyoka describes as "African spiritual disorientation."[7]

- Spirituality is also diverse: Christianity, African Independent Churches, African Traditional Religions, Islam, Hinduism, and so on, all form the landscape of modern African spirituality. In this pluralistic environment Christianity thrives. It helps to be a good student of world religions to be able to serve diverse communities better.

---

3. Mbiti, 3.

4. J. S. Mbiti, *Concepts of God in Africa* (New York: Praeger, 1970), 218.

5. Mbiti, *Concepts of God*, 244.

6. Mbiti was the first person to coin the term the "living dead," meaning "the departed who are still remembered personally by someone in their family." See Mbiti, *Concepts of God*, 179.

7. B. Musyoka, "Spiritual Disorientation: Primary Cause of African Identity Crisis and Moral Relativism," *Africa Journal of Evangelical Theology* 35, no. 2 (2016): 109–41.

- Key characteristics of African Christianity:
  - African Christians take the Bible seriously. The Bible is alive for an African Christian. The Bible speaks. African Christians read the Bible literally and believe that what it says is true. The Bible is resourced for day-to-day experiences.
  - African Christians take morality seriously. They believe that a genuine Christian must live above reproach. African Christians are firm about moral issues (e.g. homosexuality), and for many this is non-negotiable.
  - African Christians tend to take social issues seriously. They believe that the Bible and Christian faith have much to say about poverty, injustice, politics, and so on. It was the church that started schools, hospitals, agricultural demonstration centres, and so on. When African governments have failed to help their people, the church has been there to provide help. The church is deemed relevant when it is active in the day-to-day lives of God's people.
  - African Christians take community seriously. Interdependence, community, hospitality, and togetherness are all vital for existence in Africa. Likewise, you would do well to foster community in the classroom.
  - Africans take the supernatural seriously. This stands in contrast to the naturalistic worldview characteristic of Western societies and much of Western Christianity. In African understanding, the worship of God is a supernatural and experiential encounter in which God speaks to the day-to-day realities of life. There is no part of life that God does not touch. For an African person, spiritual forces are real forces. Exorcism is part of Sunday liturgy in many African churches.
- General implication: pay attention to practical issues in your teaching. Do not overemphasize academic issues at the expense of practical matters. African theology seldom engages in theoretical theologizing. African theologians are engaged in theology for transformation. Theology is for the church.

African Identity

- The African understands him- or herself as a being who exists in community. In Africa, we are all related: "Each individual is a brother-in-law, uncle or aunt, or something else to everybody else. That means that everybody is related to everybody else."[8] Community includes visible and invisible beings, the living and the dead, the unborn, and God. Bishop Desmond Tutu asserts, "Our humanity is caught up in that of all others. We are human because we belong. We are made for community, for togetherness, for family, to exist in a delicate network of interdependence."[9] Elsewhere Tutu says, "In Africa when you ask someone 'How are you?' the reply you get is in the plural even when you are speaking to one person."[10] Likewise, John Mbiti observes that the African view of humanity can be summarized in the aphorism "I am, because we are; and since we are, therefore I am."[11] Similarly, Bénézet Bujo asserts, "For Black Africa, it is not the Cartesian *cogito ergo sum* ('I think, therefore I am') but an existential *cognatus sum, ergo sumus* ('I am known, therefore we are') that is decisive."[12] To be human is, first of all, to relate with the Supreme Being (God), then to relate with people, and finally to relate with non-human creation and things.

- The person's community shapes that individual's identity through important religious events, ceremonies, rites of passage, and on occasion the exercise of discipline. Community transcends geographical location as people always carry their community wherever they go. They are never truly separated from their fundamental communal connection.

- Throughout Africa, oral rather than written communication is the main means of sharing thoughts and values.

---

8. Mbiti, *African Religions*, 104.

9. D. Tutu, *No Future without Forgiveness* (New York: Doubleday, 1999), 196. See also D. Tutu, *In God's Hands* (London: Bloomsbury, 2014), 34; and D. Tutu and J. Allen, *God Is Not a Christian: Speaking Truth in Times of Crisis* (London: Rider, 2011), 21–23.

10. D. Tutu, *God Has a Dream: A Vision of Hope for Our Time* (New York: Doubleday, 2004), 25.

11. Mbiti, *African Religions*, 106.

12. B. Bujo, *Foundations of an African Ethic: Beyond the Universal Claims of Western Morality* (New York: Crossroad, 2001), 4.

Teaching Cross-Culturally in Kenya

Rev. Dr. David Tarus, Executive Director, Association
for Christian Theological Education in Africa (ACTEA)

Social

- Kenya is blessed with a rich diversity of people groups and cultures. Kenya is a multi-ethnic country with over 47 million people classified into about forty-two distinct ethnic groups from the Bantu, Nilote, and Cushite clusters. Indian, Arab, and European immigrant communities also contribute to Kenya's ethnic diversity. This diversity is expressed in cultural and religious beliefs, music, art, celebrations, languages, and colours.

- Kenyans are very sociable people. Hospitality is a key element of African life. Among the Kalenjin of Kenya, for example, children are continuously reminded to be hospitable to strangers. This is captured in the proverb *mewong'u che eng sot* ("Never drink all the milk; spare some for the stranger"). When you are invited to have a meal in a home, please accept the invitation if possible.

Politics and Security

- Kenyan elections are held every five years. Ethnicity remains a salient element in the formation and operation of political parties in Kenya. Politicians capitalize on ethnicity to attain, retain, or control power.

- Kenyan politics are highly unpredictable. Ethnic and clan fragmentation is most evident during national elections. Sometimes ethnic conflicts have resulted in hatred, violence, and even death. Ethnic strife has been manifested in Kenya since the first election in 1961, although its severity was felt mostly from the start of multiparty politics (1991 onwards). The 2002 election was the most peaceful; the 2007 election was the most volatile. It is important to be aware of what is going on in terms of politics. Be on high alert during national elections. Try to avoid campaign crowds.

- Kenya is generally a peaceful country, but it pays to be careful. In the recent past Kenya has experienced a number of terrorist attacks. Always be alert, especially when you visit shopping malls in Nairobi, Mombasa, and Northern Kenya.
- Exercise caution when travelling to remote regions, especially those on the Kenya–Somali border.

Language

- English and Swahili are the official languages in Kenya. There are also many other indigenous languages in Kenya (more than sixty) spoken by more than forty ethnic communities.
- Especially in towns, Kenyans use Swahili in day-to-day communication. The younger generation use a blend of English and Swahili, popularly known as "Sheng."
- English is preferred in the marketplace, schools, and offices. English is the main language of instruction in the classroom but is a second or third language for most students.
- Peri-urban and rural dwellers mostly speak either Swahili or their local dialect.
- Do not call adults boys or girls, including when you teach. Kenyan men in particular are offended when they are referred to as boys or young men.

Education

- Kenya has a well-developed education system. The eight years of primary school education are free in public schools and compulsory. The four years of high school education are also free in public schools but not compulsory. There are many private schools of varying standard and cost.

- In 2017 the government introduced a new system of education called Competence Based Curriculum (CBC), which is designed to emphasize application of skills and knowledge to real-life situations.
- University undergraduate education lasts four years.
- It helps to pay attention to the institutional culture of your host school. The school's culture will impact how you teach. For example, some institutions are strict on keeping to time, while others are not. Board and staff meetings are generally on the long side.
- Every institution has its history. For seminaries, part of their history is their denominational connection. Some institutions are still very particular about keeping their traditional roots intact. Some have opened doors to other denominations. You should pay attention to the denominational and doctrinal distinctives of the institution you serve.
- Embrace a learner-centred approach to learning. As a teacher you are a facilitator of learning. Students have something meaningful to contribute. Challenge them to reflect and share ideas. Respect their input.
- Encourage your students to participate in class. You might have to call on some students, especially the shy ones, to contribute. But do not ignore their input.
- Try to understand accents. It is acceptable to ask a student to speak more slowly so that you can understand. You yourself should speak slowly so that they can understand you.
- Many Kenyan students abhor multiple-choice questions. They prefer essays. You will find remarkably interesting thoughts if you give your students the opportunity.
- It is acceptable to acknowledge that you do not understand something, or you do not have the whole answer(s). Do not seem to be an expert on African culture. Embrace an attitude of humility so that you can learn the context.
- Be wary of plagiarism. You need to reinforce the importance of originality.
- Spend time with students outside the classroom providing mentorship, guidance, and discipleship. It is appropriate to invite students to your home for a meal. They will also invite you to share a meal in their homes.

Accommodation and Food

- Kenya has a well-developed accommodation industry for Kenya's travellers and visitors, with many standards of hotel, as well as private options such as self-catering apartments, cabins, campsites, villas, and cottages. Most hotels in upmarket areas provide free wi-fi. Others provide airport pickup and drop-offs. Taxis are also available around most of the hotels in upmarket areas.

- Meals in most hotels in upmarket areas are prepared by professional chefs and served by trained waiters. Street food is also available. We encourage you to sample indigenous foods.

Health Matters

- Kenya's health-care sector is quite developed. We have public hospitals, private hospitals, and hospitals operated by NGOs. Private hospitals are the best-developed, although quite expensive.

- The government has been trying to subsidize the cost of health care by offering free services in public facilities. Maternity care is free in public facilities.

- It is prudent to get medical insurance for your time in Kenya. There are two types of health insurance provided by private insurance companies in Kenya: *in-patient* (covers hospitalization of a patient) and *out-patient* (covers medical costs for patients who do not require hospitalization).

- The biggest threat to Kenyans' health is communicable diseases such as malaria, tuberculosis, HIV/AIDS, and respiratory diseases. You should be up to date on routine vaccinations. Use mosquito nets or repellent.

Travel

- The Kenyan currency is the Kenya Shilling (KSh). Payments in some establishments can be done by visa card or Mpesa (mobile money). Some places accept foreign currency.

- Kenya is generally an easy country in terms of visa requirements. Please find out if you require a visa to travel to Kenya; some nationalities may obtain a visa on arrival. The maximum number of days a visitor may stay in Kenya on a tourist visa is six months.

- Kenya has relatively good infrastructure especially in urban areas. Rural roads may not be as good quality. You might need an off-road vehicle to travel to some regions.

- The public transport system is extensive but isn't recommended for someone who is not familiar with it. You will generally do better to use taxis. Online taxi businesses are a thriving industry in major cities like Nairobi, Mombasa, Nakuru, and Eldoret. There are several taxi companies that use mobile apps by which users can choose to be picked up from their homes.

- Kenya has a broad network of local flights. Thus, you may choose to get to your destination by air. There are two major airports in Nairobi. The leading one is Jomo Kenyatta International Airport, which is home to our local company, Kenya Airways (KQ), and services many international airlines. The second one is Wilson Airport. There are also a number of smaller regional airports. From the two major airports you can fly to some towns and the many diverse tourist destinations. Most of the local Kenyan airlines are reliable but be sure to book well in advance. There are many travel companies offering transfers, drop-offs, and pickups from the major airports, but you need to have informed them ahead of time.

- Kenya has a well-developed telecommunications industry.[1] You will need to buy and register a SIM card to be able to make calls. Roaming is always expensive. Some companies also provide mobile money transfers. There are several companies that provide Internet through fibre-optic connectivity.

- Do not bring plastic bags into Kenya. They are now illegal.

---

1. A report by Jumia Business Intelligence and GSMA Mobile notes that over 60 percent of Kenyans own a smartphone. S. Zab, "Whitepaper: The Growth of the Smartphone Market in Kenya," 2 June 2015, https://www.jumia.co.ke/blog/whitepaper-the-growth-of-the-smartphone-market-in-kenya/.

Teaching Cross-Culturally in Ethiopia

Dr. Seblewengel Daniel, Head of Academic Affairs, Ethiopian Graduate School of Theology

Note: Ethiopia is a large country with diverse cultures, traditions, and social and economic realities. While generally true, what is given below may not apply to every part of the country.

Social and Cultural

- Social relationships are very important in Ethiopia. Especially visiting the family of the dead and burying the dead is very important to community life. Students may not show up for a class if someone has died (even if the deceased is not a family member or friend, but simply lived in their neighbourhood). It is culturally expected to attend the burial and go to the family's house and sit with the bereaved for some time. This can be difficult for task-oriented people, but in Ethiopia relationships come first.
- Nearly everything is weighed against how it might affect the other. One might refrain from speaking the truth if it is feared that speaking might hurt the other. The social emphasis centres around community and belonging. Life is people-centred and holistic, not individual and compartmentalized.
- Culturally, it is improper to challenge or question seniors or leaders. The elderly are respected as those who have gained wisdom over the years. In many cases, it may be rude for a young person to look directly at an older person when being spoken to. A visiting lecturer would be assumed to be an expert. Hence, saying something "wrong" deliberately to evoke debate in class may not generate the desired effect, as students will not wish to

publicly question the teacher-leader. Yelling someone's name from far away, especially that of an older person, is seen as inappropriate.

- Dress code: both women and men should dress modestly as teachers. Outside class, wearing shorts may offend students in rural parts of Ethiopia. Urban settings may be more tolerant, but it is still best to dress conservatively. Women should avoid revealing outfits, excessive jewellery, and make-up.

- Greetings and gender relationships: shaking hands and/or kissing cheek to cheek three times is a common way of greeting persons of both the same and the opposite sex. Holding hands with a person of the same or the opposite sex is quite common and it does not have sexual undertones. Kissing in public is frowned upon even for married couples, but holding hands is a normal sign of friendship. While greeting, bowing the head is a common sign of respect. It is very common to kiss children and pick them up. This is seen as a sign of love.

- Gestures should be used sparingly since they may be misinterpreted as rude, or not understood at all. For example, it is inappropriate to receive or give something with the left hand only. Do not point directly at an older person.

- Time: Ethiopians are less time-conscious than people from the West. Being late for an appointment is common, so don't take it personally. Especially for social gatherings such as weddings or public engagements, people tend to come late.

- Hospitality and respect are strong values. Inviting people to one's house and going when invited is very important. When a visitor comes, it is very rude to talk to him or her outside the house without inviting the visitor to come in. It is also expected to serve some food (or at least to offer to serve, which the visitor may politely decline). When someone declines to come inside or eat food, the host is expected to insist. Chewing gum in front of older people, especially religious teachers, is seen as offensive. Cutlery is not used for traditional foods, which are usually eaten with the hands. Licking fingers while eating is offensive. When eating in a restaurant with a group of people, it is normal for one of the group to pay the bill. Splitting the bill is not common and may be seen as ungenerous. People take great delight in paying the bill for strangers. You have to learn to pay the bill for others and not just yourself. Eating on the streets is not common in rural areas.

- Ethiopians are reserved and do not feel comfortable talking about their family in front of strangers, so do not ask personal questions apart from the normal pleasantries. Interrupting someone while he or she is talking is perceived as offensive, so jumping into conversation is not common. Ethiopians generally listen quietly. Do not mistake this for shyness or timidity; it is a sign of respect. Breastfeeding babies in public is quite common and not offensive, but generally there is a fear of the evil eye, so bottles are covered with a piece of cloth and mothers cover babies while feeding them.

- National pride and ethnic identity: Ethiopians are intensely proud of their history as the only non-colonized nation in Africa. Be careful when talking about our ethnic differences as such discussions can be divisive and volatile. Asking about someone's ethnic background can make the person uncomfortable. Mistrust of strangers may be encountered in some parts of the country. But in most cases, foreigners are respected and protected. In fact, the society has compassion for those who live far away from their home countries, and people go out of their way to help.

- Avoid talking about politics as much as possible.

Religious

- Religion plays an important role throughout the country. The Ethiopian Orthodox Church, one of the most ancient forms of Christianity in Africa, has the majority number of Christians. Be careful to show respect for this historic church. Both women and men should put on a traditional garment (*netela*) when going to an Ethiopian Orthodox church.

- In Orthodox churches, shoes are taken off and left outside. Talking loudly inside any kind of church building can be inappropriate.

- Orthodox Christians fast on Wednesdays and Fridays and observe the Lent season. They also have numerous fasting seasons in which they refrain from dairy products. It is important to observe these practices when in Orthodox majority regions.

- In Protestant settings, expect a wide range of denominational backgrounds among your students, although the denominational barriers are not rigid in Ethiopia. You will find charismatic Baptists and charismatic Lutherans. We share ministers freely and students go to seminaries more freely. Do not bring denominational boundaries into your class. Charismatic experiences are held dear in Ethiopia, and cessationist positions sound very odd to Ethiopian Protestants.

- When going to Protestant churches, modest dressing is recommended. For preaching or teaching a jacket and tie is seen as appropriate. Preaching with one's hand in one's pocket is seen as very offensive.

- The Bible is not just any book – it is a *holy* book. Never put the Bible on the floor, and never sit on top of the Bible. Treat the physical book with respect. When preaching or teaching, handling the Bible with its cover rolled back can be offensive.

- Avoid making derogatory remarks about Islam or any form of Christianity. Keep in mind that religious diversity and mutual respect are encouraged in Ethiopia. According to the 2008 official census, Ethiopia is 43 percent Orthodox Christian, 33 percent Muslim, 18 percent Protestant, and 0.7 percent Catholic; open critique of another's faith will not be well received.

- Unlike elsewhere on the continent, African Traditional Religion (ATR) will not generally be viewed positively by Ethiopian Christians. Ancestor theology is not common, although it is now growing among some ethnic groups. Even though ATR is gaining acceptance in some ethnic groups, it often takes place under the cover of darkness, and you may not readily see its practice. Among the evangelical population, ATR rituals are usually regarded as demonic. Even though practising ATR is not openly denounced by the historic churches, there is a form of stigma attached to those who participate in it.

Educational

- Students have a high regard for teachers and will want to know what you think about any subject matter. Most notably they may expect to be given information rather than being made to find it out for themselves, because that has been their previous experience of education.
- The society is predominantly oral. You should therefore go through your instructions orally, and not simply present materials in written form.
- Do not publicly critique students. Expect students to talk around a sensitive issue rather than addressing it directly. For example, if students differ from one another in their faith perspective, they may be reticent to argue about it in class.

Language

- Try to avoid very idiomatic language. None of the European languages are lingua francas. Amharic is the official language and there are numerous other regional languages. English proficiency can be low simply because Ethiopia was never a colony of any of the European powers and English is not a market language. While communicating, keep your vocabulary as simple as possible and speak slowly and clearly. Speak in short, simple sentences.

Practical

- The weather is mild in most parts of Ethiopia. There is sunshine all year round. The rainy season can be cold but it is not unbearable.

Teaching Cross-Culturally in Francophone Africa

FATEB (Bangui Evangelical School of Theology)

If visiting faculty members come from other parts of the world to teach, they must be aware of and sensitive to the following:

Social, Cultural, and Political

- It is crucial that visiting faculty members treat national faculty and students with respect and dignity. We are all creatures in the image of God. There is a history of racism that is felt strongly by many West Africans.
- Visiting faculty members must come not just to give to the learners but with a heart of willingness to also receive and learn from them.
- It is crucial that visiting faculty be sensitive to the denominational backgrounds of learners.
- It is crucial that visiting faculty be aware of the social and political environment of students. Visiting faculty should avoid being critical of tribal or political leaders, and certainly should be affirming of existing church leadership. Discussion of politics should be left to nationals.
- Visiting faculty should be sensitive to the economic limitations of schools, faculty, staff, and students.
- Visiting faculty must avoid behaviours that are deemed negative or are forbidden in our region, so as not to shock the learners. For example, if a visiting professor arrives on the campus from the airport and begins to smoke cigarettes, this will be seen as shocking and unacceptable.

Religious

- Africans have great spiritual awareness of the surrounding environment, rooted in their traditional beliefs. This spiritual awareness resonates with what is found in the Scriptures. Visiting faculty should appreciate and be willing to learn from their students' spirituality.

Educational

- Visiting faculty should understand the educational backgrounds of the learners, while also recognizing that intellectual expression may differ from what is found in the West: for example, high levels of intelligent engagement may be expressed in narrative rather than rationalist forms.

Language

- It is important that visiting faculty discover which language to use to best communicate the message of God. For most students the language of instruction (French) may be their second or third language. Finding ways to enable students to express themselves in their heart language will greatly enhance their preparation for future ministry.

Practical

- Dress code is important to West Africans and visiting faculty should dress in a way that is respectful of the sensitivities of the nationals. Appropriate attire would usually be slacks for men (rather than jeans) and dresses and skirts for women.
- Food: nationals greatly appreciate foreign faculty who are willing to eat and enjoy the meals presented to them.

Teaching Cross-Culturally in Benin and Togo

Baptist Biblical Institute of Benin, Baptist Biblical Institute of Togo, West Africa Baptist Advanced School of Theology, Bohicon, Lomé

Religious and Political

On the political–religious level, the following elements should be remembered:

- Africans are extremely religious with a strong attachment to spirituality. You must understand that Africans did not come to know about the existence of God from the missionaries; they knew it before the missionaries came. Sensitivity to the spiritual is very strong in our cultural vision of the world.

- Africans already believe in a supreme God, but to gain access to him they go through intermediate deities. In the *fongbé* language, for example, God is designated by the expression *Sègbo lissa*, which means the "Unique Supreme," demonstrating pre-existing monotheistic understandings. He is the one supreme God who delegates his power to the lower deities to deal with humanity.

- The African religious universe can be a great obstacle to the success of cross-cultural teachers, because there are areas that can be very difficult for the visiting teacher to identify with. For example, for the Westerner shaped by so-called "Enlightenment" paradigms, the dominant thought is the individualistic "I think, therefore I am"; in contrast, Africans understand their existence as linked to something unseen. In this it would appear that biblical culture is much closer to that of Africa than to that of the West.

- Authority is still traditionally recognized in Africa and perceived as a positive quality. These vertical authority patterns contrast notably with the supposedly more horizontal "democratic" understandings of the West.

Respect for authority influences every element of society – including schools and churches.

- African politics and especially the politics of West Africa are strongly influenced by the West. African politics are generally guided from the West, whose rulers appear to manipulate African heads of state. There is a neo-colonialism decried by Africans. Sometimes white people are perceived as spies or intelligence agents – even if they are openly engaged in religious or educational activities.

- Modern politics as practised in most African countries seem to promote corruption even if this plague is criticized verbally. This stands in stark contrast to traditional African politics, in which the king was expected to genuinely care about the people. The king's ministers were trained to do their job well, otherwise they would be severely punished, even physically eliminated.

Historical

You cannot build the future by ignoring history. In Benin they have a saying, "The old rope weaves the new." This is why you should take time to understand some elements of how local history has impacted the Beninese and Togolese both individually and as a people. The following are some essential elements:

- There is a lot of strong feeling linked to colonization and slavery. Africans have developed something of an inferiority complex, and many white people still tend to think of themselves as superior to Africans. White faculty must be humble enough to touch the hearts of Africans; you must not come with a domineering posture. Africans are aware that a certain Western anthropology endures (even in the church) which considers Africans as of a lower status or rank and therefore condemned to savagery and slavery. Western teachers must be careful not to play a "civilizing" role when teaching. Humility is needed. You should never be seen to be asserting Western supremacy.

- The gulf in wealth between white and black is a huge issue. You should not flaunt your wealth, and you should be circumspect when talking about money.

- White faculty may experience being identified with the white colonizers who were involved in the destruction of our cultural, religious, geographic, and geological heritage.

- Christianity is perceived as the religion of white people by many who today work at the rehabilitation of indigenous religions. A festival of indigenous religions is celebrated every 10 January in Benin, and for many the day is a paid holiday.

- Often out of ignorance (but consciously for some) the missionaries tended to demonize all the habits and customs of the colonized countries. This has left an imprint on many Africans who today believe that the way to succeed is to become like a white person. You should avoid a posture that encourages this. Many Africans need to regain confidence in themselves in order to move forward.

- In every way you should come with an attitude of humility and equality.

Social and Cultural

A Beninese proverb says: "If you visit a place where people walk on their heads, you must also do the same." Those who want to teach must pay close attention to the content and form of their teaching and how it relates to the people for whom their teaching is intended. If teachers lack cultural sensitivity, they will miss the point. As regards the culture of Benin and Togo, the foreign teacher should take note of the following:

- Know that orality dominates in communication. You must present your material in a simple manner and in living contact with the learners. When teachers are "glued" to their notes on paper and cannot detach themselves and speak freely to the learners, this becomes an obstacle to oral learners. When the presentation sounds like a story being told, learners listen and remember more easily. Concrete examples and personal experiences (presented without appearing to be very special or superior) reinforce learning. When you are too stuck on your notes, people no longer know who is talking to them.

- Know that in communication and learning, the Beninese and Togolese prefer to use images, proverbs, songs, stories, and anecdotes, rather than direct "rationalist" speech; these more narrative forms are what anchor the message and communicate meaningfully.

- Take seriously the importance of personal greetings – which are very important for the Beninese and Togolese. You should engage the courtesies of greeting before engaging in teaching. Details are very important. When inquiring about the immediate family, church, and relatives of the learners, you should see the individual in relation to his or her family and tribal group.

- Respect for the elderly is very important in relationships. You should always take this into account when you have older students, or when dealing with senior staff and administration. This respect is demonstrated in the way you greet older people and address them. Even when you are the teacher, older students must be treated with the respect due to them. For example, you should never use the personal name of an elder. Failure to respect this principle can be a real hindrance to learning, not only for the older students but for the whole class.

- Do not require people to call you by your first name. It is very embarrassing for someone to call his or her teacher by the first name.

- Know how to behave in a way that inspires confidence, avoiding attitudes of flippancy and compromise. In Beninese and Togolese culture one does not separate thoughts from actions. What ultimately is respected is what someone does, not his or her ability to master a theory or principle. You first teach by your actions and demonstration of skills before your explanations will be taken seriously by your learners.

- Dress appropriately. This is very important for teachers in Africa. It is often perceived as positive when male teachers wear a jacket. Female teachers should dress conservatively. It is shocking to students if a female teacher puts on trousers or a revealing outfit. Certain behaviours, such as smoking or getting drunk – or even consuming alcohol at all – are strongly condemned among local Christians.

- Know that basic education is gendered: the father oversees the education of the boys and the mother oversees the education of the girls.

- Have an acceptable level of language in the medium of educational instruction. Your pronunciation is important for the communication of the ideas being delivered. If learners struggle to understand your pronunciation, they will no longer be able to focus adequately on the content that needs to be captured.

Educational

From an educational point of view, the visiting teacher must take into account the following elements:

- For the Beninese and Togolese, the concrete takes precedence over the abstract in learning. This orientation towards the concrete does not mean absence of depth or inability to reason, but rather that in communication, listening and seeing are intimately associated in the process of understanding.

- The most natural method of learning is active and interactive, not "magisterial." Watching someone do, then doing with, then doing it yourself is the royal way of education at all levels in African society, from home to official places of learning, through to the streets. Where pressures and time require it, a more authoritative approach can be used; however, it should be supported by images and visuals. A mixed method (mixture of masterful discourse, mimicry, and interaction) is ideal.

- Consequently, a more "andragogical"[1] approach is better suited to learning in a Beninese–Togolese environment. What learners already know naturally, culturally, and socially is a good foundation on which to build.

- People want to know if the person in front of them has something to give them. The academic level of the teacher is important to know, but demonstrating this level in practice is far more important. Your life experience is as important as your academic qualifications.

- The illustrations you give during your teaching should take into account the realities of the local culture and environment. For example, some elements of biblical culture are close to local African culture: to explain biblical worship to a Beninese or Togolese, you would do well to take advantage

---

1. M. Knowles, E. Holton, and R. Swanson, *The Adult Learner: The Definitive Classic in Adult Education and Human Resource Development*, 6th ed. (Amsterdam: Elsevier, 2005).

of the royal and clan tradition that forged the local culture, including royal and clan panegyrics. You would do well to tap into the cultural richness of Africa. If you don't know the culture well, allow time for students to give their own examples. Students can provide many illustrations from their own experience of such things as rules of decency and precedence, and totems, taboos, and proverbs.

- Know that encouragement plays a large role in teaching. You have to show the learners that they can succeed even when they find something difficult. It is not enough to tell them it is easy; you have to show them how they can accomplish the goal. Clear step-by-step guidance is valued. However, we must not give the impression to learners that in all cases they will succeed. In general, the fear of failing, of suffering a great loss, or of being failed for an indefinite time creates anxiety in learners. In reality, some students are able to finish their studies in three years, while others greatly exceed this time.

Teaching Cross-Culturally in Nigeria

Rev. Prof. Emiola Nihinlola, President, The Nigerian
Baptist Theological Seminary, Ogbomoso

Preamble

Cross-cultural teaching is a good cross to bear! Most evangelical theological
institutions in Nigeria (at both undergraduate and postgraduate level) that I
know will be most glad to have theological educators from other parts of Africa
and beyond to engage in short-term teaching in our institutions. We shall be
especially grateful to also have such personnel from Asia, the USA, the UK, and
Europe. Help is needed for such supplementary teaching in all major areas of
discipline/study: biblical, historical, missiological, philosophical, theological,
preaching, missions, ethics, education, and music/worship. Even where there
are resident local experts, the services of international scholars will no doubt
enrich our mutual learning.

Knowledge about African Culture

When an institution indicates interest and a teacher decides to accept the
invitation to teach in a Nigerian theological institution, it is helpful for the
teacher to read one or two articles or books on general African culture. This
should be supplemented with specific information from the appropriate leaders
and administrative office of the institution.

Understanding the Institution's Distinctives

The teacher should understand the distinctives of the institution. A good starting point is to review the school's website, where you may find such things as the vision, mission, motto, philosophy, and objectives of the school.

Before you prepare your course or seminar it is important that you know what is expected. Ask for one or two sample syllabi of similar courses used by others recently in the institution. This will provide you with helpful information about "house" style, teaching hours, volume of work, the grading system, number of students, and so on.

A gift to the institution's library of some sample copies of current books and journals relevant to the course or seminar you have been invited to facilitate is always greatly appreciated.

Cross-cultural teaching provides a great opportunity both to share and to learn. You will be enriched as you work frankly and sincerely with your host, interpreting and attempting global standards in the context of local realities!

Travel and Other Logistics

Travel arrangements will normally involve the following:

- A letter of invitation from the designated officer of the host school.
- Visa procurement, which may depend on the diplomatic relationship between Nigeria and your home country.
- Booking of your flights well in advance. This should be done in consultation with the school, to determine whether you will need to book not only international but also Nigerian domestic flights, or whether ground transport will be used to get you to the school.
- In most cases you will be expected to cover the cost of your flights. The host is responsible for airport pickup/transfers, ground transportation, and room and board.

Please respect the arrangements made by your host.

Do not be disturbed by travel advice that exaggerates insecurities in some parts of Nigeria. Take your advice rather from the leadership of the school. Nigerian theological schools have been receiving overseas visitors regularly for over one hundred years and understand the security issues. They take a high level of responsibility for their guests and will not take unnecessary risks. Keep in mind also that our security is ultimately in the hand of Almighty God in Christ Jesus.

Lodging and Food

Nigeria has dusty, warm-to-hot tropical weather. Drinking plenty of water and eating fruit will help maintain your health.

If the environment of your accommodation does not appear to be neat, please inform your host and feel free to ask for further cleaning. Your host will not be offended if you ask for insect treatment of your room. They, even more than you, do not want to run the risk of malaria and other diseases.

Feel free to ask questions about the food items you are served. Most local foods are high in carbohydrates, proteins, fats and oils, and vitamins! If your stay is longer than for modular teaching (of one or two weeks) and you are provided with facilities to do your own cooking, you will find many fresh and bottled items to buy in many local supermarkets. This will add to the fun of your "cross." Nigerian local foods are cheaper and more affordable for your host. If you want a more international cuisine, you should ensure that you pay the bill; your host will probably feel the need to pay but generally cannot afford to. Be sensitive to the limited economic situation of local leaders.

Health Matters

Inquire from your host if you are free to engage in physical exercise on the campus. Half an hour jogging daily is a good health supplement. Some campuses have a variety of sports and games facilities.

It makes practical sense to travel with your personal medication. However, if you experience unusual symptoms, please report promptly to your host. Most institutions have clinics with competent medical personnel. They can also help to arrange a quick referral.

Clothing

When teaching or attending church or at special institutional events you should err on the side of the formal: suits for men and dresses for women. In most locations more casual attire is acceptable. In most parts of Nigeria outside the large cosmopolitan centres of Lagos and Abuja, a female wearing trousers will send the wrong signal.

Hospitality

You should honour invitations to meals. Believe me, we are celebrative! It will greatly enrich your understanding of our context if you accept the invitations of your host, or even participate in social events that take place on campus during your teaching period.

Closing Pieces of Advice

Please participate joyfully in devotional activities on campus as may be requested or arranged by your host. Spiritual formation is taken seriously in Nigeria as the foundation of ministerial training and equipping.

Where you have particular needs, please feel very free to tell your hosts. Nigerian theological educators are a bundle of African and Christian hospitality mixed together. But be sensitive to the limitations of your hosts; it can be a great burden not to be able to help an honoured guest!

At the end of your stay or thereabouts, if you are given an honorarium (in cash or kind), please accept the gift with gratitude and do not reject it. However, it will also be greatly appreciated if you receive the honorarium with thanks, and then quietly return the money to the finance office as a gift towards the college's projects.

Teaching Cross-Culturally in Zambia

Justo Mwale University[1]

Culture

- Zambians are gracious people. Come with an eagerness to embrace the people and the learning experience. Be among them as a guest with the posture of an open, active learner.

- Try to learn a few phrases such as "Thank you" and "How are you?" in one of the local languages. This encourages relationships and warms people towards you. Zambians use these phrases all day long. Not saying "How are you?" to someone and not saying "Thank you" for a service is considered strange. However, Zambians do not frequently hug one another, and hugging across gender lines might be frowned upon.

- Titles are important. Even long-time friends and colleagues call one another "Professor," "Doctor," and "Reverend." If talking informally, they often call one another "Doc.," "Prof.," and "Rev." Students may address you in these ways when the atmosphere feels relaxed.

- People in Zambia value the appearance of unity and harmony. Conflict is not typically visible to outsiders. People may not look perturbed, but they can still feel hurt or angry. Zambians tend to understate problems and not speak openly or with intensity about such things. Conflict tends not to be handled directly but through a third party. It is best not to speak with intensity or get close to people's faces while stating opinions strongly. Greet them and be friendly before sharing something difficult.

---

1. Contributors: Rev. Dr. D. T. Banda, Rev. Dr. Isaac Banda, Rev. Dr. Lameck Banda, Rev. Thijs and Mrs. Marike Blok, Rev. Dr. Victor Chilenje, Rev. Dr. Dustin W. Ellington, Rev. Dr. Johann Du Plessis, Rev. Dr. Lukas R. K. Soko, and Rev. Dr. Edwin Zulu.

- Key core values which shape almost everything that happens in Zambia are hierarchy and harmony. People feel strongly and positively about hierarchy as a glue which holds groups together.
- A local proverb says, "If you don't join the hierarchy, you join the gossipers." Zambian culture cherishes hierarchy, structure, polity, and protocols. Something is considered true and will take effect when it comes from or is announced by an authority figure, and once that happens we should assume that it has been discussed and settled.
- Although great respect is shown to seniority and authority, hierarchy can at times be overruled if the community as a whole moves in a different direction. This can bring some balance to the authority of hierarchy. In a classroom situation, students will be highly respectful, but it is also possible to lose some control if the class as a whole disagrees with the content or method of the teacher.
- Zambians learn, value, and honour institutional protocols and polity in ways above and beyond what people from other regions of the world may be accustomed to. Try to pay attention to protocols and value them as much as you are able.
- Zambians speak of "soldiering on" and say they are "coping up" with difficulties. Being tolerant and forbearing are valued cultural strengths, and you will see these traits on display. Students won't likely complain, but that does not always mean everything is just fine.
- Zambian society tends to be somewhat secretive about problems. Talking openly about current personal problems or successes is somewhat unusual, though you may find that as an outsider you may be appreciated as someone to speak openly with.
- Funerals of people who may seem to you to be distant relatives or distant friends may take precedence over other aspects of life, including education. Your course may be interrupted by a funeral, and you may have students leave to attend funerals. It is best to accept this as a reality of African communal identity.
- Giving and receiving loans of money is widely practised as a normal part of life in community. There is no need to be shocked if someone you only recently met asks you for a loan. It is acceptable to be clear and frank

with the person, and say you are sorry that you are not able to make the loan. Acting as if you are unsure and saying, "I will look into it" may be interpreted as "yes" and may lead to awkward situations later.

- While Zambians value relationships and community, most tend not to talk directly or openly about topics which are very important or personal. For instance, they may not speak about their relationship to God, but that relationship may nonetheless be very important to them. Moreover, most Zambians prefer not to make comments on or state opinions to guests regarding controversial topics.

- Zambians generally do not like to deal with complicated or sensitive topics via email. They strongly prefer face-to-face conversation. If the topic is sensitive, they tend not to use phone calls, preferring to wait for face-to-face conversation.

Politics

Zambians are peaceful and free, but be aware of the following realities:
- Zambia mixes religion and politics. By constitution, it is a Christian nation, though in practice this is still under development. This combination of politics and religion presents opportunity; for example, you as a Christian scholar are welcome to visit. Democracy has developed somewhat differently in Zambia from democracy in the West, and some rights taken for granted elsewhere are limited in Zambia. For example, you should not assume the same level of "freedom of speech," and you should be careful about what you put on social media with respect to politics. Expatriates can be detained, deported, and prohibited for saying things that seem to be not in good taste. In particular, be careful when speaking about homosexuality; homosexual behaviour is illegal, and arrests can be made.

- Zambia has multiparty politics, but tribal commitments play a role. Saying something negative or positive could be associated with favouring a particular tribe. Be careful to avoid unconsciously aligning with a particular group. Commenting on political happenings in the country may be misunderstood.

- Zambians are patriotic regarding their country, so be wise how you speak about it. If you find that something disturbs you, it's best *not* to say, "If we were in my country, this could not happen."
- Zambians are genuinely interested in listening to visitors. There's a saying: "A visitor comes with a sharp knife" – that is, visitors are often thought to be wise experts who can bring needed perspective. Zambians desire foreigners as conversation partners and have special tolerance for them. However, be wise in how you handle this. Visitors should think through what they say, and they need to be careful about being construed as belonging to one side of rival groups.

Religion

- Christianity is robust in Zambia, but it is important to be aware that African Traditional Religions (ATR) and the prosperity gospel exercise influence on the practice of Christianity here.
- African Traditional Religions will tend to be a reality for your students – similar to how local languages precede English for them. Expect syncretism to be at least somewhat present. Although some magical practices are prohibited, witch doctors are approached by rich and poor alike. Traditional medicine is available and respected alongside conventional Western medicine.
- Africans believe in the spirit world, and people are concerned about its negative effects upon their lives. Many people have turned to the Christian faith to avoid harm from evil. All Christian denominations, including mainline churches, deal with demon possession. This should be treated with respect, as a reality of life.
- In recent years, Pentecostalism has heavily influenced the practice of Christianity in Zambia, and the prosperity gospel and Pentecostalism tend to go together here. You will notice the influence of prosperity teaching upon evangelical, mainline, and Catholic churches, not just Pentecostal.
- Many people tend to live with a feeling of insecurity and are looking for solutions. The atmosphere of poverty and vulnerability may help

you sympathize with the attraction of the prosperity gospel for religion in Zambia.

- People commonly think of any religion, including Christianity, as a way to move forward materially and economically. They generally say that if you want to do well in life, you first need to be part of a church. A common belief is: "There's no prosperity outside the church." Christians here tend to interpret theological words in a more material-oriented way than Christians from outside Africa. If you are not from Africa, your words may be taken as more material-oriented than you realize. For instance, the word "blessing" tends to have material and monetary connotations. It is good to help students see that blessings (and other theological words) may not be material or monetary in meaning. Many Zambians who experience poverty also wonder if they are genuine Christians, since it is commonly believed that a lack of prosperity means one is not truly Christian or a child of God. People tend to see being Christian as a material guarantee; you can help students see this is not always the case.
- Zambia is highly Christian but tolerant and respectful of other religions, including Islam, even though Islam may be growing. A visiting teacher should not insult or speak disrespectfully of any religion.

Education

- Before starting to teach, try to get some orientation to the particular school and its history and situation. Ask your hosts what they would like you to know, and what particular dos and don'ts they would like you to be aware of.
- Upon entering class, address students respectfully as adults. You may notice that Zambians usually call one another by their surnames, because they tend to consider using someone's last name as more respectful than using that person's first name. Calling someone by an honorific (such as "Mr.," "Mrs.," "Dr.," or "Rev.") with the last name is how people most like to be addressed. However, Zambians sometimes use first names and they graciously allow foreigners to use their first names if that seems easier.

Cultivating an atmosphere of respect in the classroom is more important than which names you use.

- Your students bring a wealth of life experience and informal knowledge as well as formal education. They are not children. Respect their background and acknowledge that they don't come empty or blank. It is best not to approach your subject by merely pouring out information, with the idea that education is only from the top down. Interact and listen. Invite students to participate, which will help you understand them and help them to grasp the subject.

- Since Zambia is a former British colony, speaking English is the norm for education. However, different accents can be difficult for people to understand; therefore, speak slowly and simply at first so the students can get accustomed to the way you talk. Keep in mind that English may be their second or third language. Also, while your students may be excellent at speaking and listening, they may find composing English for written assignments difficult, depending on their educational background. If you are very critical of people's English, as though it is the one language that matters, that can offend. Also, there may be students from other African countries present with somewhat different amounts of English in their educational backgrounds.

- Be mindful as an expatriate lecturer that students may struggle with the way you present the material. Try to be very clear. Keep in mind that your students come with a different worldview from yours, so they may be wrestling with how your material suits their context. Moreover, out of respect for you, students may say they understand when they do not. Because of their backgrounds, they may feel it is impolite to ask you questions about what you are saying. You may not learn that the students have misunderstood you until you receive written assignments or examinations from them. Treat small assignments and quizzes along the way as valuable feedback.

- Zambian education has been shaped by traditional British and South African norms. The teacher is in authority and is treated with respect. Creativity and critical thinking are valued, but these are not typically seen as important as doing well in examinations. People think of good exam results as leading to a good future. It is valuable to teach critical thinking skills, but be patient because it can be strange and difficult for students to be critical of what they read or hear from an expert.

- Zambian theological schools are making strides towards gender equality and sensitivity, and you as a foreigner can also help in this area if you model listening to women's voices and treating female students with value, respect, and dignity.

- Due to the influence of communal thinking, grading tends to be not too high and not too low. Student grades tend to cluster together close to "average" and "good," and grades may be moderated after you submit them so that the results will cluster together. Depending on the institution, a distinction (excellent) may go from 75 to around 85. Failure tends to be below 50, but anyone receiving 35 to 50 may get a second chance.

- Plagiarism is common and Zambian institutions are working to correct the problem. Some students may see plagiarism as a form of working with and getting help from others. They may not feel plagiarism is cheating, even if they know it breaks the rules. Look to the school's leadership regarding how to enforce rules regarding plagiarism.

- The students generally prefer to hide success and failure for fear of provoking others or being excluded by them. Be careful not to draw much attention to an individual student's excellence or shortcomings during class, which can lead to exclusion or jealousy. Students feel sensitive about instances of comparison, so try to avoid it.

Final Practical Considerations

- Zambia is blessed with lovely weather. However, consider avoiding October, when the heat is intense. Unless you stay at a nice lodge or hotel, you will not likely have air conditioning, and water and electricity may be scarce during and around October.

- Guests should exercise sensitivity in taking pictures and ask their hosts about what is appropriate for photographs.

- Zambians are gracious, welcoming, polite, and respectful. They value harmony and hierarchy, and you can have an especially good experience with them if you are polite and respectful.

Teaching Cross-Culturally in Zimbabwe

Theological College of Zimbabwe

Social and Cultural

- The typical Zimbabwean worldview is summed up in the statement "I am because we are." Hence, the social emphasis centres on community and belonging. Life is people-centred and holistic, not individual and compartmentalized.

- Culturally, it is improper to challenge or question your seniors or leaders. The elderly are respected as those who have gained wisdom over the years. In many cases, it may be rude for a young person to look directly at an older person when being spoken to, especially in a discipline or rebuke situation.

- In gender relationships, be aware of what is appropriate and inappropriate behaviour between members of the opposite sex, and between members of the same sex. For example, shaking hands with a person of the opposite sex is appropriate, but embracing or hugging a person of the opposite sex may be inappropriate in public. However, Christians may embrace briefly (or touch shoulders). Kissing in public is frowned upon, but men (or women) holding hands is a normal sign of friendship and does not have sexual overtones.

- Because of the emphasis on relationships, time is not considered important. Thus, punctuality is not regarded highly; it is much more important to be at the event than "on time" for it. If a relationship issue is the cause of the lateness (e.g. meeting an important relative after a long absence) it is quite acceptable to be late. Hence, events will often start late, even if that disrupts the carefully planned program.

- Gestures should be used sparingly since they may be misinterpreted as rude, or not understood at all. For example, do not receive something with the left hand only; that is inappropriate. Do not point directly at an older person. When indicating the age or size of, say, a child, do not place your palm downwards; that is rude.

- As in many other regions, poverty shapes identity. Irrespective of how you view yourself, students will see you as wealthy. You should be very cautious about flaunting your comparative wealth, as this may lead to requests for financial help (on the basis of a relationship), which could become a nuisance.

- In a communal setting, "things" – including children – "belong" to everyone. Hence, items can be borrowed without necessarily seeking permission from the owner; this is not classified as stealing. Children can be disciplined by any responsible adult in the community without incurring the wrath of the parents. Very often, if a crime (e.g. stealing) is not seen or does not directly harm the community, it is not considered wrong. This has implications for ethics, including such educational issues as plagiarism and cheating: stealing someone's intellectual property is difficult to understand.

- Because community is fundamental, relationships are all-important – even over and above some ethical or moral issues. Thus, it is acceptable to tell a lie to protect a family member or a close friend because maintaining the relationship is often more important than the truth. This leads naturally to nepotism, affects power relationships ("You scratch my back and I'll scratch yours"; "I did this for you, so you owe me"), and often quashes individual and independent initiative.

Language

- There are sixteen official ethnic languages in Zimbabwe, but chiShona and SiNdebele are the two predominant vernacular languages, while English is the main lingua franca for business and education. For many, English would be their second language or, in some cases, their third or fourth. The population is estimated at about 13 million, of which around 70 percent are Shona speakers. However, approximately 2 to 3 million people have fled economic and political oppression in the last two decades.

Political

- Politically, Zimbabwe is a multiparty constitutional democracy, with parliamentary and judicial systems modelled on those in the UK and Roman-Dutch law. Presently, there are two main political parties: ZANU PF, which has a majority in Parliament, and the opposition Movement for Democratic Change (MDC).
- Visiting instructors should be aware of sensitive issues. It is illegal to criticize the president. Criticizing the government and/or the ruling party can be problematic. The *Gukuruhundi* (Shona for "the wind that blows away the chaff") massacres of the 1980s, in which an estimated 20,000 mainly Ndebele-related people were killed, are deeply resented in Matabeleland and mentioning them evokes strong reactions.
- Homosexuality is illegal and culturally frowned upon, as are abortion and transgenderism.

Religious

- Spiritually, Zimbabwe, as part of Southern Africa, has a cultural and spiritual background of African Traditional Religion (ATR), which is ancestor-centred. The spirit world – both good and bad spirits – is sensed very strongly. The spirits are responsible for everything. Appeasing the spirits is crucial and, hence, fear and fatalism tend to predominate.
- Witchcraft and its rituals are an important influence, even for many Christians. The *n'anga* (witch doctor) or some traditional healers are important members of society who explain events, prophesy, and heal. Syncretism with ATR is a major problem, as are false gospels that resonate with ATR. False prophets and false concepts of church – and, thus, false expectations of Christianity – are all influenced by the ATR background.
- Many rural folk have some direct experience of ATR rituals and practices, but many urban people, while not practising ATR directly, are still

subconsciously influenced. Socialization with ATR influences is widespread in the towns and cities. There is increasing evidence of ATR influences shaping the Christian church.

- A majority of Zimbabweans would identify themselves as "Christian," but most would be nominal. It is estimated that less than a quarter of the population are churchgoers. Although there is freedom of worship, the government is increasingly concerned about the mushrooming of local, independent "churches" based on the prosperity gospel and which seem to exist just to make money.

- While the Christian church is well established, syncretism has seen the establishment and rise of African Independent Churches (AICs) or Zionist or Apostolic movements. Many Christians seek help from these prophets, "witch doctors," and traditional healers using ATR means.

- The ATR influence means that there is always a spiritual cause or reason for something happening: sickness, mishaps, accidents, and especially death always have a reason behind them – and often someone (in the extended family or elsewhere) will be identified as being responsible (through "witchcraft"). This means, typically, that one is never to blame directly, nor should one necessarily accept accountability: someone or something else is always the problem.

Educational

- Educationally, Zimbabwe has the roots of a sound educational system (based on the colonial English approach), but recent political and economic events have decimated this sector. Nevertheless, literacy is still higher than in many other African countries. The first national school examination is held at the end of Grade 7 (Standard Five in primary school), followed four years later (Form Four in high school) by Ordinary Level exams, which are the basic entry requirement for most employment and training programs, followed two years later (Form Six) by Advanced Level, which is the basic university entrance requirement.

- There are currently fifteen universities, both state and private, secular and Christian. However, with an estimated 90 percent unemployment and a de-industrialized and informalized economy, very few graduates are able to find meaningful employment. Many students enter university with the hope that better qualifications will assist them to find employment, but end up "qualifying" with degrees that they are not really interested in or that appear to serve no economic purpose.

- The school system has very much a rote and regurgitation approach with a view to passing exams. This has built a culture of grades and paper (certificates) being all-important. Even some nursery schools now have "graduation" ceremonies with caps and gowns. The mindset is often: "If I have the piece of paper, then I have learned." Or, "If I fail to get a passing grade, it is the teacher's fault, not mine." Yet competence in doing the work may be lacking. Critical thinking is not expressly taught or expected. Thus, at tertiary level, instructors should work intentionally to help students begin to think for themselves. Sometimes, instructors may find students reluctant to answer questions, not because they don't know, but because they expect to be told the answer(s). Often, what is written on the board is copied down; what is said is not.

- A visiting lecturer would be assumed to be "the expert." Hence, saying something "wrong" deliberately to evoke debate in class is unlikely to be questioned, at least in public.

- Africans are primarily oral learners who process information differently from literate learners. Even though the educational system is literate in approach, some students may struggle to produce "useful" class notes. They may appear disrespectful to the lecturer or uninterested, but they are merely processing the information differently. Encouraging them to discuss issues – both in and out of class – can help greatly in the learning process.

- Using small groups in class is often a new phenomenon for first-year college or university students because this is not typical in the school system. However, given the centrality of relationships it is beneficial to have learners discuss issues among themselves and to appreciate that others may have alternative views.

- It is important to give very detailed, step-by-step guidelines to help students to accept approaches they may not have encountered previously.

- Instructors should be aware that, as their relationship with the students grows, so will the students' expectation that the lecturer will "help" them to pass. A failing grade may well be viewed negatively, not as a learning failure but as a relationship failure.

- Because of the relationship factor, be careful how you ask for student assessment of your work: you are likely to be told what you want to hear, not what you may actually need for self-improvement. Students will not critique you directly. It is important to explain the distinction between critique (positive) and criticism (negative). Students will often find such evaluation difficult.

- In some cases, translation may be necessary. Assume that you will cover less than half of your normal content because of the time needed for translation. If possible, provide the text of your teaching notes in advance to the translator so that he or she can be prepared. Prepare supplemental teaching aids to support your verbal delivery. Keep your vocabulary as simple as possible, and speak slowly and clearly. Speak in short, simple sentences. Use complete sentences as far as possible. Avoid using excessive sub-clauses.

- Be aware that foreign accents may take time to be "heard." Speak slowly, deliberately, and clearly. Avoid mumbling. Speak to the students, not to the board. In exceptional cases, it may be necessary to have a student repeat what you say.

- Be careful with idioms, proverbs, and illustrations. Foreign idioms may not "work," while some proverbs may need explaining. It is often useful to ask students to think of vernacular equivalents as well. Western illustrations – places, people, and events – should be chosen carefully, assuming that your audience is unfamiliar with them. If the background to an illustration requires explanation, it is best not used; the illustration should be simple enough to be understood directly.

- Both men and women should dress neatly. Men are often expected to wear a jacket and tie with long trousers, with shoes and socks (not just sandals); however, a smart shirt is often acceptable. Shorts are considered inappropriate for a teacher. Women should not wear trousers, and tops should be modest and not revealing. Avoid excessive jewellery and make-up.

- Depending on the setting, expect a range of denominational backgrounds among your students. Please do not try to press your own theological beliefs too much. Many students will be aware of the general doctrinal position of their church, but may not know the historical or theological background to, or reasons for, those beliefs. In general, the Zimbabwean church is theologically conservative.

Teaching Cross-Culturally in Mozambique

Dr. Verena Schafroth, Academic Dean,
Instituto Teológico de Lichinga

Social and Cultural

- Mozambique was a Portuguese colony until it gained independence in 1975. It has retained Portuguese as the official national language, but most Mozambicans also speak a variety of Bantu languages. English is little spoken or understood outside the capital, Maputo, or the tourist areas along the coastline.

- Agriculture makes up 81 percent of the country's production and is mainly done by small-plot farmers in poor rural areas. Many families have their own field, called *machamba*, and for most pastors in rural areas this usually is the primary source of income.

- Hospitality is highly valued in Mozambique and even a poor family will delight in providing for a visitor. Part of this hospitality is also to yield the pulpit to a foreign visitor at church, and it is therefore recommended to always have a sermon outline handy wherever one goes.

- The general recommendation regarding dress would be to overdress rather than assume a more casual attire. Men should wear long trousers and a shirt (shorts are not acceptable), and women a skirt and top. The traditional clothing for women is a long cotton cloth called *capulana*, which is wrapped around the waist and tucked in to make a skirt.

- There is a marked regional difference in Mozambique, often referred to as the south–north division, which also coincides with a rural–urban divide. Starting in Maputo in the south, the further one goes north, the less developed the country becomes. Patrilineal cultures in the south give way to matrilineal cultures in the north.

- As a foreigner, you will be considered rich irrespective of how wealthy or poor you see yourself, and people in church and school will ask you for help. The general rule follows the common belief "there is no shame in asking – and there is no shame in saying no."

Political

- Independence resulted from a coup in Portugal on 25 April 1974 which led in July 1975 to the independence of Mozambique. Mozambique was ruled by FRELIMO (Frente de Libertação de Moçambique – Mozambique Liberation Front) as a one-party state until 1990.
- Communism was adopted shortly after independence, but a poor agriculture plan, in addition to sustained drought for some years, resulted in a growing food crisis in the country and a breakdown of the economy in the 1980s. In response to this, RENAMO (Resistência Nacional Moçambicana – Mozambican National Resistance) was founded as an anti-communist political movement and a civil war ensued.
- By the end of the 1980s, the economy was at an all-time low after years of fighting. This caused a change of attitude: FRELIMO turned from their communist stance, opened up to the West, and signed a peace agreement with RENAMO in 1992. In 1994, the first multiparty elections were held, with FRELIMO and RENAMO as the front runners, but also with many smaller parties. Ever since, FRELIMO has governed Mozambique and RENAMO has been the main opposition. This "co-existence" has not always been peaceful and in recent years there have been armed skirmishes between RENAMO and FRELIMO soldiers, although these have mostly been limited to the centre of the country in the Gorongosa area.[1]

---

1. Dr. J. Hanlon, a social scientist based in the UK, writes a regular political update called "Mozambique News Reports and Clippings." You can subscribe to it at http://www3.open.ac.uk/forms/subscribe-Mozambique-English/.

Religion

- The country is host to a number of religions – according to recent statistics, about 32 percent Catholic, 21 percent Protestant, 19 percent Muslim, as well as other traditional faiths.

- There are currently more than 300 Christian denominations operating in Mozambique, with the Catholic Church being the largest. Ecumenism is well established through the Christian Council of Mozambique, and the churches generally have a good reputation.

- African Traditional Religion (ATR) is still very much alive in Mozambique, with the belief that whatever happens in a person's life always has a spiritual reason. Hence, people might go to the hospital to seek treatment, but they will also go to the *curandeiro* (traditional healer or witch doctor) to seek answers as to why something has happened.

- Most evangelical churches strongly oppose going to the *curandeiro*, but do not tend to offer a credible alternative solution or theology for dealing with people's fears and suffering in general. Hence, many Christians still seek out the traditional healers in secret in times of misfortune or illness.

- There is a marked geographical movement as far as religion is concerned. The south is predominantly Christian, but the further north one goes, the more Muslim the culture becomes. ATR is common practice in most villages.

- Muslims and Christians live together peacefully in Mozambique, with the exception of the province of Cabo Delgado in the north-east close to the border with Tanzania. A fundamentalist Islamic group often called Al-Shabaab has radicalized some areas to the north of Pemba and there has been a level of armed conflict. This has been a local issue, probably also to do with unemployment and poverty, and has not spread beyond the north of Cabo Delgado.

Education

- Primary education is free and compulsory and offered in the various local languages, but secondary education is optional, comes with school fees, and is done in Portuguese. There are only eighty-two secondary schools in the whole country.

- The level of education follows the south–north and urban–rural divide, with Maputo in the south providing the most opportunities for secondary and higher education, including theological education. As you move north and out of the cities, education levels drop drastically.

- Education is very important to most Mozambicans, but the general education system cannot cope with the number of pupils enrolled. Teachers do not tend to be well educated or well paid, and "sex for good grades" sometimes occurs. Sadly, many people finish eight or nine years in school without ever having learned to read and write well.

- Nationwide, only about 7 percent of pupils enrol in secondary school, which then makes tertiary education a privilege for the few and wealthy. There is high competition for the small number of existing university places and, unfortunately, a degree does not guarantee a job after graduation.

- Even with good education, most Mozambicans are oral-preference learners and enjoy group discussions and working in groups. Providing a full set of notes also makes it easier for them to follow in class so that they are not distracted by having to take notes.

- Unless you are fluent in Portuguese, you should expect to use an interpreter in class. Unfortunately, this will cut your time in half and will also make it difficult to convey more complex ideas. In this case, it helps to plan well and make more use of small groups in which students can discuss things in their own language(s) and then report back.

- Written tests tend to be a source of great stress for Mozambicans as they remind them of their school years when pupils are often shamed for not performing well. Therefore, most will underperform in written tests. Students often do better in demonstrating what they have really learned when they can present orally or work in their own time at home.

- Few Mozambicans have a personal computer at home or access to good Internet as a research tool. Technology might be more common in Maputo, but even there it should not be expected. At many Bible schools, homework is submitted handwritten.

- Mozambique follows a point system for grading: 20–19 = A; 18–17 = B; 16–14 = C; 13–10 = D; below 10 is a fail. This can take some getting used to, so it is advisable to consult in advance with the administration of the receiving Bible school.

- Being punctual in Mozambique often means arriving within an hour of the scheduled time. This is also because life is less plannable, and heavy rains or public transport without regular timetables makes it hard to be on time. A combination of showing grace in the rainy season (December to April) and setting firm rules often does the trick.

- Due to Mozambique's communist past, religious studies of any faith still cannot be found in higher education at universities. The government leaves this up to the church denominations and mosques. This has made it very hard for Bible schools to have their degrees recognized by the government. So far, only two Bible schools have succeeded in doing so, mainly because they also offer secular degrees.

Practical

- Maputo is the political and economic centre of the country. The currency used is the Mozambican Metical and ATMs can be found in most towns and cities. However, if you go to rural areas, make sure to take plenty of cash with you.

- Tourist visas are available on arrival to most foreign nationals on submission of a return ticket and confirmation of accommodation and/ or an invitation letter.

- Keep your passport and related documents with you at all times. In the major cities, frequent police checks are common, and the police have a bit of a reputation for making life difficult. Always stay polite and calm, and seek help from your local contacts.

- If someone in authority tells you *boas festas*, it is a guarded way of asking for a bribe. Be polite and calmly say "no." If necessary, explain that you work with the church and therefore cannot simply "give" something.

Teaching Cross-Culturally in Guatemala

Seminário Teológico Centroamericano (SETECA)[1]

Culture and Society

- There are wide cultural differences within the same country, most notably in the contrast between *latinos* and *indígenas* (indigenous, pre-Columbian ethnic groups).

- Racism (in particular against the *indígenas*) is present in explicit and implicit ways. Discrimination is observed in society (and the church) but it would appear to be lessening in the academic environment.

- In many places in Guatemala (and in Latin America in general) you will find that Spanish is the second language, the first language being indigenous.

- Guatemala is one of the countries with the greatest power distance[2] in the world, and this relationship of power distance is very present in the classroom. In indigenous cultures the hierarchical structure of society is even more pronounced.

- Although there are some who will come directly and speak what they think, in general Guatemalans are very indirect in expressing their opinions.

- The intangible "trust" factor: things will get accomplished or be blocked depending on the participants' trust (or lack thereof) in the person and/or the process. The need for trust-building applies equally to the classroom, and profoundly affects student participation and commitment.

---

1. SETECA has an unusually multicultural environment – there are students from at least twenty-five countries on campus. Even the faculty includes many foreigners, mostly from other Central American countries.

2. G. Hofstede and G. Hofstede, *Cultures and Organizations: Software of the Mind*, 3rd ed. (New York: McGraw-Hill, 2010), 61.

- *Machismo* (strong or aggressive masculine pride) may limit the participation of some women as students and create challenges for women as teachers.
- In Guatemala and elsewhere in Central America there is a history of living under dictatorship. This has led to people feeling somewhat insecure and can make them more reserved in revealing their opinions and personal feelings.
- There is a high number of disintegrated families, often due to absent fathers (migration, war, violence).
- Demographically, Guatemala is a young population, and you should expect a large presence of young students in your classes.
- In the younger population there is a steady weakening of strict denominational ties. Younger believers will tend to have a deeper connection to certain leaders, not necessarily to a denomination.

Educational

- The public school system is not generally of a high quality, and there is a high degree of attrition at every level. Private schools offer a better schooling, but access to these schools is restricted and expensive.
- However, do not underestimate your students. Do not assume that, because you are coming to a Majority World country, you should lower your academic expectations. Here in Guatemala we have all too often seen professors coming from outside with an assumption that students will have a low academic level, but when students are given space they demonstrate excellent levels of thinking. In particular, you should avoid taking a paternalistic approach when dealing with indigenous students.
- You should get to know the institutional culture of the school where you are teaching. There are differences, especially in terms of doctrine, among seminaries in the same country, in the same region, and even in the same city. You may need to be open to dialogue in a context which you perceive as more or less conservative than your own.

- Inquire as to what is expected from you. Are you expected to give lectures or conferences to larger audiences or to teach in small settings in a more dialogical manner?

- Take into consideration the level of the program where you are teaching. Undergraduate classes or events opened to lay people in the church will generally be less open to dialogue between perspectives, and you should be more careful not to push people away with provocative ideas. In some cases, the students will expect to have their beliefs confirmed or explained better; in other situations, students may even expect to be told what to do or believe. In graduate programs, there is generally a good context for dialogue, which allows for a higher level of provocative ideas and interaction. This may also depend on the background of the students, some of whom come from a "banking" approach to learning, while others have more experience in critical participation in discussion.

- While it is an oversimplified generalization, in Latin America you can expect to find those from South America more willing to participate in dialogue than those from Central America, where many will expect the teacher to tell them "what to believe" and find the ambiguity of several options to be disquieting and even unacceptable.

- If you expect discussion, you will have to adjust your methodology to create safe spaces for it. Quality discussion can happen in the classroom, but the best opportunities may take place outside the formal lesson, in informal spaces and conversations.

- Do not display or show knowledge in an arrogant way.

- Do not assume the methodology you used in another place will work here.

General

- Before going to the host school, you should be intentional in collecting information about the school and the country through websites, news channels, and the like. However, even if you study your host culture carefully, collect quality information, and prepare as best you can before you get there, you still need to have flexibility and openness to the realities of the context itself.

- Make sure that you interact in advance with those who have invited you. Rely on them for information.
- Go out of your way to show respect to students. Learn what might offend and avoid doing or saying things that may upset students or staff. Consult in advance and while on campus with leaders of the host school.
- In many schools in the West attention has been given to the strengthening of minority groups on campus. If you come to a country in Latin America, you may meet students or staff from countries you have previously encountered on your home campus. Building relationships with these people supports your teaching.
- There is a long history of "educational imperialism" in Guatemala. Sometimes the support of a visiting professor is accepted for diplomatic or economic reasons, but it does not always respond to a felt or real need of the seminary. Some schools receive offers from speakers or organizations and feel they have no power to say "no." You should ensure that you are not imposing yourself on the school.
- Above all else, avoid a "saviour" attitude. You are not being invited to "save" the school and the students, but to support an excellent work that people are already doing.

Teaching Cross-Culturally in Costa Rica

Seminario Esepa

Political

- Costa Rica has a strong heritage of "peace," without army or a history of warfare. The independence of Costa Rica was established peacefully. This is part of the "being" of the *tico* (Costa Rican). If you want to be relevant with your "illustrations," you should avoid military ones because the army is a distant and little-understood subject. That said, societal violence and crime are growing.

- National events quickly become the object of teasing or jokes. Ask about them because these can be used as very good "hooks" to start conversations. Some examples might be when we lose a football match or when a politician is denounced for a corruption issue.

- The *ticos* feel proud of their culture, and have a lot of love for Costa Rica, believing they are superior to their Central American neighbours. They may be xenophobic with respect to certain nations. However, Costa Ricans may also defer to and show preference for North Americans or Europeans.

- There is still something of a self-perception that we are poor, and many Costa Ricans expect things to be given for free. In fact, even if a person is in a solid economic condition, he or she will not necessarily demonstrate it.

Social and Cultural

- The *tico* greets effusively. It is not strange to greet each other with a hug or a kiss. Personal space is smaller than in North America or Europe. However, you should keep a respectful distance from the opposite sex. If physical contact is difficult for you, try a handshake. It is very important that you greet everyone when you enter and say goodbye to everyone when you leave.

- People will apologize for things that in another cultural context would not be seen as needing an apology.

- Costa Rica lives on coffee and food. Many things happen around a cup of coffee, and food will be a central part of meetings. Before talking about "business," the Costa Rican wants to eat and drink coffee. Costa Rica is not a wealthy country. Be considerate and grateful for what you are offered to eat.

- There are some important dates and celebrations for the country; be sure to ask about these and make reference to them as necessary. For example, 15 August is Mothers' Day, when you are expected to congratulate mothers, and 15 September is Independence Day.

- Costa Rica is a *macho* but matriarchal society. The mother has a leading role in many families, often due to the absence of fathers. Women today have more "modern" understandings than the older generation, speaking more naturally about issues such as feminism and gender rights. Women retain their surnames despite being married. So, if a couple is legally married, don't be surprised if the woman has a different last name from her husband's.

- Family is very important and a big deal is made of family celebrations. It is natural for children to live at home until they get married, and children often remain at home until well into their twenties. Do not see this as immaturity; it is a sign of strong family ties.

- Soccer is very important in Costa Rica. There are differences between the various teams. Ask about it to have contact points during your preaching or teaching.

- Costa Ricans are less individualistic than North Americans or Europeans, but much more individualistic than Asians, Africans, and South Americans.

- Indigenous populations: although we still have indigenous communities in rural settings, they are a minority (only 3 percent of the total population). People live mostly in cities and villages. There is access to electricity, technology, and clean water throughout virtually the entire country.

Religious

- Costa Rica is a very religious country, so you need to be sensitive to its religious heritage. Be particularly aware of the Catholic heritage. People are faithful to their Catholicism, especially among the older generations. Even though many Catholics come to evangelical churches, they are nonetheless sensitive to their Catholicism. So be careful and don't attack or make jokes about the Catholic religion or make comments about the Virgin Mary that might offend.

- The *tico* is superstitious, especially in rural areas. Mysticism is consequently strong. These superstitions also contribute to the widespread playing of the lottery.

- The churches of Costa Rica are very fragmented, and there are significant differences between them. Try to become familiar with the "dress code" of each church represented by your students, and make sure you know the expectations of churches you attend. Different churches "demand" different types of clothing when you teach. Some are quite formal, even expecting male professors to wear a coat and tie. The most widely used version of the Bible in most evangelical churches is the *Reina Valera 60*, although the use of the *Nueva Versión Internacional* (New International Version) has been growing. Ask in advance and make sure that you use the preferred version in your notes or audiovisual support.

- In many parts of the country pastors are bivocational: they work in the church and also have a second job because of the lack of resources that congregations can offer them. Many have minimal if any formal training. Only 1 in 10 pastors has ever attended a seminary or Bible school.

- "Prosperity gospel" theology has grown significantly in some sections of the country. In particular, the local Christian television network ENLACE promotes the prosperity gospel. Be aware of the popularity of this position when teaching, and check when visiting local churches you have been invited to.

- For young people in Costa Rica, the truth is often seen as relative in the midst of a culture that is believed to be "modern." However, what is lived in practice often seems to reflect more of a pre-modern mentality, with religion still seen as of the utmost importance.

- Fundamentalist Christianity is strong in the evangelical world of Costa Rica. Be aware and respectful.

Educational

- Education is important in Costa Rica. For historical reasons, education has been prioritized in the country. Therefore, compared with the rest of Latin America, you will find a good level of literacy in Costa Rica. However, education has traditionally been based on rote memorization with little encouragement of critical thinking.
- Communication: the *tico* is not confrontational. People do not speak directly, and frequently go "walking around the bush." They may take five hundred words to say what could have been said in fifty. In professional situations, Costa Ricans will often spend a lot of time asking questions about your family and matters of a personal nature.
- Since people are not confrontational, they can easily take offence when they are made to see something bad that they have said or done. We recommend setting clear limits from the beginning. The *tico* needs affirmation. Think of positive things you can highlight, whether from the activity, the place where you are staying, the food, and so on.
- While there is a high level of respect for a teacher or speakers, Costa Ricans will also feel confident to speak out and express their thoughts. Moreover, a student may confidently challenge the grade he or she has received. This horizontal approach to communication is possibly more common in Costa Rica than in other Latin American countries, due to the country's strong democratic history and an egalitarian mentality that is translated into the educational space.
- The average *tico* is unpunctual, with only minimal structure to life. Costa Ricans function on "*tico* time." Be sure to check the start times and be patient when people are late. Many Costa Ricans will be unpunctual in the completion of homework. You should not be surprised if you are asked for more time to deliver a task or final job, even if you gave them the date with enough time to deliver.

Language

- The *tico* frequently uses humorous sayings and phrases that should not be taken literally. If translators are used, make sure they are Costa Rican or at least know these sayings or phrases.

- The *tico* tends to exaggerate and generalize without seeing any problem with this. When Costa Ricans relate a life story or reference "facts," it is worthwhile double-checking their veracity. But it is important to do this without dishonouring the local.

- If you speak Spanish it is preferable when addressing students and church people that you use *usted* (the formal "you") or *vos* (a little closer). Avoid the very familiar *tu* – although you may hear it because of the Mexican influence on television.

Practical

- Clothing: the weather in general is warm but moderate without extremes. There are areas in the mountains that can be cold, but we don't experience snow or extreme cold. It is common for women to dress in a way that would be perceived as "sexy" in other parts of the world. Do not necessarily think they are unchristian or non-believers. It is simply a matter of culture and all should be treated with respect.

- Security: in the past we have been a trustworthy and trusting community, and we went out into the streets without fear. Unfortunately, crime has increased. Try not to walk around with valuable objects in sight (cameras, phones, etc.). If you do not stand out in the crowd and walk quietly and confidently, you should have few difficulties in Costa Rica.

- Transportation: at least in the main cities, traffic can be chaotic and public transport is slow and even unpredictable. Buses do not have fixed schedules. Be sure to leave early and coordinate well with the people who are going to take you or pick you up – even more so if you are going to use a public bus. That said, there is easy access to transportation, including to some digital platforms like Uber.

Teaching Cross-Culturally in the Caribbean

Dr. Errol E. Joseph and the Caribbean
Group (David Corbin, Sheldon Campbell,
Cherisse Forde, and Mark Lawrence)

History and Culture

- The Caribbean region has four major language groups — English, Spanish, French, and Dutch. The language spoken is indicative of the country which previously ruled them. As a result, English is spoken in Jamaica, Spanish in Cuba, French in Haiti, Dutch in Curaçao, and so forth. The colonial history impacts our language, culture, and education.

- Regarding Caribbean culture, Jamaica is known for reggae music, Trinidad and Tobago for calypso music, and so forth.

- Caribbean countries generally have had a significantly high number of people from African descent – from the time of slavery until now. There is also a noticeable population of Indians and Chinese, many of whose ancestors were brought to the region as indentured workers when slavery was abolished. The Indians and Chinese have done fairly well economically and many own shops and establishments. As a result, there is great diversity, even within individual countries.

Education

- Adult literacy in the Caribbean averages about 90 percent. In Jamaica and Guyana literacy is about 90 percent, while in Trinidad and Tobago and Cuba it is almost 100 percent. In Dutch countries such as Aruba, Bonaire,

260 Teaching across Cultures

and Curaçao (ABC), it is about 97 percent, while in French-speaking Haiti it is about 60 percent.

- The moderate unemployment rates in some Caribbean countries has led to something of a "brain drain," with the best educated and qualified often opting to work in Minority World countries such as the USA, Canada, and the UK, capitalizing on the work opportunities offered in these countries.

Religion

- Former Spanish and French countries generally have a strong Catholic influence. Former Dutch countries have Catholicism and the Dutch Reformed Church. The former English countries are generally Protestants (Anglicans, Baptists, Methodists, and so forth) with greater diversity.
- Cults and false religions are common in the Caribbean, often influenced by the African heritage. For example, Jamaica has Rastafarianism, Haiti has Voodoo, and so forth.

Political

- There are typically two main political parties in each Caribbean country. Political parties are sometimes responsible for high levels of corruption and crime and violence.

Post-colonial

- It is clear from the attitudes and content expressed in the music of our people that we still need to address some of the consequences of our being former colonies of Europe. Poverty is an issue for many Caribbean countries, even when official statistics indicate otherwise. For example, while Jamaica is a high category B country according to the World Bank and United Nations standards, this results from a high disparity in income: a small proportion of the population owns most of the financial resources or capital, while the majority have to seek innovative ways to provide for themselves. The similarity with the old plantation economy is notable. The disparity between rich and poor contributes to high rates of crime and violence, as well as a significant drug culture, with some seeking to make money through selling drugs.

Jamaica

- Ensure that your entry is to do volunteer work. Volunteerism should take care of the issue of remuneration and taxes.
- Having an official letter of invitation is helpful at every port of entry. When completing immigration forms, you should identify yourself as an educator. Using the local home address of a Jamaican comes across better than giving a hotel as your place of residence.

St. Lucia

If faculty members need to visit St. Lucia, they should first contact a key leader directly for advice on the documents it will be necessary for them to have on their person, in order to follow all requirements for working or teaching in St. Lucia.

Some observations on St. Lucia:

- St. Lucians are very warm and friendly people, very open and jovial, respectful and helpful.
- The society is very laid-back, so, in order to get people to do anything, it may be necessary to give frequent reminders and a gentle push towards accomplishing tasks. These reminders should be gentle and gracious, as otherwise they may upset the students and backfire.
- Witchcraft is commonplace in St. Lucia. Often, witchcraft is practised out of jealousy within a family or community.
- People tend to treat pastors as political leaders. The pastors are seen as being there to do whatever the congregation wants.
- The average St. Lucian is not an ardent reader, nor very tech-savvy in terms of study.

- St. Lucians are also not givers by nature. Because of this, some of them are very poor at paying their tuition fees.
- Insect repellent is absolutely necessary as the country is plagued by sandflies, which cause allergic reactions on some people's skin or may simply leave annoying marks.
- In terms of shopping, there is very little variety in anything in St. Lucia, so if you require a particular brand of a product for health or personal reasons, you should bring it with you.
- Health care is not free in St. Lucia. You should ensure you have travel insurance before coming.

Trinidad

- Trinidad is notable for our warm climate, as well as for our warmth as a people, our love of music, and our love just to have a good time.
- Visiting teachers need to be aware of the impact of slavery in the region. We don't want to be patronized. We want to be seen as equals.
- Do not judge our work ethic. We don't like to be treated as slaves, but we do work. We like good-quality work, so give us good quality.
- Do not underestimate where we are on the learning curve. We are an intelligent people.

Teaching Cross-Culturally in Colombia

Fundación Universitaria Seminario Bíblico de Colombia

Official Business

- Upon entering the country, always present an official letter of invitation. Don't merely turn up.
- Observe the simple security protocols that are given to you. You'll be safe here if you trust us.
- Be proactive in letting us know about food or other allergies. Frankly, we don't have as many available goods as there may be in your home country. But we want to take care of you.
- Let us know explicitly whether we are free to film or record your lectures.

Respecting the Context

- Pay attention to local expectations regarding style of dress and personal cleanliness. Your temporary context may be more formal than the one to which you've become accustomed. Host institutions may have written guidelines to help you.
- Don't assume that you'll find only poverty in Colombia. We have the whole continuum of wealth and poverty.
- Leave the themes of sexuality, gender, and family to local experts. You don't know enough to know what you don't know about local cultural patterns and understandings.
- Be honest when it comes to food and other very concrete matters of culture. If you can't eat something, say so, ask for your hosts' pardon, and move on.

- Perhaps unlike where you come from, a person here can be a respected researcher, professor, or teacher and not have earned a doctorate.

- Be ready and willing to learn from people even of the lowest social standing.

- It may be a little awkward for you to be honoured the way we want to honour you. Just go with it. It's how we do things.

- Spend a little time learning some simple ways to give and receive greetings.

- Ask local leaders about appropriate relationships between members of the opposite sex and err on the conservative side.

- When it comes to alcoholic beverages, realize that these matters are tricky in specific contexts of churches and denominations. Our country and our region has a variety of views about such things. Don't generalize. Use common sense.

- Come to us eager to learn. Things here are different, but not necessarily bad. Don't expect people to act as you would.

- Be aware that the relationship in our region between the Catholic Church and Protestants has a long and often tough history. When you assign readings, use good judgment and an instinct for theological dialogue. Some Protestants have strong reservations about anything that is Roman Catholic. Just be aware. Images, expressions, and certain religious behaviour carry a lot of historical baggage.

- Many of our health and education services are quite good. Don't assume otherwise.

- Read a book about us before you arrive. But remember: you've only read one book.

- There's a good chance we're more punctual than what you're used to. Or less. Roll with us.

- Be politically aware. If you're American, there's a good chance your military or the CIA has been here and done damage. We're not all eager to celebrate that. And be aware that our country has a lot more going for it than drug traffickers, no matter what the Western media think. Don't joke about our politics and history. You don't know them well enough. Still, we like you.

- We want to learn from your politics and your history, if you'll help us to understand them. Just be careful. Christians here may lean in different political directions from how you anticipate.

Communicate Like a Grown-Up

- Be clear about the education level of the people you've been invited to address. Don't assume that people don't already know something about your topic.
- Don't be arrogant. Realize that we may *expect* you to be arrogant. Disarm us with genuine humility.
- Don't make unnecessary comparisons that pretend to show the superiority of your culture. Avoid criticizing the culture you're visiting. You haven't yet earned the right to do so, nor do you yet know when you're comparing apples with apples and when you are not.
- Don't be offended if we interrupt. Sometimes it's not rudeness, but rather a function of the spirited conversation in which you've been invited to participate. On the other hand, don't even think about throwing anything at anyone!
- Our regional language (Spanish) is actually *many* dialects. Realize that the same word may be ordinary in one country and offensive in another. When you don't know, ask!
- Rely on your translator. Seek his or her input ahead of time. Use images and anecdotes that make sense in your hosts' experience.
- Realize that your way of seeing things and your sense of humour are neither the only possible ones nor the points of reference from which all others are derivations.
- Don't pass out effusive compliments as though the simplest achievement by one of us deserves a Nobel Prize.
- Be careful about making off-the-cuff comments about Pentecostals. A lot of us are one.

Teaching Cross-Culturally in Andean Peru

Instituto Bíblico Sinodal de Arequipa [IBSA]
de la Iglesia Evangélica Peruana [IEP]

Social and Cultural

- Andean context and culture are still substantially animistic, and this will influence the worldview of your students.
- There is not "one leader," but pretty much everything is done in the context of community. Consequently, Andean students expect to be helped by the community (teacher and other students).
- There's a huge power distance in the wider culture; this is often reflected within the church as well.
- Andean regions tend to be fairly closed and conservative communities.

Political

- Bureaucratic tasks are often very tedious for churches and theological institutions.
- Corruption is a huge problem in Peruvian politics and bureaucracy.
- Marches and political campaigns are quite regularly on the agenda of Peruvian life.

Religious

- There is a wave of neo-Pentecostalism sweeping across the continent, and this is impacting Andean Peru.

- While evangelicalism is strong in cities such as Lima, it is still quite weak in Andean regions.
- The predominance of the Roman Catholic Church and its beliefs and practices are felt heavily throughout Peru.
- Roman Catholicism in Peru today often seems to reflect the kind of institution the Reformers in the sixteenth century were reacting against.
- A variety of religious cults and movements are evident in Peru, including Jehovah's Witnesses and Mormons.

Educational

- Andean students tend to prefer pastoral and practical aspects of theological education; when the classes are too "theological," the students tend to create distance.
- Students feel an enormous pressure from the local churches to be the "know-all" once they return from seminary. Hence the desire for everything to be immediately applicable.
- It is best to show how the Scriptures themselves espouse the content of the classes. That is, the students like to read the Scriptures and have the Scriptures shape what is being taught.
- Many students come from oral communities. Consequently, narratives and stories tend to make a deeper impression than abstract ideas.
- In the past, within the Andean classroom jokes were not viewed favourably, and boys were not allowed to talk to girls. These understandings are changing, but slowly.
- It is not uncommon in theological programs to have enormous diversity in levels of education, perhaps having classes in which some have difficulty in reading while others have completed university.
- The education system in Peru is traditional with an emphasis on rote learning. Students are not encouraged in reflection or critical thinking. The expectation in the school system is that when a teacher asks a question, students are to repeat word for word what has been said previously. Teachers need much patience in developing reflection skills.

Language

- While classes are generally held in Spanish, Quechua is the heart language of most.
- Because the language of instruction differs from the spoken language, students often have difficulties with technical terms and complex literature.

Teaching Cross-Culturally in Brazil

Faculdade de Teologia de São Paulo da Igreja Presbiteriana Independente do Brasil – FATIPI

General Observations

- The Brazilian context is different from other Majority World countries, and there is only rarely an actual need for a Western missionary to come to teach a class in a seminary or college.

- A substantial part of our literature base is already translations from English or German. The main priority today, therefore, is to get a closer correlation to the Brazilian context, rather than the presentation of propositional ideas along classic Western lines.

- We question the ability of scholars coming from the North for a short period of time to understand adequately our context and plan a course or series of presentations that appropriately takes into consideration factors that Brazilian and Latin American theology understands as foundational, such as issues of inequality, poverty, human suffering, and power. If scholars come to Brazil they should come as learners, with great humility and awareness of their limited understanding of the context.

- This does not mean that we think there is nothing for us to learn from colleagues from the North. But so often an international lecturer comes only to reaffirm what he or she has already written in his or her latest book.

- At many congresses and events there is the celebrity factor – a famous international scholar (usually from the West) is invited as a sort of advertisement for the event to attract a larger audience. There is a certain colonial perspective even coming from ourselves, in which we value somebody from the West more than our fellow Brazilian colleagues.

- Such factors add to our perception that in many cases an international professor from the North coming to teach in Brazil often devalues the local professors – often with economic factors playing a part. This does not necessarily result in a gain for the school or the students.

- On the other hand, we long for collaboration with colleagues from Asia, Africa, Eastern Europe, and other parts of Latin America, as they share many of our concerns and priorities. In terms of Latin America, there is a mutual ignorance between the two parts of the continent – Spanish-speaking and the Portuguese-speaking Latin America – and we still have much work to do in terms of building a meaningful exchange.

Theological Education in Brazil

- Among other standard cultural and regional differences, our context is different from most other parts of Latin America in that theological studies have been accredited by the Brazilian Ministry of Education since 1999. Even before that, theological studies in the country had a history, going back at least 140 years.

- As a consequence, we have officially accredited schools offering more than 250 undergraduate-level programs – evangelical, mainline Protestant, and Catholic. We also have programs offered by institutions that are not accredited by the Ministry of Education, including at least sixty institutions which are members of AETAL (the Latin American branch of ICETE). Many others are just unaffiliated or associated with particular organizations.

- Throughout Brazil there is a robust field of theological education, with many scholars holding doctoral degrees, specialized in their fields, but often isolated from the global community of scholars due to the issue of language, as they publish mostly in Portuguese.

- Online education has been growing steadily, perhaps to capacity. In Brazilian higher education in general, there are now more students in online than in face-to-face programs. Theological education is heading in the same direction.

Religious

- Brazil is still mostly a Catholic country, although this has been changing rapidly over the last couple of decades with the astonishing growth of the Protestant church, including mainline Protestant, Pentecostal, neo-Pentecostal, Reformed, and evangelicals. In general, in Brazil the term "evangelical" is used to refer to any Protestant church.

- There is an overwhelming presence of "neo-Pentecostal" groups, which have a marked emphasis on the prosperity gospel and a strong presence in the media, especially network and satellite television.

- Be mindful that even in a denominational institution your students may come from very different groups. For example, you may be teaching in a Presbyterian college, but find students in your class from all the groups mentioned above!

- Both the evangelical church and the general society are profoundly polarized in terms of political issues and public policies regarding issues such as abortion and gender. As an outsider, it is best that you avoid these topics and leave discussion of sensitive issues to national Brazilian teachers.

Educational

The following are some important insights for an international scholar who comes to teach in Brazil:

- When you come to teach or lecture, attend to the specific need presented by your host institution; do not simply present what you already have.

- You should take into account our local Portuguese bibliographic resources. In virtually any subject area we have a solid bibliography. While it is perhaps not as extensive as that available in English, if you want to teach in Brazil you should know what is available and include local texts in your course bibliography. Generally, the school librarian can help you discover what is available in Portuguese. It can also be worthwhile to contact local Brazilian professors who teach in the same area of study as you will be teaching.

- Remember we speak Portuguese, not Spanish! Our capital city is Brasilia, not Buenos Aires (as a former US president once said!). Spanish-speaking Latin America is fragmented into many different countries, but Brazil remained united as a single large Portuguese-speaking "island." However, bear in mind that there are huge regional differences within the country.

- Contrasts occur not only inter-regionally but also locally. São Paulo, for example, is a city of 12 million people housing billionaires and at least 25,000 homeless people.

- Your students at undergraduate level will most likely be from lower-mid to lower strata of society; at graduate level, from the middle classes. Socio-economic background affects basic schooling and the ability to read and write. Students at undergraduate level may not always be able to keep up with assigned readings, and you should adapt accordingly.

- The south and south-east parts of the country hold almost 60 percent of the population in about 15 percent of the country's territory. They also hold most of the institutions offering theological education, and it is likely that you will be invited to this area.

Practical

In São Paulo and most of the other large Brazilian cities, the following common characteristics may be found:

- There are fairly good public transportation systems in place in the larger cities, although your host will probably take you to places.

- When you are working out logistics, always factor in traffic, as it is often an issue. You can rely on apps such as Waze or Google Maps to give you a good estimate of the time you will spend getting from one location to another. You should expect a number of late (and very late) arrivals at your classes and conferences, but people generally try to be on time for meetings.

- As in many other places, there are areas of the city you should avoid. The best thing is to be guided by a local, since the difference between safety and danger is sometimes a single block. You should avoid having your mobile phone visible while out in the street.

Teaching Cross-Culturally in Paraguay

Instituto Bíblico Asunción

Social and Cultural

- Paraguay has a bilingual culture, with both Spanish and Guaraní as official languages. Spanish is the language for education and business. Guaraní is spoken by a large majority of the population and is used in more colloquial contexts.
- Soccer is very important to Paraguayans, and commonly used as an "ice breaker."
- Greetings: relationships are very important in Paraguay. A greeting between men is by means of a handshake or, when there is a lot of trust, with hugs. Greetings between men and women are done with a handshake and without hugs, especially in evangelical contexts.

Political and Historical

- Paraguayan democracy is relatively young. The dictatorial past of the country has shaped and serves to shape many idiosyncratic aspects of Paraguayan culture. It is important that teachers from other cultures have a general awareness of this impact to better understand Paraguayan students.
- Knowing some specific events in the history of Paraguay, such as the wars against neighbouring countries, will be important for those who wish to better understand the vision that the Paraguayans have for themselves – their sense of national pride, and their regrets, pains, and doubts.

Religious

- Religion and religiosity are an important part of Paraguayan culture. The large majority of the population have a nominal Catholic faith, but still consider themselves Christian.
- Evangelicals are still a minority, but they have a strong presence in educational settings (schools, colleges, biblical seminaries, and a university). There are sporadic evangelical appearances at the political, cultural, and social levels. In general, evangelicals are theologically "conservative."
- There is a growing sense of unity, cooperation, and belonging among evangelical denominations.

Educational

- In general, Paraguayan students are quite introverted in the classroom context. In most cases, they will hesitate to ask questions or to respond to questions before their classmates. Trust develops better in small groups where students can open up and ask questions about topics related to the class.
- Paraguayan students have a deep-rooted oral culture. You need to take this into account when teaching, even in administrative details. For example, while instructions may be clearly written in detail as part of the lesson plan or syllabus, students will still need to hear the instructions given orally by the teacher. It can be a challenge to lead students towards greater independence and personal management of their studies.
- In general, Paraguayans are very open and friendly towards foreigners. While they may not pay attention to details as desired by the foreigner, there will always be a positive attitude of reception and friendship towards people from other countries.
- Assessment: the relational dimension is crucial, so do not expect students to make any direct assessment of your work. If you want to strengthen your teaching, you should give opportunity for anonymous written assessment – especially in educational settings. You need to expect that your students will also receive your assessment relationally, so you should avoid public critique of their work.
- Dress: in general, semi-formal dress is expected from professors and guests.

Teaching Cross-Culturally in Greece

Myrto Theocharous, the Greek Bible
College, Athens, Greece

Your Attitude

- Don't overestimate the greatness of your contribution. You are going on a trip for one to two weeks to teach, and then you are out, which is an enormous difference from those who keep the school and programs going year-round. Be aware of your limitations and keep humble about your contribution.

- Be aware of the danger of cultural arrogance. There may be subtle ways in which you are communicating the idea that you are the foreign expert who "knows," teaching the less privileged. In fact, some of the local students you teach may be more intelligent and informed than you expect. Greeks tend to read a lot and are generally well informed. Many students in Greece enter biblical-theological education after they have finished their first degrees in areas such as literature, philosophy, and classics.

- In addition to the above, ask yourself whether you are really contributing something that is needed. If you think that you will make a great contribution because you can slap a course together by using three to five commentaries on 1 Corinthians, be aware that more than likely there are people in the country who can easily do that (and without the need of a translator). So are you bringing a real expertise to the table? People in Greece are usually interested in new ideas and approaches, and while the more "sermonic" style is valued, they appreciate and are able to recognize good scholarship.

- Ask yourself whether there are public relations or financial factors that are the reasons for your being asked (or accepted) to teach somewhere. Is the church you pastor supporting a missionary who now feels a sense of obligation to you or your church? Might this actually influence the interpersonal dynamics in the field? At the end of the day, is the actual curriculum and training of students truly served by your coming, or was it somehow inserted into the program because of financial or public relations factors? Churches that are minorities in a country, such as the evangelical church in Greece, tend to need strong bonds with institutions in the United States or other countries with a strong evangelical presence, and this can lead to situations of obligation rather than need or desire.

Social, Cultural, and Religious

- Be aware that while you may be coming from a context where your faith is accepted and even celebrated, evangelicals in Greece are a tiny minority that has experienced until quite recently discrimination and even a level of persecution. Consequently, some things may be a given in your mind but not in the mind of Greek students.
- It is okay to compliment people on their culture and express admiration for it, but realize that their culture is not the touristy thing that you did yesterday. A better way to say it is: "Yes, yesterday I did the standard thing that tourists do in your country. I went to the Acropolis and then I ate at Plaka and shopped at Monastiraki. But, to be honest with you, I want to get beyond that. I am excited to meet you all and to be introduced by you to deeper levels of your culture." Don't pretend you somehow "learned" their culture after only two days there. The local students themselves probably rarely if ever go to the touristy places you may visit.
- Observe the style of professors and especially preachers. What works in your context to grab attention may be ridiculous or irritating to the Greeks. For example, if people are gentle and/or serious in their preaching, do not attempt to introduce a new style, such as jumping up and down and being wildly animated. Sometimes it is cute, but it rarely works. Things may be

tolerated by the culture if the content one brings is unique and brilliant, but that is rarely the case.

- Ask what the normal and acceptable ways of evangelism are and what the proselytization laws for the country are. Ask the locals how they do evangelism, and if you plan a certain style make sure you ask if any Greek would do it this way or if any Greek would participate in something you organize. Missionaries often have the idea of a prayer walk around neighbourhoods, praying and laying on hands on buildings. This would strike the locals as extremely odd and would not inspire credibility. Instead, a walk around the square to clean the streets of garbage would have a much greater impact and be an immediate witness. One could pray quietly while cleaning the streets.

Political

- People are probably aware of the politics in your home country, and most likely will ask you about your position on certain issues. Do not idolize your own culture. Be aware that the majority of people in Greece are anti-American and anti-capitalist, and you should try not to be defensive about your political structures and leaders. Rather, be quick to offer criticism of your own culture and political situation. People have more respect for individuals who have a "prophetic voice" in their own home country before coming to another context.
- Be aware and sensitive about various national issues such as with North Macedonia. We don't expect you to call this country Skopjia, but please use its legal title correctly and with awareness.

Educational

- Realize that some cultures listen to a teacher with attentiveness as though everything the teacher says is unquestionable, while in other cultures (such as Greece) it is customary to continually raise questions and challenge the professor. Greeks are generally very talkative and sometimes opinionated. They tend to filter things and question everything they hear, and do not trust easily. Be aware of the audience you will be facing, and don't take the students' confrontational approach personally.

- Realize that some things get lost in translation. Consequently, you should send in technical terms early on to your translator. Avoid puns and acronyms; they are difficult to translate. Remember that jokes can have a cultural flavour; they can also assume a wealthy economic status.

- Come with an attitude of learning. You may be teaching material that you have taught many times in your home country, but when you teach in another context you have a great opportunity to become aware of your hidden presuppositions and perhaps even prejudices. Students in this new context may challenge even what you thought was self-evident.

- Your role is to assist the local community and support indigenous theology. Familiarize yourself with the greatest novelists or poets of the country, even with major Greek Orthodox theologians whose writings may relate to your teaching. It is important to demonstrate that your teaching connects and converses with local thought. The school librarian or national faculty members should be able to help you to discover key materials in Greek or written in English by Greeks.

- Certain theological debates may be extremely important in your own context but they might not be a problem in the context you are asked to serve. The issue of "the inerrancy of Scripture," for example, was never a major debate in the Greek Orthodox context. Sometimes visiting scholars "import" theological problems into another context unnecessarily.

- Remember, you are there to take off people's shoulders some of the overload they are already experiencing. Try not to add extra work and take away lots of their valuable time. We often find that local churches or colleges get more tired when visitors come because visitors expect airport pick-ups, tours of the sights, dinners in local cuisine, and so on. Unless the locals insist, make sure you plan ahead for your own transportation, sightseeing, and so on. Do not burden locals with questions about the best hotels or restaurants. Locals rarely stay in hotels so it is better to consult a website like TripAdvisor or Booking.com.

Teaching Cross-Culturally in Czech Republic

Vyšší Odborná Škola Misijní a Teologická, Kolín (VOŠMT)

Social and Cultural

- Agnosticism has become the dominant worldview in Czech Republic.

- Czechs are direct in speech and serious in their relations. For example, if you greet Czechs with "How are you?," they generally take your question literally and believe you are genuinely interested in their current state or situation.

- Czechs tend to be reserved in the expression of their feelings. Consequently, it can take longer to get responses to questions and feedback from the class as a whole.

- Czechs are very cautious about making long-term commitments.

- Czechs will often "close ranks" in times of crisis, express solidarity, and if necessary collect money to help those in need – both nationally for regions damaged by disasters, or personally to help someone pay for special medical treatment.

Political and Historical

- The Czech Republic is a small nation and Czechs do not tend to see their country as "the greatest in the world."

- The Czech Republic is West-oriented and an active member of the European Union and NATO. However, there are also strong "Eurosceptic" opinions among politicians.

- Czechs are proud of their cultural heritage and appreciate outsiders who are aware of Czech "heroes" such as Comenius, Bata, and T. G. Masaryk.
- Key events in Czech history:
    - 863: Arrival of missionaries Constantin and Methodius from Thessaloniki and the acceptance of Christianity as a state religion.
    - 1415: Burning of Master John Hus.
    - 1613: Translation of Kralice Bible, the translation similar to KJV which is still used today.
    - 1621: Execution of twenty-seven representatives of Protestantism, disappointment of Protestant hopes, and the beginning of systematic re-Catholicization.
    - 1722: Revival in German Herrnhut, where Czechs and Moravians had emigrated, and the emergence of the Moravian Brethren mission.
    - 1780s: Josephine era influenced by the Enlightenment; the birth of scepticism towards Catholicism as well as to religion in general.
    - 1918: Emergence of an independent Czechoslovak republic; separation from the Austro-Hungarian Empire.
    - 1948: Communists win the parliamentary elections and take power, applying Stalinist policies.
    - 1968: The attempt to reform communism (so-called "communism with a human face"), which was suppressed by the invasion of Warsaw Pact armies.
    - 1989: "Velvet Revolution," when communists gave up their power, and the emergence of a democratic regime.

Religious

- The church is differentiated regionally: Moravia and Silesia are more religious and more conservative than Bohemia.
- Today's ministers enter ministry only hesitantly.

Educational

- The Czech system has nine years of obligatory elementary education. Then pupils can choose either four years' gymnasium of high-school education ended by *maturita* (i.e. public state examinations), or three years' vocational education ended by professional examinations.

- The condition for continuing at university is high-school education ended by *maturita*.

- University education has two parts: three years of bachelor studies (Bc.) followed by two years of master's study (Mgr., Ing.).

- Bachelor education is strongly professionally oriented as a preparation for a specific master's study.

- During the communist era (1948–89) university education was regulated, as the regime was afraid of overeducation, and only 17 percent of the population completed university education. After the "Velvet Revolution" of 1989 a massification of university education took place, and now everybody wants at least a bachelor-level degree. This has negatively influenced the quality of secondary schools. As everybody wants *maturita* to be able to continue at university, vocational schools without *maturita* have experienced a decrease in applicants. This has led to a national decrease in the number of much-needed tradespeople, which in turn has opened the door to immigrants – particularly from former communist countries.

- In the past the Czech approach to education was very much biased towards memorization, with only a small emphasis on the development of critical thinking. Czech students are used to cramming for examinations and memorizing information, and often struggle to work independently and present their opinions. However, this is gradually changing.

- With the increase in technology many students are being distracted by their notebooks and smartphones and often only pretend to focus in class.

Teaching Cross-Culturally in Ukraine

Odessa Theological Seminary

Political and Historical

- Ukraine is an independent country that was once a republic in the Soviet Union. It is the second-largest country in Europe. Ukraine is probably best known in the West for its nuclear accident at the Chernobyl Nuclear Power Plant in a city located a little more than seventy miles north of Kiev. The conflict between Russia and Ukraine that began in 2014 is an ongoing tragedy, but it largely goes "unnoticed" for many living outside the conflict area.

- Ukraine is a typical postcolonial country with the consequent issues and challenges. Some key texts that can help you understand recent Ukrainian history are Anna Reid's *Borderland*, Serhii Plokhy's *Gates of Europe*, Anne Applebaum's *Red Famine*, Timothy Snyder's *Bloodlands: Europe between Hitler and Stalin*, and, for a wider cultural perspective, Brogi Bercoff's *Ukraine and Europe: Cultural Encounters and Negotiations*.

Social and Cultural

- Language: the official language of Ukraine is Ukrainian. Nevertheless, if one travels from the centre of Ukraine eastwards one mainly encounters the Russian language. West of Kiev, the capital, one usually encounters the Ukrainian language. The farther one travels in either direction from the centre, east or west, the more one encounters primarily Russian or Ukrainian vernacular.

- Relationships are very important for Ukrainians, and Ukrainians are a very gracious people. When you ask for permission to do something, you may find that your Ukrainian host will often answer in the affirmative to "save face," even though the host may not understand the request, or (worse) does not know how, or is unable, to do what you ask. If possible, seek advice from a trusted local advisor or long-term missionaries. Be sensitive to the cultural mores, and focus on being people-oriented rather than task-oriented.

- Ukrainians often give gifts when they go to someone's house as a guest, whether it be a friend or a relative. Flowers, boxed chocolates, or fruit are common. When giving flowers, be sure the number of flowers you give is odd; an even number of flowers is given only to commemorate the death of a loved one.

- Do not be late to organized events, or at least if you are late make sure it is not your fault. Try to be precise and punctual. Ten minutes late is still within the "normal" time. Half an hour late is not normal unless a person has warned that he or she will be late due to particular circumstances. At the same time, understand that nationals may be late. Do not become tense if one or more of your national colleagues do not arrive at the set time. The keyword of your trip needs to be "flexibility."

- Do not put your feet up on a table or chair, as this is very offensive to a Ukrainian. Be sure to remove your shoes when entering a residence.

Religious

- The Ukrainian Orthodox Church is considered the church of the land, although there are a number of Protestant groups. Evangelicals are said to make up 1 percent of the population in some areas. The Orthodox Church is opposed to the idea of "the separation of church and state" and is often opposed to foreign missionary activity in "their" country. Be very polite and never disparaging when talking about Orthodox "traditions"; many people whom you may consider "lost" view themselves as very religious.

- As a general rule, Protestant church services last for about two hours. The order of service varies but often includes two to four sermons, congregational singing, choir or worship group specials, solos, poetry, greetings, prayers, invitation, and announcements. The final pastor may "correct errors" and clarify misunderstandings in the sermons preached by you and those who preached earlier in the service.

- A few songs may have familiar tunes but humming or singing loudly in English during a Ukrainian song may be considered disruptive to the congregation. There is no clapping in Ukrainian churches. The choir occupies a central place in the worship service. It is usually in the centre of the stage and has a very prominent place in the heart of the people.

- The Lord's Supper is typically served on the first Sunday of the month. Real wine is used and is often served from a common cup. Out of consideration for those who struggle with alcoholism, some churches do offer juice instead of wine. Most Protestant churches follow a "high church" approach to the Lord's Supper, but there are nuances. If you know that you will be celebrating the Lord's Supper, it is best to ask your host or translator what to expect.

- In smaller churches, foreigners will often be asked to preach or bring a greeting, but this request will often be made just before the beginning of the service. Be prepared! In larger churches, particularly in urban settings, if the foreigner is asked to preach the invitation will probably come during the planning phase of the visit.

- Typically, a preacher signals the end of a sermon by saying "Amen." This will generally be followed by a time for "greetings." Especially as a foreign visitor, you will be expected to give a greeting from your church as a sign of fellowship and respect. You should stand and wait to be acknowledged by the pastor. Your greeting should be short and sincere and given while standing. A simple statement is sufficient, along the lines of "It is my great joy to bring you a sincere greeting from the church in . . . "

- Ukrainians stand and pray before and after meals.

- Unless they are physically unable to do so, Ukrainians stand or kneel every time they pray.

- Protestant Christians in Ukraine do not consume alcoholic beverages or any form of tobacco. If Ukrainian Christians do so, they will likely be excommunicated from their church.

Educational

- Stories or personalized narratives are very significant for the communication of your point. Ukrainian folk culture in general has strong visual and musical components. One of the foundational national myths points to the importance of visual and musical elements: when Prince Volodymyr of Kyiv chose the Orthodox faith based on the reports of his envoys who attended liturgy in Hagia Sophia in Constantinople, the sights and sounds were key factors.

- Ukrainians can learn both in groups and individually. However, communal learning is preferred, and individuals in general have a level of interdependency in decisions and judgments. Authority is duly respected but with some level of critical assessment.

- Younger Ukrainians are mostly visual learners due to the "smartphonization" of society and the popularity of movies and television series.

- The higher the educational level of the students, the more interactive the learning should be. For certificate and diploma level a lecture approach is still common. However, at the bachelor level, seminars and group assignments are very helpful. At master's level the primary methodology should be seminars and discussions in class coupled with individual research or reading assignments outside class.

- Photocopying takes time and needs prior arrangement. The earlier you send notes, handouts, and outlines, the more likely your class will run smoothly. If you want to avoid problems and miscues, it may be better for you to bring complete copies of the translated materials with you.

- Books are a nice gift for students. Many books may be purchased in Ukraine or brought from your home country.

- It is a good idea to invite your students to your room for tea after class to get to know them.

- When you first meet your students, begin with the word of God rather than personal greetings. Once the Scriptures have been presented you can present your greetings – telling the students how happy you are to be in Ukraine, how good the food has been, how great the singing is, and how you bring greetings from all the churches in your home country.

Translation

- Unless your Russian or Ukrainian is very good, you will be using a translator, and therefore typed notes are helpful. It is best to go over your classroom notes with your translator at least one day before your class session.

- Handouts, PowerPoint presentations, reading materials, and outlines should be submitted several weeks before class begins for translation and photocopying. Keep in mind that translation of materials is costly and time-consuming, and so you should try to minimize translation of materials as much as is feasible. It is best (if possible) to consult with the school's librarian as to what materials on the subject are available in Ukrainian or Russian, and build your assignments around these local resources.

- Keep in mind that everything you say in English will take twice as long through translation. Plan to reduce the material you are trying to cover.

- Speak in complete sentences. Word order in Russian and Ukrainian is flexible, and it is often impossible to translate a thought until the translator has heard the entire sentence.

- Keep your sentences short and simple. Complex terms and ideas are often difficult to translate. Avoid idioms and colloquialisms. Be aware that jokes do not readily translate.

- Give your translator time to translate. Finish your thought, let him or her translate, and move on. Try to get into a rhythm.

- If your translator does not understand a sentence, do not repeat it more slowly. Rather, restate the sentence using synonyms, as there was probably a key term with which the translator was not familiar.

- If someone is asking a question through translation and you are not sure you understand, take the time to ask for clarification. This is better than compounding misunderstandings later.

- Don't read Scripture passages in English, as this wastes time. Ask your translator to read the Scriptures directly in the language of instruction

Practical

- Water: it is not recommended that you drink the tap water in Ukraine. Ukrainians boil the water for hot tea, which usually makes it safe for drinking. Bottled water is widely available in carbonated and non-carbonated varieties.

- Eating in homes: your host knows your concerns and will not serve you anything that is harmful. You will also be served far more than it is possible to eat. Eat, enjoy, and expect to stay a while at the table. At times, there are seven to ten courses at the main meal. Be aware that the same type of food may be served for all three meals each day.

- Many Ukrainians are not accustomed to "eating out." Dining out can cost from $1 to $60 per person and you will be expected to cover this cost for all who accompany you. If you choose to eat out, tipping in the past has been rare and you may find that the waiter or waitress attempts to return your "overpayment." However, increasingly a 3–5 percent tip is appreciated.

- Jewellery: Ukrainians, especially Christians, generally wear less jewellery than people from other regions of the world. You may do well to leave most of your jewellery at home. A wedding band is a notable exception. It is not necessary to change yours, but most Ukrainians wear their wedding band on the right hand.

- Do not play cards. Ukrainian believers think that only the heathen play cards.

- Personal security: it is impossible to hide the fact that you are a foreigner. However, avoid being perceived as a "foolish foreigner" and thus becoming a target. Ukrainians are generally quieter in public than most Westerners, especially in crowds. Try not to talk loudly in public. It is not advisable to walk alone after dark.

- Police and officials: these agents of the state may be helpful in emergencies, but they are not "public servants" as understood in many countries of the world. Be sure you do not expose all of your money to a policeman; fines have been known to fluctuate widely.

- Be careful not to give any promises to anyone, unless you are absolutely planning on being the one to follow through. This means if you even hint at sending money or support, time, or volunteer groups, you yourself must be willing to take on the full responsibility of the promise.

- Leaving: many visitors bring things they think they will need but do not intend to take back home. These things may include extra pieces of luggage, medical supplies, snacks, paper, clothes, toiletry items, tools, or unused ministry items. These items are often a welcome help to nationals. However, make sure the items you leave are of good quality, and ask your host or translator if the items will be useful and if he or she can give them to someone. Do not leave items with no explanation, or leave low-quality merchandise. This may be taken as an insult.

Afterword

The experience of teaching cross-culturally can be one of the most transformative opportunities in a person's life. This collection has sought to sensitize you to some of the key issues that you may encounter when you cross cultures, as well as providing a wealth of practical suggestions, not least in the material that comes from leaders in specific local contexts.

This collection was built largely during the period of the COVID-19 pandemic. We recognize that the long-term impact of that crisis on global theological education was not clear at the time of writing. We sensed that many schools would likely embrace a higher role of technology in their delivery, although how extensive this would be in the long term was yet to be seen. Nonetheless, the need for cross-cultural teachers will most probably continue in the years ahead, and consequently the issues discussed in this book will remain significant and strategic.

It is worthwhile as an afterword to summarize some of the key themes that run through this collection. They include the following:

- The importance of affirming local people, and in particular the students' life experiences and ways of thinking and acting. In cross-cultural teaching trust is critical, and respect is the gateway to winning trust. This means having the willingness to adapt both your content and your methodology in such a way that the emerging leaders in your care will be better prepared to serve meaningfully in their own context.
- The importance of quality preparation. Early contact with the school. Providing your materials well in advance – particularly when translation is involved. Reading about the context – its history and contemporary challenges. Praying for the school, the students, and the communities they serve. These all require time and effort

but will ultimately be rewarded when you reach the location and begin teaching.

- Respect for the school and its leadership. Particularly in the country pieces there is a call for visiting instructors to serve the vision and priorities of the institution where they are teaching, rather than coming with a personal agenda or pre-packaged product. Quality cross-cultural teaching goes far beyond simply delivering the same material that has been taught in the home country. Rather, you need to listen and adapt to the local contextual needs. You also need to abide by the school's curricular expectations in terms of hours of engagement and assessment.

- An acknowledgment that our cross-cultural teaching has a *political* dimension, but should not get into *politics*. That is, there is an undeniable element of social-political and power dynamics in this situation. However, be sure not to get into the specific aspects of local politics.

- An openness to learn from your mistakes. You will make mistakes. Everyone does. Your response to these mistakes can model to your students that failure is a friend and can be a bridge to quality learning and enhanced relationships.

- Joy and a sense of humour. The ability to laugh at yourself and a joyful appreciation of all you see and hear are attitudes that are appreciated and reciprocated.

Above all, the theme that dominates this collection is a posture of humble learning. If you come with a recognition of how little you know, and teach from below rather than from above, it is then that you are positioned to provide a "third space" for mutual transformative learning. May God grant you wisdom and grace on this remarkable journey.

For Further Reading

Amorim, L. "Intercultural Learning." Community Foundation Transatlantic Fellowship Orientation Session, European Foundation Centre, 2–4 June 2001, Washington, DC. http://www.angelfire.com/empire/sdebate/TCFF-Intercultural-Learning.pdf.

Amstutz, D. D. "Adult Learning: Moving toward More Inclusive Theories and Practices." *New Directions for Adult & Continuing Education* 1999, no. 82 (1999): 19–32. doi:10.1002/ace.8202.

Ango, S. "Lessons for Effective Christian Education in Golmo: An African Traditional Approach to Teaching and Learning." *Christian Education Journal Series* 4, no. 1 (2007): 17–33.

Apfelthaler, G., K. Hansen, S. Keuchel, C. Mueller, M. Neubauer, S. H. Ong, and N. Tapachai. "Cross-Cultural Differences in Learning and Education: Stereotypes, Myths and Realities." In *Learning and Teaching across Cultures in Higher Education*. Edited by D. Palfreyman and D. L. McBride, 15–35. New York: Palgrave Macmillan, 2007. doi:10.1057/9780230590427_2.

Apple, M. W. *Official Knowledge: Democratic Education in a Conservative Age*. New York: Routledge, 2000.

Banks, J., and C. McGee Banks. *Multicultural Education: Issues and Perspectives*. Hoboken: Wiley, 2010.

Bass, G., and M. Lawrence-Riddell. "UDL: A Powerful Framework." *Faculty Focus*, 6 January 2020. https://www.facultyfocus.com/articles/course-design-ideas/universal-design-for-learning.

Bauman, C. W., and L. J. Skitka. "Ethnic Group Differences in Lay Philosophies of Behavior in the United States." *Journal of Cross-Cultural Psychology* 37, no. 4 (2006): 438–45.

Behera, M. "Inequality in Theological Education between the North and the South." In *Reflecting on and Equipping for Christian Mission*. Edited by S. Bevans, T. Chai, J. N. Jennings, K. Jørgensen, and D. Werner, 116–28. Oxford: Regnum, 2015. doi:10.2307/j.ctv1ddcmcd.14.

Black, S. "Scholarship in Our Own Words: Intercultural Rhetoric in Academic Writing and Reporting." In *Challenging Tradition: Innovation in Advanced Theological Education*. Edited by P. Shaw and H. Dharamraj, 127–43. Carlisle: Langham Global Library, 2018.

Blake, N., and J. Masschelein. "Critical Theory and Critical Pedagogy." In *The Blackwell Guide to the Philosophy of Education*. Edited by N. Blake, P. Smeyers, R. Smith, and P. Standish, 38–56. Malden: Blackwell, 2003. doi:10.1002/9780470996294.

Bliss, A. "Rhetorical Structures for Multilingual and Multicultural Students." In *Contrastive Rhetoric Revisited and Redefined*. Edited by C. Panetta, 15–30. New York: Routledge, 2008.

Bosch, D. *Transforming Mission: Paradigm Shifts in Theology of Mission*. Maryknoll: Orbis, 1991.

Brookfield, S. *Becoming a Critically Reflective Teacher*. San Francisco: Jossey-Bass, 1995.

———. *Discussion As a Way of Teaching*. San Francisco: Jossey-Bass, 2005.

———. *The Skillfull Teacher: On Technique, Trust and Responsiveness*. San Francisco: Jossey-Bass, 1990.

Bujo, B. *Foundations of an African Ethic: Beyond the Universal Claims of Western Morality*. New York: Crossroad, 2001.

Caldwell, L. W. "How Asian Is Asian Theological Education?" In *Tending the Seedbeds: Educational Perspectives on Theological Education in Asia*. Edited by A. Harkness, 23–45. Quezon City: Asia Theological Association, 2010.

Canagarajah, A. *A Geopolitics of Academic Writing*. Pittsburgh: University of Pittsburgh, 2002. doi:10.2307/j.ctt5hjn6c.

Chan, H. M., and H. K. T. Yan. "Is There a Geography of Thought for East–West Differences? Why or Why Not?" In *Critical Thinking and Learning*. Edited by M. Mason, 44–64. Oxford: Blackwell, 2009.

Choi, H.-S., J.-G. Seo, J. Hyun, and M. Bechtoldt. "Collectivistic Independence Promotes Group Creativity by Reducing Idea Fixation." *Small Group Research* 50, no. 3 (2019): 381–407.

Connor, U. *Intercultural Rhetoric in the Writing Classroom*. Ann Arbor: University of Michigan, 2011. doi:10.3998/mpub.3488851.

Costas, O. "Conversion As a Complex Experience: A Hispanic Case Study." *Occasional Essays* 5, no. 1 (1980): 21–44.

Cranton, P. *Understanding and Promoting Transformative Learning: A Guide for Educators of Adults*. San Francisco: Jossey-Bass, 2006.

Cushner, K., and S. Brennan, eds. *Intercultural Student Teaching: A Bridge to Global Competence*. Lanham: Rowman & Littlefield Education, 2007.

Dahlfred, K. "Ten Tips on Teaching through Translation." Karl & Sun Dahlfred, 16 February 2011. Accessed 5 March 2019. https://www.dahlfred.com/en/blogs/gleanings-from-the-field/440-ten-tips-on-teaching-through-translation.

Dasen, P., and A. Akkari, eds. *Educational Theories and Practices from the Majority World*. New Delhi: Sage, 2008. doi:10.4135/9788132100683.

Dei, G. "Rethinking the Role of Indigenous Knowledges in the Academy." *International Journal of Inclusive Education* 4, no. 2 (2000): 111–32. doi:10.1080/136031100284849.

Dietz, G. *Multiculturalism, Interculturality and Diversity in Education: An Anthropological Approach*. Münster: Waxmann Verlag, 2009.

Dyrness, W., and O. García-Johnson. *Theology without Borders: An Introduction to Global Conversations*. Grand Rapids: Baker, 2015.

Egege, S., and S. Kutieleh. "Critical Thinking: Teaching Foreign Notions to Foreign Students." *International Education Journal* 4, no. 4 (2004): 1–11.

Eisner, E. *The Educational Imagination: On the Design and Evaluation of School Programs*. New York: Macmillan, 1985.

Elmer, D. *Cross-Cultural Connections: Stepping Out and Fitting in around the World*. Downers Grove: IVP, 2009.

———. *Cross-Cultural Servanthood: Serving the World in Christlike Humility*. Downers Grove: IVP, 2009.

Enns, M. "Theological Education in Light of Cultural Variations of Reasoning: Some Educational Issues." *Common Ground Journal* 3, no. 1 (Fall 2005): 76–87.

Epstein, D. *Geographies of Knowledge, Geometries of Power: Future of Higher Education*. New York: Routledge, 2007.

Escobar, S. *The New Global Mission: The Gospel from Everywhere to Everyone*. Downers Grove: IVP, 2013.

Fisher, M., Jr. "Student Assessment in Teaching and Learning." Vanderbilt University, Center for Teaching, 2020. https://cft.vanderbilt.edu/student-assessment-in-teaching-and-learning/.

Foucault, M. *Power/Knowledge: Selected Interviews and Other Writings, 1972–1977*. Brighton: Harvester, 1980.

Freire, P. *Pedagogy of Freedom: Ethics, Democracy, and Civic Courage*. Critical Perspectives Series. Lanham: Rowman & Littlefield, 1998.

Georges, J., and D. Baker. *Ministering in Honor–Shame Cultures: Biblical Foundations and Practical Essentials*. Downers Grove: IVP, 2016.

Goleman, P. "Communicating in the Intercultural Classroom." *IEEE Transactions on Professional Communication* 46, no. 3 (2003): 231–35. doi:10.1109/TPC.2003.816786.

Gorski, P. C. "Good Intentions Are Not Enough: A Decolonizing Intercultural Education." *Intercultural Education* 19, no. 6 (2008): 515–25. doi:10.1080/14675980802568319.

Gudykunst, W. "Individualistic and Collectivistic Perspectives on Communication." *International Journal of Intercultural Relations* 22, no. 2 (1998): 107–34.

Gudykunst, W. B., S. Ting-Toomey, and T. Nishida, eds. *Communication in Personal Relationships across Cultures.* Thousand Oaks: Sage, 1996.

Gutchess, A. H., R. C. Welsh, A. Boduroglu, and D. C. Park. "Cultural Differences in Neural Function Associated with Object Processing." *Cognitive, Affective and Behavioral Neuroscience* 6, no. 2 (2006): 102–9.

Hall, E. T. *Beyond Culture.* New York: Doubleday, 1976.

Hampden-Turner, C., and F. Trompenaars. *Riding the Waves of Culture: Understanding Diversity in Global Business.* New York: McGraw-Hill, 1997.

Hiebert, P. *Anthropological Insights for Missionaries.* Grand Rapids: Baker, 1985.

———. *Anthropological Reflections on Missiological Issues.* Grand Rapids: Baker, 1994.

———. *Transforming Worldviews: An Anthropological Understanding of How People Change.* Grand Rapids: Baker, 2008.

Higuera-Smith, K., J. Lalitha, and L. D. Hawk. *Evangelical Postcolonial Conversations.* Downers Grove: IVP, 2014.

Hill, G. *Global Church: Reshaping Our Conversations, Renewing Our Mission, Revitalizing Our Churches.* Downers Grove: IVP, 2016.

Hodges, C., S. Moore, B. Lockee, T. Trust, and A. Bond. "The Difference between Emergency Remote Teaching and Online Learning." *Educause Review*, 27 March 2020. https://er.educause.edu/articles/2020/3/the-difference-between-emergency-remote-teaching-and-online-learning.

Hodgetts, R., and F. Luthans. *International Management: Culture, Strategy, and Behavior.* 10th ed. Boston: McGraw-Hill, 2017.

Hofer, B., and L. Bendixen. "Personal Epistemology: Theory, Research, and Future Directions." In *Personal Epistemology: The Psychology of Beliefs about Knowledge and Knowing.* Edited by B. Hofer and P. Pintrich, 227–56. New York: Routledge, 2012. doi:10.4324/9780203424964.

Hofstede, G. "Cultural Differences in Teaching and Learning." *International Journal of Intercultural Relations* 10, no. 3 (1986): 301–20. doi:10.1016/0147-1767(86)90015-5.

Hofstede, G., and G. Hofstede. *Cultures and Organizations: Software of the Mind.* 3rd ed. New York: McGraw-Hill, 2010.

House, R., P. Hanges, M. Javidan, P. Dorfman, and V. Gupta, eds. *Culture, Leadership, and Organizations: The GLOBE Study of 62 Societies.* Thousand Oaks: Sage, 2004.

Howell, B., and J. Paris. *Introducing Cultural Anthropology: A Christian Perspective.* Grand Rapids: Baker, 2019.

Jackson, M. *Minima Ethnographica: Intersubjectivity and the Anthropological Project*. Chicago: University of Chicago Press, 1998.

Jegede, O. J., and G. S. Aikenhead. "Transcending Cultural Borders: Implications for Science Teaching." *Research in Science & Technological Education* 17, no. 1 (1999): 45–66. doi:10.1080/0263514990170104.

Jenkins, P. *The Next Christendom: The Coming of Global Christianity*. 3rd ed. Oxford: OUP, 2011.

Jin, A., M. Cooper, and B. Golding. "Cross-Cultural Communication in Teacher Education." *Australian Journal of Teacher Education* 41, no. 6 (2016): 20–34. doi:10.14221/ajte.2016v41n6.2.

Jones, G., and S. Paulsell, eds. *The Scope of Our Art: The Vocation of the Theological Teacher*. Grand Rapids: Eerdmans, 2002.

Kang, N. "Envisioning Postcolonial Theological Education: Dilemmas and Possibilities." In *Handbook of Theological Education in World Christianity: Theological Perspectives, Regional Surveys, Ecumenical Trends*. Edited by D. Werner, D. Esterline, N. Kang, and J. Raja, 30–41. Eugene: Wipf and Stock, 2010.

Kaplan, R. "Cultural Thought-Patterns in Inter-Cultural Education." In *Landmark Essays on ESL Writing*. Edited by T. J. Silva and P. K. Matsuda, 11–26. Mahwah: Erlbaum, 2001.

Kim, S., and K. Kim. *Christianity as a World Religion: An Introduction*. Sydney: Bloomsbury, 2016.

Knowles, M., E. Holton, and R. Swanson. *The Adult Learner: The Definitive Classic in Adult Education and Human Resource Development*. 6th ed. Amsterdam: Elsevier, 2005.

Leask, B. "Plagiarism, Cultural Diversity and Metaphor: Implications for Academic Staff Development." *Assessment & Evaluation in Higher Education* 31, no. 2 (2006): 183–99. doi:10.1080/02602930500262486.

Leask, B., and J. Carroll. "Good Practice Principles in Practice: Teaching across Cultures." *International Education Association of Australia*. October 2013. https://www.ieaa.org.au/documents/item/125.

Lee, K. "Teacher–Student in Multicultural Theological Education: Pedagogy of Collaborative Inquiry." *Journal of Supervision and Training in Ministry* 22 (2002): 81–99.

Levine, R. *The Geography of Time*. New York: Basic, 1997.

Lingenfelter S., and M. Mayers, *Ministering Cross-Culturally: An Incarnational Model for Personal Relationships*. Grand Rapids: Baker, 1986. Repr. 2016.

Livermore, D. *Cultural Intelligence: Improving Your CQ to Engage Our Multicultural World*. Grand Rapids: Baker, 2009.

Loh, C., and T. Teo. "Understanding Asian Students Learning Styles, Cultural Influence and Learning Strategies." *Journal of Education and Social Policy* 7, no. 1 (2017): 194–210.

Lopes, C. "Nurturing Emancipatory Local Knowledges." In *Challenging Tradition: Innovation in Advanced Theological Education*. Edited by P. Shaw and H. Dharamraj, 145–65. Carlisle: Langham Global Library, 2018.

Lustig, M. W., and J. Koester. *Intercultural Competence: Interpersonal Communication across Cultures*. Boston: Allyn and Bacon, 2003.

Marshall, E. O. *Christians in the Public Square*. Eugene: Wipf and Stock, 2008.

Mbiti, J. S. *African Religions and Philosophy*. 2nd ed. London: Heinemann, 1989.

———. *Concepts of God in Africa*. New York: Praeger, 1970.

McArthur, J. "Time to Look Anew: Critical Pedagogy and Disciplines within Higher Education." *Studies in Higher Education* 35, no. 3 (2010): 301–15. doi:10.1080/03075070903062856.

McCroskey, J., and V. Richmond. *Fundamentals of Human Communication: An Interpersonal Perspective*. Prospect Heights: Waveland, 1995.

Mendieta, E. *Global Fragments: Globalizations, Latinamericanisms, and Critical Theory*. Albany: State University of New York, 2007.

Merriam, S. B., and Associates. *Non-Western Perspectives on Learning and Knowing*. Malabar: Krieger, 2007.

Merriam, S., R. S. Caffarella, and L. M. Baumgartner. *Learning in Adulthood: A Comprehensive Guide*. San Francisco: Jossey-Bass, 2007.

Mezirow, J. *Transformative Dimensions of Adult Learning*. San Francisco: Jossey-Bass, 1991.

Moreau, S., E. Campbell, and S. Greener. *Effective Intercultural Communication: A Christian Perspective*. Grand Rapids: Baker, 2014.

Morrow, R. A., and C. Alberto Torres. *Reading Freire and Habermas: Critical Pedagogy and Transformative Social Change*. New York: Teachers College, 2002.

Musyoka, B. "Spiritual Disorientation: Primary Cause of African Identity Crisis and Moral Relativism." *Africa Journal of Evangelical Theology* 35, no. 2 (2016): 109–41.

Na, J., I. Choi, and S. Sul. "I Like You Because You Think in the 'Right' Way: Culture and Ideal Thinking." *Social Cognition* 31, no. 3 (2013): 390–404. doi:10.1521/soco.2013.31.3.390.

Nakane, I. "Negotiating Silence and Speech in the Classroom." *Multilingua* 24, no. 1 (part 2) (2005): 75–100. doi:10.1515/mult.24.1part2.75.

Nashon, S., D. Anderson, and H. Wright. "Editorial Introduction: African Ways of Knowing, Worldviews and Pedagogy." *Journal of Contemporary Issues in Education* 2, no. 2 (2007): 1–6.

Nieto, S. M. "Profoundly Multicultural Questions." *Educational Leadership* 60, no. 4 (2002): 6–10.

Nisbett, R. *The Geography of Thought: How Asians and Westerners Think Differently . . . And Why.* New York: Free Press, 2003.

Nisbett, R. E., K. Peng, I. Choi, and A. Norenzayan. "Culture and Systems of Thought: Holistic versus Analytic Cognition." *Psychological Review* 108, no. 2 (Apr. 2001): 291–310. doi:10.1037/0033-295X.108.2.291. PMID:11381831.

Ntseane, P. "Culturally Sensitive Transformational Learning: Incorporating the Afrocentric Paradigm and African Feminism." *Adult Education Quarterly* 61, no. 4 (2011): 307–23. doi:10.1177/0741713610389781.

Ott, C., and H. Netland, eds. *Globalizing Theology: Belief and Practice in an Era of World Christianity.* Grand Rapids: Baker, 2006.

Panetta, C., ed. *Contrastive Rhetoric Revisited and Redefined.* New York: Routledge, 2008.

Peterson, B. *Cultural Intelligence: A Guide to Working with People from Other Cultures.* Yarmouth: Intercultural, 2004.

Plueddemann, J. E. *Leading across Cultures: Effective Ministry and Mission in the Global Church.* Downers Grove: IVP, 2009.

———. *Teaching across Cultures: Contextualizing Education for Global Mission.* Downers Grove: IVP, 2018.

Pratt-Johnson, Y. "Communicating Cross-Culturally: What Teachers Should Know." *The Internet TESL Journal* 12, no. 2 (Feb. 2006). http://iteslj.org/Articles/Pratt-Johnson-CrossCultural.html.

Quezada, R., and C. Alfaro. "Developing Biliteracy Teachers: Moving toward Culture and Linguistic Global Competence in Teacher Education." In *Intercultural Student Teaching: A Bridge to Global Competence.* Edited by K. Cushner and S. Brennan. Lanham: Rowman & Littlefield Education, 2007.

Ramachandra, V. *Subverting Global Myths: Theology and the Public Issues Shaping Our World.* Downers Grove: IVP, 2008.

Reagan, T. *Non-Western Educational Traditions: Indigenous Approaches to Educational Thought and Practice.* Mahwah: Erlbaum, 2005.

Richards, R., and B. O'Brien. *Misreading Scripture with Western Eyes: Removing Cultural Blinders to Better Understand the Bible.* Downers Grove: IVP, 2012.

Riebe-Estrella, G. "Engaging Borders: Lifting up Difference and Unmasking Division." *Theological Education* 45, no. 1 (2009): 19–26.

Rockwell, E. "Recovering History in the Anthropology of Education." In *A Companion to the Anthropology of Education*. Edited by B. A. Levinson and M. Pollock, 65–80. Chichester: Wiley-Blackwell, 2011. doi:10.1002/9781444396713.ch5.

Rosenblatt, A. "Committing to Ungrading, in an Emergency and After." *The Chronicle*, Duke University, 27 March 2020. https://www.dukechronicle.com/article/2020/03/duke-university-gradin-coronavirus-covid-19-public-health-crisis-emergency-thinking-ungrading-pass-fail?

Ryan, J. "Improving Teaching and Learning Practices for International Students: Implications for Curriculum, Pedagogy and Assessment." In *Teaching International Students: Improving Learning for All*. Edited by J. Carroll and J. Ryan, 92–100. Abingdon: Routledge, 2005.

Sanders, Paul. "Evangelical Theological Education in a Globalised World." Presentation delivered at Centre for Theological Education, Belfast, Northern Ireland, 17 November 2009.

Schwartz, S. H. "Universals in the Content and Structure of Values: Theoretical Advances and Empirical Tests in 20 Countries." In *Advances in Experimental Social Psychology*. Edited by M. Zanna, 1–65. Orlando: Academic Press, 1992.

Semali, L., and J. Kincheloe. *What Is Indigenous Knowledge?* New York: Falmer, 1999.

Shaw, K. "All in the Family: Nepotism and Mission?" *Evangelical Missions Quarterly* 49, no. 4 (Oct. 2013): 134–35.

Shaw, P. "Culture, Gender, and Diversity in Advanced Theological Studies." In *Challenging Tradition: Innovation in Advanced Theological Education*. Edited by P. Shaw and H. Dharamraj, 89–108. Carlisle: Langham Global Library, 2018.

———. "Moving from Critical to Constructive Thinking." *Evangelical Review of Theology* 45, no. 2 (2021): 128–40.

———. "Patronage, Exemption, and Institutional Policy." *Evangelical Missions Quarterly* 49, no. 1 (Jan. 2013): 8–13.

———. "Westerners and Middle Easterners Serving Together: Potential Sources of Misunderstanding." *Evangelical Missions Quarterly* 46, no. 1 (2010): 14–20.

Shaw, P., and H. Dharamraj, eds. *Challenging Tradition: Innovation in Advanced Theological Education*. Carlisle: Langham Global Library, 2018.

Sleeter, C., and P. McLaren. *Multicultural Education and Critical Pedagogy: The Politics of Difference*. New York: SUNY, 1995.

Smith, D., and P. Dykstra-Pruim. *Christians and Cultural Difference*. Grand Rapids: Calvin College, 2016.

Storti, C. *Figuring Foreigners Out: Understanding the World's Cultures*. Boston: Nicholas Brealey, 2011.

Tennent, T. C. "New Paradigm for Twenty-First-Century Mission: Missiological Reflections in Honor of George K. Chavanikamannil." In *Remapping Mission Discourse*. Edited by S. Samuel and P. V. Joseph, 185–203. Delhi: ISPCK, 2008.

———. *Theology in the Context of World Christianity: How the Global Church Is Influencing the Way We Think about and Discuss Theology*. Grand Rapids: Zondervan, 2009.

Thomas, D., and K. Inkson. *Cultural Intelligence: People Skills for Global Business*. San Francisco: Berrett-Koehler, 2004.

Thompson, S., ed. *Encyclopedia of Diversity and Social Justice*. Lanham: Rowman & Littlefield, 2014.

Tracy, D. *Plurality and Ambiguity*. San Francisco: Harper & Row, 1987.

Triandis, H. C. "The Self and Social Behavior in Differing Cultural Contexts." *Psychological Review* 96 (1989): 506–20.

Trompenaars, F., and E. Voerman. *Servant-Leadership across Cultures: Harnessing the Strength of the World's Most Powerful Management Philosophy*. New York: McGraw-Hill, 2010.

Tutu, D. *God Has a Dream: A Vision of Hope for Our Time*. New York: Doubleday, 2004.

———. *In God's Hands*. London: Bloomsbury, 2014.

———. *No Future without Forgiveness*. New York: Doubleday, 1999. doi:10.1111/j.1540 -5842.1999.tb00012.x.

Tutu, D., and J. Allen. *God Is Not a Christian: Speaking Truth in Times of Crisis*. London: Rider, 2011.

Vella, J. *Taking Learning to Task: Creative Strategies for Teaching Adults*. San Francisco: Jossey-Bass, 2000.

Vella, J., P. Berardinelli, and J. Burrow. *How Do They Know They Know?* San Francisco: Jossey-Bass, 1998.

Werner, D., D. Esterline, N. Kang, and J. Raja, eds. *Handbook of Theological Education in World Christianity: Theological Perspectives, Regional Surveys, Ecumenical Trends*. Eugene: Wipf and Stock, 2010.

WestEd. "Culture and Assessment: Discovering What Students Really Know." *R&D Alert* 11, no. 2 (2010). https://www.wested.org/resources/culture-and-assessment-discovering-what-students-really-know/.

Wiggins, G., and J. McTighe. *Understanding by Design*. Alexandria: Association for Supervision and Curriculum Development, 2005.

Yung, H. "Critical Issues Facing Theological Education in Asia." *Transformation (Durban)* 12, no. 4 (1995): 1–6. doi:10.1177/026537889501200401.

Zab, S. "Whitepaper: The Growth of the Smartphone Market in Kenya." 2 June 2015. https://www.jumia.co.ke/blog/whitepaper-the-growth-of-the-smartphone-market-in-kenya/.

Zahneis, M. "For International Students, Academic Dishonesty Numbers Don't Tell the Full Story." *The Miami Student*, 2 May 2017. https://www.miamistudent.net/article/2017/05/for-international-students-academic-dishonesty-numbers-dont-tell-the-full-story.

Zhongshe, L., and L. Lan. "Rhetorical Diversity and the Implications for Teaching Academic English." *Asian Journal of Applied Linguistics* 3, no. 1 (2016): 101–13.

Zimmerman, Jennifer. "Thinking Critically." PowerPoint presentation. Academic Resource Centre, Mercer University. https://slideplayer.com/slide/3932290/.

Author Biographies

Perry Shaw (EdD) is Researcher in Residence at Morling College, Sydney. Prior to moving to Australia, Perry served in the Middle East from 1990–2019, the final decade of which was as Professor of Education at the Arab Baptist Theological Seminary, Beirut, Lebanon. Through his time in the Middle East and in consultation work across the globe Perry has been concerned by the legion of complaints he has heard from leaders of Majority World schools as to the perceived "arrogance" of visiting lecturers. He has also cringed at the various culturally inappropriate practices observed in visiting teachers – some of which he himself has fallen into in his own experiences of cross-cultural teaching. Perry's commitment to this collection is related to his desire to counter these concerns by promoting a humble learning posture in cross-cultural teaching encounters.

Joanna Feliciano-Soberano (PhD) is the Academic Dean at Asian Theological Seminary in Manila, the institution she has served as faculty for Christian Education for over twenty years. Joanna is also the Regional Director (RD) for Southeast Asia–Overseas Council and has been a GATE Associate (Global Associates for Transformational Education) since 2012. Her work as a GATE associate and as RD for Southeast Asia has provided an added perspective on classrooms in local contexts and the role of international faculty, as well on the reality of the scarcity of women in theological education and leadership. Her continuing passion is transformative learning in multi-cultural classrooms, as well as helping to break the "glass ceiling" for women leadership in the Majority World. This twin passion is reflected in this book.

César Lopes (PhD) serves as President of the Community for Interdisciplinary Theological Studies – CETI (Costa Rica) and also as Dean of Online Studies at the São Paulo School of Theology (Brazil). For the last twenty years he has been working in pastoral and academic environments with a focus on holistic mission and transformation. Both while hosting international lecturers in Brazil and in teaching experiences through courses and lectures in different international contexts, César has seen and made enough mistakes in terms of cross-cultural exchanges. He believes the kind of active and humble listening this collection promotes is fundamental in making these exchanges a blessing for both guests and hosts, including in the growing South to South collaborations.

Bob Heaton (PhD) has served at the Theological College of Zimbabwe (TCZ) in Bulawayo since 1990, first as Acting President for nine years, then as Academic Dean. He is also head of the Practical Theology Department. TCZ is a multi-cultural, non-denominational college, where Bob is passionate about teaching students what the gospel means, what it means to be a Christian in the Zimbabwean context, and developing Christian leaders. His teaching career has largely been cross-cultural to an ethnically wide range of Zimbabwean students, as well as some Mozambicans and Zambians. In that context, he has made many blunders and learned the importance of paying attention to other people's cultural and theological views with humility and empathy. Bob's contribution to this collection is part of a desire to help fellow travellers in the teaching-learning journey to avoid some of the mistakes he has made along the way.

ICETE International Council for Evangelical Theological Education
strengthening evangelical theological education through international cooperation

ICETE is a global community, sponsored by nine regional networks of theological schools, to enable international interaction and collaboration among all those engaged in strengthening and developing evangelical theological education and Christian leadership development worldwide.

The purpose of ICETE is:
1. To promote the enhancement of evangelical theological education worldwide.
2. To serve as a forum for interaction, partnership and collaboration among those involved in evangelical theological education and leadership development, for mutual assistance, stimulation and enrichment.
3. To provide networking and support services for regional associations of evangelical theological schools worldwide.
4. To facilitate among these bodies the advancement of their services to evangelical theological education within their regions.

Sponsoring associations include:

Africa: Association for Christian Theological Education in Africa (ACTEA)

Asia: Asia Theological Association (ATA)

Caribbean: Caribbean Evangelical Theological Association (CETA)

Europe: European Evangelical Accrediting Association (EEAA)

Euro-Asia: Euro-Asian Accrediting Association (E-AAA)

Latin America: Association for Evangelical Theological Education in Latin America (AETAL)

Middle East and North Africa: Middle East Association for Theological Education (MEATE)

North America: Association for Biblical Higher Education (ABHE)

South Pacific: South Pacific Association of Evangelical Colleges (SPAEC)

www.icete-edu.org

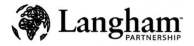 **Langham**
PARTNERSHIP

Langham Literature and its imprints are a ministry of Langham Partnership.

Langham Partnership is a global fellowship working in pursuit of the vision God entrusted to its founder John Stott –

> *to facilitate the growth of the church in maturity and Christ-likeness through raising the standards of biblical preaching and teaching.*

Our vision is to see churches in the Majority World equipped for mission and growing to maturity in Christ through the ministry of pastors and leaders who believe, teach and live by the word of God.

Our mission is to strengthen the ministry of the word of God through:
- nurturing national movements for biblical preaching
- fostering the creation and distribution of evangelical literature
- enhancing evangelical theological education

especially in countries where churches are under-resourced.

Our ministry

Langham Preaching partners with national leaders to nurture indigenous biblical preaching movements for pastors and lay preachers all around the world. With the support of a team of trainers from many countries, a multi-level programme of seminars provides practical training, and is followed by a programme for training local facilitators. Local preachers' groups and national and regional networks ensure continuity and ongoing development, seeking to build vigorous movements committed to Bible exposition.

Langham Literature provides Majority World preachers, scholars and seminary libraries with evangelical books and electronic resources through publishing and distribution, grants and discounts. The programme also fosters the creation of indigenous evangelical books in many languages, through writer's grants, strengthening local evangelical publishing houses, and investment in major regional literature projects, such as one volume Bible commentaries like *The Africa Bible Commentary* and *The South Asia Bible Commentary*.

Langham Scholars provides financial support for evangelical doctoral students from the Majority World so that, when they return home, they may train pastors and other Christian leaders with sound, biblical and theological teaching. This programme equips those who equip others. Langham Scholars also works in partnership with Majority World seminaries in strengthening evangelical theological education. A growing number of Langham Scholars study in high quality doctoral programmes in the Majority World itself. As well as teaching the next generation of pastors, graduated Langham Scholars exercise significant influence through their writing and leadership.

To learn more about Langham Partnership and the work we do visit **langham.org**